BY THE AUTO EDITORS OF CONSUMER GUIDE®

Corvette
America's Sports Car

JAY KOBLENZ

BEEKMAN HOUSE
New York

CONTENTS

Manufactured in the United States of America
10 9 8 7 6 5 4 3 2 1

Library of Congress Catalog Card Number: 83-63595

ISBN: 0-517-42463-0

This edition published by:
Beekman House
Distributed by Crown Publishers, Inc.
One Park Avenue
New York, New York 10016

Principal Author
Jay Koblenz

Photography
William L. Bailey
Becky Bodnar
Chevrolet Motor Division
David Gooley
Floyd Joliet, GM Design Staff
Charles M. Jordan, Director
 of Design, GM Design Staff
Bud Juneau
Richard M. Langworth

Douglas J. Mitchel
Nicky Wright

Special thanks to Suzanne Kane, Chevrolet Motor Division and to C. Jacks Car Capitol (owner: Dana Mecum; sales manager: Denny Lemonds) for their assistance with color photography. Appreciation is extended to these Corvette owners, whose cars are featured in the color sections: Pat Bachrodt (silver 1975 roadster), Mike Biederman (white '63 roadster), Pete Bogard (red '57 roadster), Joseph E. Bortz (turquoise '57 roadster), Gary Kuzma (red '60 roadster), Mike Massillo (red '67 roadster), Santo Scafide (red '63 roadster), Dave Stefun (red '55 roadster), Gary Wallem (silver '63 coupe), Scott Wallem (blue '66 coupe).

INTRODUCTION

Last of a great line: The 1967 Corvette Sting Ray coupe

Around the time of the Corvette's 25th anniversary in 1978, the auto editors of CONSUMER GUIDE® issued *Corvette: America's Only True Sports Car.* In the introduction we mused on the origins, success, and historical significance of this very special Chevrolet, and many of those words are just as valid today:

"For a quarter century now, the Corvette has carried Detroit's banner on competition surfaces everywhere—from Le Mans to Sebring, from SCCA to IMSA, from the 24-hour endurance race to the quarter-mile. It has captured the imagination of thousands of owners and drivers. With few exceptions, each new model Corvette has been an outstanding success...

"Yet the Corvette has for years been misunderstood. Because it is built by a company with [more assets than the government of] France, purists have derided it from the start. Nothing, they said, could ever be worthwhile if it came from General Motors. Because it is a big, heavy sports car, some have insisted that it is a contradiction in terms, possessing none of the lightness and agility they consider necessary to be worthy of the term 'sports car.'

"But the Corvette has endured. It has kept winning races and finding buyers all these years...because it is a car de-signed and built by car lovers—not some committee's evaluation of the ultimate compromise."

Happily for all car lovers, that tradition continues in the 1984 Corvette. It's the most modern, the most sophisticated car ever to wear the crossed-flags insignia. It also stands as vivid evidence that car lovers are still alive and well within the design centers of Detroit—and are still able to create machines the equal of anything built anywhere else in the world. The Corvette has always been one of the best expressions of the innovativeness and determination that have characterized the American auto industry from the very beginning. And if those qualities now seem in short supply, it's fitting that a new Corvette should arrive to re-affirm them in a dramatic and exciting fashion.

It's sobering to realize that a good many of today's Corvette fans were not yet born when the first 1953 models burst on the scene. Yet these younger enthusiasts have been no less affected by the Corvette mystique than those of us who grew up with the car. There are many facets to this mystique: the undeniably individualistic character of the cars, the colorful people who created them, the drama of the Corvette's troubled early years, the triumph of the later ones, and the allure of a proven winner on the showroom floors, the race tracks of the world, and on the main streets of America. The Corvette has endured, yes; but it has also grown and improved, attracting an ever wider following whose interest and devotion swelled with each new model, each race victory, each glamorous show car bearing the Corvette name. It is this charisma and the vast enthusiasm it inspires that makes the Corvette unique in the annals of automotive history. It remains arguably the best-known, best-loved single model ever to come from Detroit. And for millions all over the globe, it is still the symbol of the brightest and best in American automobiles.

This book is primarily the story of the Corvette through its 30-year evolution and of the people who played key roles in it. But it is just as much the story of the Corvette phenomenon and you, the many 'Vette fans who have made this car a legend in its own time. It's not easy capturing a legend—or telling afresh a story already so thoroughly documented. However, we've tried to inject new information wherever possible and to give a different perspective on familiar events in order to make the Corvette saga come alive for readers young and old.

We begin by setting the stage for the birth of America's sports car. The Corvette wasn't the first quick two-seater built in this country, though it would prove the most successful. But the Corvette might never have been born were it not for a series of developments stretching back to before World War I. In the opening chapter we review these earlier efforts, the literal foundations of the first Corvette.

The next sections trace the Corvette's history through its successive design generations. The first, spanning model years 1953-55, would be the most troubled, but it did produce the rarest and most valuable Corvettes of all. These were the "plastic bathtub" models with their six-cylinder engine, Power-glide transmission, mesh headlamp stone guards, crude side curtains, and radical fiberglass bodywork. A significant turning point came in 1955 with introduction of a lively new V-8 that would help save the Corvette from extinction. The brilliant second generation of 1956-57 is perhaps the most memorable of the early models, with sharp new styling, much improved roadability, and even more performance, courtesy of fuel injection and larger engine displacement. This basic design was given wider sales appeal in the third generation of 1958-62, which saw the Corvette become a profit-maker able to "earn its keep" for the first time. The last of the "four-lamp" cars, the 1961-62 models, are treated separately as a distinct bridge between 'Vettes of the '50s and '60s. The fourth generation followed, the brilliant 1963-67 Sting Ray cars that seem no less sensational today than they did a generation ago. This basic design would have the shortest life of any Corvette series, but its successor would have the longest. The fifth generation would run from 1968 to 1977 with only minor alterations and, with a restyled roof, from the 'Vette's 25th anniversary year through 1982. We cover it in two detailed chapters. Bringing the story up to date is the advanced sixth-generation 1984 design, which seems destined for an equally long and successful life.

These chapters are followed by in-depth interviews conducted especially for this book with four personalities vital to the Corvette story. They are William L. Mitchell, former Director of the General Motors Design Staff and the man responsible for Corvette styling from 1961 through his retirement in 1977; Zora Arkus-Duntov, widely regarded as the Corvette's "father" and now retired as chief engineer for the car; David R. McLellan, Duntov's successor and the man behind the nuts and bolts and computer chips of the '84 Corvette; and Jerry Palmer, head of Chevrolet Studio Three and the man who created the new model's stunning aerodynamic styling. Our thanks to all of them for shedding new light on Corvette history with their candid comments.

No Corvette book would be complete without a look at the many show cars and experimentals created over the years. You'll find them described and illustrated in an extensive chapter. Similarly, the Corvette's competition history is profiled from the early factory-supported efforts, including the assault on Sebring, through Bill Mitchell's privately campaigned Stingray racer and on through the literally hundreds of modified cars entered in all forms of motor-sports by independent enthusiast racers. Last but not least, we report on one of the most visible parts of the long-running Corvette phenomenon, the mini-industry that serves Corvette owners with parts, accessories, and racing gear. Interspersed throughout the book are four color portfolios with original and recent portraits of production models from most every year.

Although it is no longer, strictly speaking, "America's only true sports car," there is still no other car more revered. For its millions of fans, the Corvette has been—and always will be— the only sports car that matters.

BEFORE THE CORVETTE:
50 YEARS OF
SPORTS CARS

Old and new: The original 1953 Motorama Corvette show car poses with that year's standard Chevy Bel Air four-door sedan.

People had been playing around with sports cars—for fun if not always profit—long before Chevrolet produced its first Corvette. In fact, the sports car idea was probably born along with the automobile itself well before the turn of the century. "Automobiling" was then more a sport than a necessity of daily life and cars were uncommon novelties, rarely seen objects of wonder and curiosity. The tink-erers and inventors who cobbled up the early horseless carriages hoped to make their fortunes selling them, of course. And many realized, perhaps instinc-tively, that one of the best ways to do that was to demonstrate the speed and reliability of their wares in contests with other cars.

Speed runs, durability trials, and cross-country marathons were the main forms of com-petition in those days. Of course, it did little good to compete if you didn't win; so, right from the start, racing cars were most al-ways specially prepared vehicles. Many had cut-down bodywork to reduce weight and thus increase speed, and had the most power-ful and durable engines their makers could devise. And most, though by no means all, were far more agile and maneuverable than the standard article—all the better for outdistancing opponents in turns. These characteristics—less weight, better performance, and more responsive handling—would become basic to the sports car idea.

Although largely experimental, the embryonic racers of the early 1900s—the first sports cars—stirred the emotions of many "automobilists," some of whom began demanding the same qualities in cars they could buy and drive on normal roads every day. This led to the notion of dual purpose, or "race and ride," as we would later term it. One of the earliest examples of this concept was the original Mercedes of 1901. It was conceived primarily as a more competitive racer at the behest of Emil Jellinek, a member of the board at Daimler Motor Works in Germany, who also happened to run one of the firm's most profitable distributorships. Partly through his influence, Daimler engineers wasted little time adapting the advanced design of this 35-bhp racer to a new line of road cars that would firmly establish the Mercedes marque as a leader in the European industry. Soon, companies in the United States like Simplex, Lozier, Locomobile, and Chadwick were offering better-than-average performance in sporting tourers and runabouts, though these were large, clumsy brutes compared to cars like the Mercedes.

Undoubtedly the spiritual ancestor of America's sports car was the legendary Mercer Type 35 Raceabout. Introduced in 1911, it was the very essence of the sports car idea in its day. Its bodywork was natty and dashing, with a pair of snug bucket seats slung low ahead of a large cylindrical fuel tank. Ahead was a long steering column mounting a distinctive "monocle" windshield. Wheels and tires were large in relation to the body, and

7

this plus the sharply angled cycle-type fenders gave the car an eager, ready-to-run look.

The Raceabout lived up to its looks and its name. At just 2450 pounds it was a lightweight, and its engine was an unusually powerful 300-cubic-inch T-head four built with exacting precision. Rated at 58 horsepower and coupled to an advanced three-speed selective-shift transmission, this powerplant could see a Raceabout to a top speed of at least 75 miles per hour—sensational go for the Brass Age. The gearbox shifted easily, though synchromesh was years away, and the whole car was manageable and easy to drive. The chassis was quite modern, with a full-floating rear axle located by radius rods and with semi-elliptic leaf springs at each corner made of sturdy vanadium-alloy steel. There was even a pull-up handbrake for the rear wheels to supplement the mostly ineffective foot-actuated service brake that acted on the transmission.

Priced at $2150—more than twice the cost of the most expensive Model T Ford, for example—the Raceabout was not the sort of car everyone could afford, another characteristic of sports cars that persists to this day. But its jaunty air and jackrabbit quickness captivated the nation. It's still one of the most sought-after models among antique-car collectors.

The Raceabout quickly proved its mettle in competition, winning the important Panama-Pacific Light Car Race in San Francisco in February 1911. Later that year, two Mercers were literally driven in off the street and ran flat out to finish 12th and 14th at the Indianapolis 500. They averaged 63 mph and, according to many reports, were so trouble-free that their hoods weren't opened even once during the race. Afterwards, in what would become traditional for sports car racing in a later era, drivers Hughie Hughes of England and Charles

Bigelow (who'd won at San Francisco) simply drove their Raceabouts off the track and on home. It was a spectacular showing for an unmodified automobile. The next year, a Raceabout finished third at the Brickyard, averaging 76.3 mph.

Though it went on to score many more victories in the hands of speed merchants like Ralph DePalma, Eddie Pullen, and Spencer Wishart, the Raceabout didn't last long. The last ones were built in 1915. Just before that, however, a rival company introduced a new model that would be even more celebrated. It was the Stutz Bearcat, the car synonymous with sheiks and flappers and all the other razzmatazz of the Roaring '20s.

Designed as a "sportsman's car," the Bearcat was the road-going equivalent of the famous T-head Stutz racers that had scored many wins of their own against the Mercers. Its chassis and four- and six-cylinder engines came from the Stutz F Series passenger models, a kind of "derivative" engineering that would be commonly employed for many later sports cars, including the Corvette. However, its wheelbase was considerably shorter, its stance much lower. Though it was far less graceful and more ponderous than the athletic Raceabout (which it initially resembled), the Bearcat had superior roadholding, and its overall performance was thrilling.

The Bearcat progressed through a pretty restyle in 1917, when it also gained a more powerful 80-bhp, 360-cid engine with a 16-valve cylinder head. In this form it was capable of an astonishing 85 mph. The car was reworked again for 1920 and continued to sell well for another couple of years. The final 88-bhp model with 3.00:1 rear axle could hit almost 90 mph, but it wasn't enough to counteract the sales slide and the Bearcat was phased out in 1923.

America's automakers created a number of memorable sporty-

looking models in the years between World War I and World War II. But, by and large, they were not the sort of compact, nimble, dual-purpose machines we now associate with the term sports car. To be sure, there were romantic roadsters and convertibles, and some of them, like the elegant Auburn 856 boattail speedsters and the futuristic Cord 810, have long been recognized as among the greats from the automobile's "Golden Age." But cars like these were more *gran turismo* than sports car—comfortable and fast, but too large and heavy to be entertaining over a challenging country road. Others, like the Millers and early Duesenbergs, were more competition car than road machine—too powerful, too unwieldy to be practical for the vast majority of motorists in everyday use. Besides, they were built in tiny numbers and cost a fortune. The same was true of the later SJ Duesenbergs, which were purely luxury tourers. America, it seemed, had given up on the sports car idea.

But not completely. In the late Twenties we began hearing about enthusiasts who called themselves "hot rodders." These backyard mechanics, blessed with dreams and a native intelligence but not much cash, began rebuilding old worn-out wrecks into very personalized automobiles. Hot rods were supposed to look good on the street and be fast on something called a dragstrip. Model T and Model A Fords were the favored starting points because, even then, they were cheap and available, and their simple basic engineering was amenable to all manner of modifications. The most common ones were to discard the fenders and running boards, lower the body, maybe bend some

Top: The legendary Mercedes-Benz SSK of 1928 could reach near 120 mph with its supercharged 7.1-liter straight six. Bottom: The MG TC of 1947 helped spark sports car fever in postwar America.

sheet metal, fiddle with the suspension and, naturally, wring more horsepower from the engine.

In a way, the early hot rodders were after the same things the pioneer automakers sought in their racers: more speed, more agility, more distinctive looks. Though their approach was certainly different—low-budget, one-of-a-kind machines built from a crazy-quilt of production-car pieces—hot rods were nonetheless quite faithful to the "race-and-ride" ideal, sports cars in the best sense.

Meanwhile, the sports car idea was being pursued in Europe along several different lines. Bugatti in France put the emphasis on small, almost delicate open-wheel racers and two-place road cars built unhurriedly, one at a time. From Germany came the imperious bellow of the heavyweight, supercharged Mercedes-Benz—the imposing S/SS/SSK roadsters of the late '20s/early '30s and the more civilized 500/540K sports tourers of 1935-39. Down in Italy, companies like Maserati and Alfa Romeo were building race-bred performance and technical sophistication into curvaceous open two-seaters that marked a new peak in coachbuilt artistry. But it was left to England to define the classic sports car as we would come to know it. The exemplars were lithe, lovely roadsters like the Squire, the four-wheel Morgans, the sleek SS 100 (forerunner of the Jaguar) and—most of all—the cars from Morris Garages.

MG has long been credited as the marque that introduced sports cars to America. One model in particular kindled the fascination that swept the country in the early postwar years, the sports car fever that would be an impetus for the future Corvette. It was, as everyone knows, the MG TC, introduced in 1945. As writer T.C. Browne put it, this car became "one of the most beloved British exports ever to reach these shores, rival-ing Scots Whiskey in its popularity among Americans. . .[But the TC] was to become admired all out of proportion to its numbers (few) or its technical virtues (fewer). In fact, the TC was all but indistinguishable from its immediate prewar predecessor, and a typical British enthusiast regarded the earlier PB as a measurably superior motorcar. Legends are seldom born of logic."

Nevertheless, GIs stationed in England fell in love with this humble little piece of iron-mongery. They brought some of them home, and the word spread. What did the TC have that was so special? Charm for one thing. It was cute, but somehow it looked right—nifty and, well, sporty. It was also appealingly quaint: vintage '30s styling, diabolical folding top mechanism, cozy two-seat cockpit, conveniences notable by their absence—the whole package. The flexible ladder-type chassis and crude solid-axle suspension were anachronisms a decade before, and the ride was stiff and joggly. Yet the TC's agility was a revelation to Yanks raised on workaday Fords and Chevys. With its implausibly small, 1250cc four producing just 54 bhp, the TC was hardly fast—well under 80 mph tops—but it showed power-hungry colonials that a car needn't have a big-inch engine to be fun. And, like those Model A Fords so popular with the hot rodders, this MG was about as simple as an anvil. But perhaps the TC's greatest significance was that it combined all the elements basic to the sports car idea evolved over the previous 50 years. That it had a folding top and only two seats seemed almost super-fluous. The stage was set for the sports car revolution in the postwar era.

But the revolution took a long time to get rolling, and there was no immediate rush to sports cars in the U.S. The end of war had brought the promise of a prosperity unknown since before the Depression, and the public mood was expansive. After four long years without new cars, buyers were eager to snap up anything and everything Detroit could turn out, even if they were only warmed-over versions of 1942 designs. Gas was still cheap. Many GIs returned home to begin raising families, and tiny two-seaters just didn't make much sense. Most U.S. auto-makers unveiled their first completely new postwar models for 1949, and they mirrored the state of the nation perfectly. They were the longest, lowest, widest, flashiest cars in history—and they sold like crazy. So while a great many people were interested in sports cars, not many people bought them at first.

Interestingly, the postwar boom convinced a number of enterprising individuals that now was the time to break into the auto business. Most saw the best way to succeed was to offer something a little different, something buyers couldn't get from Detroit. What could be better than a sports car?

This hopeful but faulty reasoning led to a good many small-scale attempts at an American-style sports car in the Fifties and late Forties. In the main, these were hastily conceived hybrids consisting of a special body hiding an assortment of mass-production hardware, including—almost invariably—the engine and—frequently—the chassis. Some of these efforts never went beyond the prototype stage—if that far—while others saw only miniscule production. The main problem with these cars was the companies behind them: shoe-string operations for the most part, with insufficient capital, design talent, manufacturing know-how, facilities, or some combination of these. Of course, all were needed for success in the postwar market. Just being different wasn't enough. Not surprisingly, most of these out-fits and their cars didn't last

The diminutive Crosley Super Sports and its doorless Hot Shot companion had good go and were quite adaptable for racing but were doomed due to slow sales of Crosley's mainline.

long, a year or two at best.

Two established American independents got in the sports car game early on, though neither produced a real sales winner. One was Crosley, which for 1949 fielded a spartan little roadster called the Hot Shot. It was followed a year later by the Super Sports, the same car but with opening doors instead of cut-outs in the body. Weighing only about 1200 pounds, these were tiny two-seaters built on an 85-inch-wheelbase chassis with a primitive solid-axle suspension at each end. Crosley's curious 44-cid four had but 26.5 bhp, but it was enough to make these bantamweights quite quick—and a number of accessory

houses offered enough hop-up equipment to make them into vest-pocket racers. Even in stock form they cornered like roller skates, and one modified car showed its ruggedness by winning the Index of Performance at the 1950 Sebring 12 Hours of Endurance. Ultimately, however, the Hot Shot and Super Sports were doomed by sagging sales of their economy-car sisters, which had no place in the "bigger-is-better" atmosphere of early-Fifties America. Founder Powel Crosley, Jr. got out of the car business soon afterwards, in 1952.

A more mature effort was the Nash-Healey, an Anglo-American concoction first suggested at a chance meeting in 1949 between Nash president George Mason and British sports car designer Donald Healey. This was a smooth, aluminum-bodied road-

ster on a 102-inch wheelbase and powered by a tuned version of the 235-cid ohv Nash six with 125 bhp. The transmission was a three-speed overdrive manual unit from Borg-Warner. The N-H was a pleasant machine on the road. It also did well in competition. A prototype finished fourth at Le Mans in 1950, and a stock-bodied '51 placed sixth overall and fourth in class the following year. High price— $4063 in 1951—put the damper on sales, and only 104 cars were sold that year. Mason then went to Italy's Pinin Farina for a restyle, but this only added to production costs and thus price. For 1953 a 253-cid engine with 135 bhp was specified, but sales remained meager despite this and the addition of the pretty Le Mans coupe model on a longer 108-inch wheelbase. Altogether, only 506

11

Nash-Healeys were completed before Nash abandoned the effort after 1954.

Such failures only reflected the tiny demand for sports cars in the early fifties. In 1952, for example, only 11,199 were sold, a near invisible 0.27 percent of the more than 4 million cars registered in the U.S. that year. But the sports car phenomenon was growing. The Sports Car Club of America had been formed, and was already organizing road races and a new type of motorsports called rallying. On the highway, sports car drivers were waving and honking at one another as kindred spirits, and many enjoyed playing tag with the larger, more powerful American cars. A steady stream of new models from overseas only fueled their enthusiasm. As if to announce its postwar recovery, England sent over the exquisite Jaguar XK-120 in 1949. This curvy, envelope-bodied roadster and coupe were powered by a 160/180-bhp twincam six, and were capable of flying at up to two miles a minute. They were quite expensive—$3500 or so in 1951—but the XK-120s were the cars every MG owner aspired to. MG itself issued an improved version of the TC in 1950, the TD. A few years later, the price and performance gap was bridged by the Triumph TR2, offering 90-mph performance for around $2300, and the handsome Austin-Healey 100-4, a genuine 100-mph roadster priced about $500 higher.

The nation's motoring press had been quick to spread the sports car gospel, and kept urging Detroit to keep the faith. Pioneer auto journalist Ken Purdy set the tone early in a 1949 article for *True* magazine titled "The Two-Seater Comes Back." He predicted that sports car engineering would soon filter down to ordinary family models, which would offer not just speed and style but also safety and—something new—driver enjoyment. Purdy was a bit premature, but a few people in the industry seemed sympathetic. One was a Belgian-born engineer newly arrived at the Chevrolet Division of General Motors. Said Zora Arkus-Duntov at a 1953 meeting of the Society of Automotive Engineers: "Considering the statistics, the American public does not want a sports car at all. But do the statistics give a true picture? As far as the American market is concerned, it is still an unknown quantity, since an American sports car catering to American tastes, roads, ways of living, and national character has not yet been on the market."

The voluptuous Jaguar XK-120 caused a sensation when it appeared in 1949.

A key stepping stone on the way to America's sports car was the advent of the kit car business. It began in trendy Southern California around 1950 with a small group of companies that specialized in making bodies designed to fit existing chassis. Usually they were sold with the necessary hardware for a do-it-yourself type to build a complete car at home. Kit cars were very much in the tradition of the early hot rods, but they would not have been possible were it not for the advent of a cheap, versatile material that lent itself easily to low-volume production. Its name: fiberglass.

Fiberglass, or glass-reinforced plastic (GRP) as it was originally known, had been developed during World War II. One of its first applications was in housings for certain military installations, which tended to be rendered invisible to enemy radar owing to GRP's radiowave "transparency." (Incidentally, this is what makes Corvettes and other fiberglass-bodied cars so resistant to police radar today.) When peace returned, it didn't take long for a number of individuals and firms to find new uses for the stuff. The Owens-Corning Company, for example, became one of the first fiberglass manufacturers, and applied it to an automobile as early as 1946, when it assisted engineer William Stout in building one of his rear-engine Scarab experimentals.

In 1950 a young California boat builder named William Tritt formed the Glasspar Company to fabricate fiberglass hulls. It quickly became a leader in its field. One day, Tritt was approached by Air Force Major Kenneth B. Brooks with a request to design a body in fiberglass that would fit a standard Detroit chassis, thus creating a possible substitute for the rugged Jeep. Tritt accepted.

The following year, Tritt's design was shown at the Los Angeles Motorama along with three other proposals for plastic bodies compatible with production-car frames. The Lancer was designed by Eric Irwin to fit big luxury-car chassis. The Skorpion by Jack Wills and Ralph Roberts was conceived with the Crosley in mind. The Wasp was also an economy-car idea. But the Tritt design—called the Brooks Boxer—was the only one sized for wheelbases of 100-110 inches—exactly the same as the wheelbases of Detroit's most popular cars.

Glasspar was doing business with the U.S. Rubber Company, which supplied some of the raw materials for GRP, and Tritt's Boxer caught the eye of some of that firm's engineers and executives through one of its West Coast sales engineers, Bud Crawford. Ultimately, Glasspar and U.S. Rubber's Naugatuck, Connecticut division agreed to joint production of GRP car bodies sized for 100-inch-wheelbase chassis and priced at about $650 each. The bodies would all be two-seaters with provision for folding fabric or vinyl tops. The kit car was in business.

U.S. Rubber's public relations pro managed to interest *Life* magazine in the story, and a feature entitled "Plastic Bodies for Autos" ran in the February 25, 1952 issue. The response was tremendous. Soon, Glasspar bodies were being bolted onto all kinds of chassis—everything from Crosleys to Henry Js to Fords. People in the industry also took note. One of them was a prosperous car dealer in Downey, California, B.R. "Woody" Woodill. The Aero-Willys, introduced in 1951, would make a great basis for a sports car, he thought—especially its solid, reliable 161-cid F-head six. Woodill contacted Tritt, who agreed to design a new body and to supply a separate chassis as well (the Willys used unit construction).

The result was the Woodill Wildfire, a slinky two-seat roadster appearing in 1952 with Willys drivetrain and front and rear suspension. It was offered as a complete car priced initially at $2900 (it later rose as high as $4500) or as a kit for between $1000 and $1200. Some 300 were built between 1953 and 1956, though Woodill says only 15 were "factory assembled" at his small shop. Minor components like instruments, bumpers, steering wheels, mirrors, and seats came from a variety of sources, and few Wildfires were built exactly alike. Woodill also engaged freelance engineer and hot rodder "Shorty" Post to design a new frame to accept the Ford/Mercury flathead V-8, for which dozens of bolt-on modifications were available at the time. In this form the car was a veritable rocket, but even the Willys-engine versions were quite fast. Though it's only a footnote in automotive history today, Woodill's venture is important because it demonstrated the economic feasibility of fiberglass for low-volume production.

The Wildfire might have been made in far greater numbers had Willys-Overland not been bought by Kaiser-Frazer. Back in 1942, K-F founder Henry J. Kaiser had envisioned a tiny economy car with a GRP body, and his consultant designer, Howard "Dutch" Darrin, had created a full-size fiberglass convertible in 1946 with an eye to series production. Neither of these saw the light of day, but Henry Kaiser remained fascinated with both economy cars and the new plastic material.

Ultimately, the two came together in a unique fiberglass-bodied sports car first shown in 1952. This was the Kaiser-Darrin, designated DKF-161 because it employed the same Willys six that so appealed to Woody Woodill. The 100-inch-wheelbase chassis came from K-F's economy model, the Henry J, introduced in 1951. Over this, Darrin laid a ground-hugging roadster body bereft of chrome gee-gaws and featuring unique sliding doors. Another new wrinkle was the three-way folding top that could be left half up to create a "lan-

dau" or town car effect. Standard equipment included the by-then obligatory full instrumentation, and most Darrins were fitted with a three-speed floorshift transmission with overdrive. Though fuel economy was as high as 30 mpg, a Darrin could scoot through the 0-60 mph run in about 13 seconds and approach 100 mph flat out.

After 62 preproduction prototypes, Kaiser-Darrin production began officially in December 1953. Advertised base price was $3668, well into Jaguar territory and too high to attract more than a handful of buyers. K-F was deep in financial hot water by this time, however, and the Darrin was a casualty of the firm's withdrawal from the American market after model year 1955. Only 435 were completed. The project was a big disappointment to Dutch Darrin, who bought about 100 factory

leftovers, fitted some with Cadillac V-8s, and sold them at his Los Angeles showroom for $4350 apiece. The rarest of a rare breed, these cars were capable of 140 mph maximum, with similarly vivid off-the-line acceleration.

The Darrin, the Nash-Healey, the Wildfire, the success of Bill Tritt and Glasspar, the general high interest in sports cars. In Detroit, executives, stylists, and engineers at the Big Three automakers followed these and other developments with keen interest. Yet there was little sign that any of them were about to produce a sports car of their own. Of course, advanced design concepts were always on the drawing boards, and some of them were for two- and four-place models with definite sporting overtones. Still, the prevailing attitude was "let's wait and see."

Opposite page, top: The 1954 Kaiser-Darrin, a contemporary of the first Corvette. Center: The Anglo-American Nash-Healey, 1953. Above: Chrysler's Ghia-bodied K-310 experimental, 1951.

There were reasons for this. Ford was fighting for its very survival in the postwar period, struggling to wrest its traditional spot as the number-two producer away from Chrysler. The firm had poured almost all its resources into the new 1949 Fords, Lincolns, and Mercurys, which had to sell well for the company to make it, and there simply wasn't much left for developing a sports car that company planners knew wouldn't be a high profit-maker. Chrysler had just been through a management crisis following the death of Walter P. Chrysler in 1947. His successor was the con-

15

servative K.T. Keller, a man much more interested in boxy, practical family sedans than low-slung sports cars. True, Chrysler had developed the innovative Thunderbolt show car back in 1941, a two-seat roadster with such advanced features as hidden headlamps and a metal top that completely retracted. More recently it had collaborated with Ghia of Italy on the four-seat K-310 and C-200 *gran turismos,* displayed in 1951. But these projects were strictly speculation. Chrysler continued to play with such concepts in the Fifties, but the company's up-and-down sales throughout the decade always made these low-priority items.

Things were different at General Motors. The mighty colossus had emerged from the war mightier than ever thanks to fat government contracts. Though temporarily eclipsed by Studebaker's all-new 1947 models, GM reclaimed its position as industry styling leader with the tailfinned Cadillacs and "Futuramic" Oldsmobiles of 1948. The next year saw the birth of the modern, efficient, high-compression overhead-valve V-8, and the hardtop-convertible body style, inaugurated at Buick, Ca-

dillac, and Olds, which met with overwhelming acceptance. As the Fifties opened, sales seemed headed only one way: straight up. If anybody was going to make a serious attempt at a home-grown sports car, it would be GM.

A key figure in GM's high success during these years was Harley J. Earl, founder and head of the firm's Art & Colour Section, the industry's first in-house styling department. Earl not only loved cars but also was very imaginative, and he had the good sense to surround himself with equally talented assistants for whom he provided the most stimulating and creative work environment possible. Earl had almost singlehandedly "invented" the dream car with his predictive Buick Y-Job, a long, low two-seat convertible first displayed in 1938. This car not only set the design themes for the company's styling in the immediate prewar and postwar years, it also proved the value of giving the public a "sneak preview" of things to come. This, in turn, led to the Motoramas, those exciting extravaganzas of chrome, chorines, and choreography that thrilled visitors in cities and towns all over the

Above: Another early Chrysler/Ghia effort was the C-200 four-seat convertible, 1951. Opposite page: Harley Earl's trend-setting Buick Y-Job of 1938, the first "dream car."

country between 1949 and 1961.

Earl was eager to get back to experimental projects after the war. And once the corporation's new 1949-50 models had been wrapped up, he did. Significantly, his first postwar dream cars were two-seaters, the aircraft-inspired LeSabre of 1951 and the Buick XP-300 shown a year later. Both featured ideas advanced for the day, like wraparound windshields, folding tops hidden just aft of the cockpit under metal covers, sculptured rear decks with prominent tailfins, and a low, ground-hugging stance.

But Harley had something else on his mind. As writer Karl Ludvigsen tells it: "As an antidote to post-LeSabre creative depression, Earl began thinking seriously about a low-priced sporty car during the late fall of 1951. He'd do this in his office on the eleventh floor of the anonymous-looking brick structure on the south side of Milwaukee Avenue, opposite the imposing GM Building. Then

16

he'd wander...down to the ninth floor. There, in a small enclosure adjacent to the main Body Development Studio, Earl could work privately with a personal crew on projects—like this one—that he wanted to shield from premature exposure. Earl was well aware of the perishable quality of a new idea." That new idea was the genesis of the Corvette.

The first sketches and scale models for Earl's pet project were, as Ludvigsen describes, "most like an amalgam of the classic British sports cars and the [Willys] Jeepster, for Earl had in mind a very simple car, one that could be priced at only $1850—about as much as a Ford, Chevy, or Studebaker sedan in 1952. A price this moderate meant that the design had to be based on a more or less stock chassis, and that's the way the first tentative studies went." New inspiration came from a car displayed for a time in GM's Styling auditorium. Called "Alembic I," it was essentially

the original Bill Tritt design for U.S. Rubber Company, which had purchased it and loaned it to GM. Earl now stepped up the pace, and work proceeded as "Project Opel." This name was chosen perhaps to confuse outsiders, although Chevy frequently did advanced studies for GM's German subsidiary in those days. It was all very hush-hush, limited only to those with a "need to know." If an employee wasn't directly involved with the "Opel" program, chances are he would never have heard about it.

It was at about this time that Edward N. Cole was transferred from Cadillac Division to Chevrolet, where he took over as chief engineer. Cole would be another key figure in Corvette history, but his list of credits was already impressive. He had come to Cadillac in 1933 after taking part in a work-study program at the GM Institute. His first assignments involved designing military vehicles such as light tanks for the Army. After the war he worked on rear-engine

prototypes for both Cadillac and Chevrolet, then concentrated on engines, helping Cadillac's John Gordon develop that division's short-stroke ohv V-8 for 1949. Cole then managed Cadillac's Cleveland plant for 30 months before taking his new job at Chevy. Once installed, he more than doubled the engineering staff, from 850 to 2900, then turned to designing a new V-8 for Chevy. This was the legendary small-block 265-cid unit introduced for 1955.

Meantime, Earl had tapped a young sports car enthusiast with degrees from Cal Tech in both engineering and industrial design to come up with a basic layout for Project Opel. Though assured he couldn't do it this way, Robert F. McLean started from the back, not the front, as was usual practice. With the rear axle as a reference point, he placed the passenger and engine compartments as close to it as possible, the goal being the balanced 50/50 weight distribution desirable in a sports car for op-

timum handling. (The actual figure worked out to a still-creditable 53/47 percent.) Wheelbase was pegged at 102 inches, the same as that of the Jaguar XK-120, one of Harley Earl's favorite cars. Track dimensions would be 57/59 inches front/rear, wider than the Jaguar's but not as wide proportionally as on the funny-looking little rear-engine Porsches.

Styling work was by now being coordinated with the engineering effort, and Earl's staff began incorporating ideas from his LeSabre and XP-300 show cars into the body for Project Opel. At this point, Earl's sports car was still only a proposal—a dream car for the Motorama maybe, but a long way from production. Yet, as Ludvigsen notes, Earl "envisioned new popularity for sports car racing throughout America with [his] car readily available, saying expansively that people would soon forget about those English cars as soon

as these sporty Chevys were on the market." Not surprisingly, and with examples like the "Alembic I" at hand, he looked to fiberglass as the best means for holding the line on body tooling expenses. As for the chassis, McLean's layout would somehow have to be realized with existing Chevy hardware, some of which might be modified to suit the new platform. There was simply no other choice.

But there were still two big unanswered questions about fiberglass. Would it provide the requisite body strength and how would it work in actual production? The second could not be answered without a production go-ahead, of course, but the first question was answered dramatically in an "accidental" fashion. Chevy had built a full-size convertible with a GRP body strictly for investigative R&D purposes in early 1952. During high-speed testing at the proving grounds the driver accidentally rolled the

car, but emerged unhurt. Even more amazing, the body suffered no severe damage. Now Earl was more convinced than ever that fiberglass was the way to go.

By mid-1952 the basic outlines of the new sports car had been laid down, Ed Cole was aboard as Chevy's new engineering chief, and Harley Earl was working toward completion in time for the 1953 Motorama. Cole became one of the first people within Chevy Division to see what Earl was up to. Ludvigsen records that, according to one eyewitness at the showing, Cole "literally jumped up and down" and promised to support Earl in his efforts to win production approval all the way to the Fourteenth Floor of GM headquarters.

There was but one thing left to do: a pre-selling job on GM president Harlow Curtice. A few weeks after Cole had seen that full-size plaster model, Earl set it up in the Styling auditorium

Above: The Motorama Corvette show car, alias EX-122, as it appeared at the Waldorf in January 1953. Right: An unidentified GM exec examines the show car.

to show his boss and Chevy Division general manager Thomas H. Keating. The curtain flew up with a flourish. Then, Earl led the two men around the car, explaining enthusiastically that here was not only a profitable new product but a car that would add much-needed sparkle to the Chevy line. His persuasiveness worked: it was agreed to show the car at the first Motorama of 1953, scheduled for the grand ballroom of New York's Waldorf-Astoria Hotel the following January. Meantime, engineering work with a view to eventual production would proceed as Project EX-122, with the final go/no-go decision based largely on showgoers' reactions.

Earl was delighted. The Corvette was on its way.

1953-55:
HIGH HOPES,
FALSE STARTS

Corvette? What's a Corvette? Difficult as it may be to believe now, there was a time when that name was almost completely unknown in America. Yet there it was on the nose and tail of a low, gleaming white roadster occupying pride of place at the first Motorama of 1953. Reporters got a sneak preview of GM's latest "dream car" on January 16th, the day before the official opening. In a press release, Myron Scott of Chevrolet's public relations staff explained that a "corvette" was a type of small, agile 19th-century warship, and that lately the term had been applied to describe small convoy vessels and sub chasers in World War II. Interestingly, one of these early press statements introduced the car with the English spelling "Courvette."

Top GM officials were on hand, and anxiously awaited the reactions of those who streamed into the grand ballroom at the Waldorf-Astoria to look at the two-seater. In the weeks leading up to this first showing, Harley Earl's sports car had created much excitement within Chevrolet Division. Production engineering was proceeding at full steam, and hopes were high that the public would like the car enough to buy copies—many copies. "It's made of what?" some showgoers must have wondered. "Fiberglass? That's that new

plastic, isn't it?" Others probably asked, "You say it's got the Chevy six and Powerglide? How fast'll it go?" But most people simply wanted to know two things: "When can I get one and how much is it gonna cost?"

An estimated four million people saw the Motorama Corvette, and their response was overwhelmingly positive. Even so, it's clear from drawings and dates that those most responsible for the Corvette, Harley Earl and Ed Cole, never doubted the car would see production. Certainly there was no objection from Chevrolet general manager Thomas Keating or GM president Harlow Curtice. Production would commence at the earliest possible date, and the new sports car would be available from neighborhood Chevy dealers at a suggested retail price of $3513.

Work on productionizing the Corvette had actually begun in mid-June of 1952 when long-time Chevy suspension engineer Maurice Olley sketched a chassis for "Project Opel" that was quite close to the eventual production design. His main challenge—and success—was getting a collection of off-the-shelf Chevy parts to fit under Earl's tightly drawn body. While many of the mechanical modifications made for the first Corvette were aimed toward performance, it was actually packaging that dictated most of them.

John R. Bond described the Corvette's basic chassis layout for *Road & Track* readers in June 1954: "In general, the chassis components were adapted from Chevrolet parts, but Hotchkiss [open] drive was essential, since the short wheelbase [102 inches] would have required a torque tube so short as to produce excessive change of wheel speed on rough roads.

Since the open body would contribute nothing to overall rigidity, a completely special frame was designed using box-section side rails and a [central] X-member. The X-member is low enough to allow the driveline to run above it, giving a very strong, solid junction at the 'X.' The low frame also required outboard rear spring mountings, which places them close to the wheels, for stability. Weight of the complete frame is 213 pounds." Those rear springs were the usual semi-elliptic leafs, and their outrigger location would be adopted for Chevy's all-new 1955 passenger models.

"The front suspension," Bond continued, "uses many standard parts but is stiffer in roll by virtue of a larger-diameter stabilizer bar. The coil springs are special because of the reduced load, but their rate appears to be the

same as the stock sedan. However, the sprung weight is less
than stock, giving the effect of
'stiffer' springs..." The steering
was GM's conventional Saginaw
recirculating-ball system with a
faster 16:1 ratio. "We are aware
of a preference in some quarters
for a rack-and-pinion steering
on cars of this type," said Olley.
"However, this involves a steering ratio on the order of 9 or 10
to 1. We regard this as too fast
even for a sports car..." As
noted earlier, the Corvette's static front/rear weight distribution
worked out to 53/47 percent. The
center of gravity was quite low,
just 18 inches off the ground. So,
although the Corvette chassis
borrowed much from Chevy's
mundane sedans, it was quite a
departure in many respects.

The same was true of the engine. The only available choice
was the dead-reliable but deadly
dull "Stovebolt" six, a 235-cid

overhead-valve unit then
producing a meager 105 bhp
with manual shift or 115 bhp
when tuned for optional Powerglide automatic. Chevy engineers thought the new sports car
should have a lot more oomph,
however, which led to some hot
rod-style tweaks. A high-lift,
long-duration camshaft, similar
to that of the 261-cid Chevy
truck engine, was added, and
hydraulic valve lifters were replaced with solid lifters. Dual
valve springs went in to cope
with the higher rpm capability
of the revised engine, and a fiber
gear used at the end of the
crankshaft was replaced by one
made of steel. Though aluminum pistons were being readied
in 1953, the Motorama Corvette
had conventional cast-iron pistons. The head casting was
modified a bit to increase compression, bringing it up from
7.5:1 to 8.0:1. For better cooling,

*One of the most famous early
Corvette publicity shots is this phan-
tom view of the 1953-54 chassis and
driveline. Note rearward positioning
of the Blue Flame six, angled propshaft, and the long steering column.*

the water pump flow capacity
was increased, and the pump
was relocated lower at the front
of the block so the large four-
blade fan could clear the low
hoodline.

The most obvious visual
change on the Corvette's "Blue
Flame" six involved induction. A
special aluminum intake manifold was mounted on the left
carrying three Carter "YH" side-
draft carburetors. Each carb fed
two cylinders continuously and
each had its own automatic
choke. Some thought had been
given to progressive carb linkage, but during testing it proved

23

Left: The Corvette body drop at St. Louis, photographed in December 1953, shortly after production was transferred from Flint. Right: The Corvette's Blue Flame six as seen in an early chassis mockup.

difficult to synchronize all three chokes and have them warm at the same rate. Thus, while the Motorama car had the progressive linkage, the production Corvette made do with manual chokes. Nash had managed an acceptable dual-carb setup on its Nash-Healey, but this was one of the few times anybody had tried three. Another change dictated by the Corvette's low hoodline was a redesigned rocker arm cover. It looked similar to the stock item but was lower at the front, and the "hat sections" were turned inside out. The oil filler was relocated to the rear for the same reason. The exhaust system was also modified, with dual outlets for improved power and a more burly sound.

The result of all this was 150 horsepower peaking at 4500 rpm and 223 lbs/ft of torque produced at a lazy 2400 rpm. The Motorama Corvette differed from the production version in having many chrome-finished underhood components, a fan shroud, and pancake-type air cleaners instead of the small, individual cylindrical units ultimately adopted.

Purists were quick to criticize the humble origins of the 'Vette engine, not to mention its advanced age. Noted John Bond: "Many people like to point out that 'Chevrolet hasn't changed their engine since 1937.' This is, however, a compliment, for it attests to the excellence of a design which, though perhaps not exciting or dramatic, has stood the test of time. Actually, very little of the original design is left."

Equally controversial was the lack of a manual transmission. This was a casualty of the crash engineering effort and the need to use as many stock components as possible, what with cost considerations ever more critical as production loomed closer. The main problem, again, was space. The Blue Flame six sat 13 inches farther back in the Corvette than in the standard Chevys, and the existing three-speed manual gearbox would have interfered with the rearmost carburetor. So there was no choice but to go with two-speed Powerglide automatic. This offered an unexpected bonus: easy conversion to floorshift operation. Shift points were raised to match the greater power and torque of the Corvette engine, and the transmission oil cooler was omitted because tests had shown it simply wasn't needed due to the sports car's livelier acceleration.

As for the critics who questioned whether any car worthy of the name could have a "slush-box," Maurice Olley replied: "The answer is that the typical sports car enthusiast, like the 'average man' or the square root of minus one, is an imaginary quantity. Also, as the sports car appeals to a wider and wider section of the public, the center of gravity of this theoretical individual is shifting from the austerity of the pioneer towards the luxury of modern ideas...There is no need to apologize for the performance of this car with its automatic transmission."

Olley's use of the word "luxury" is significant. *Automobile Quarterly* pointed out in a 1969 retrospective that "during 1952 the Corvette evolved entirely away from the simple roadster originally visualized by Earl...[and] by January 1953...had become a 'luxury' machine." This plus the rigid time and cost targets imposed on the development program go a long way toward explaining why the first Corvette emerged as a curious combination of the crude and the civilized. For example, Powerglide was probably chosen at least as much to satisfy

Chevy's marketing boffins (one of Olley's "modern ideas") as it was to save time and money for the engineers. Earl's body design, though clean and appealing, was still gimmicky for some tastes, especially the rocket-like rear fenders with their tiny fins, the dazzling vertical grille teeth, and the sunken headlamps covered by mesh stone guards. The top was neatly concealed under a flush-fitting metal cover and could be raised or lowered fairly easily by one person. But the clip-in side curtains, perhaps favored over roll-down windows as a cost-cutting measure, were every bit as anachronistic as they were on British roadsters of the period. The license plate was housed in a modern-looking recess covered by plastic—which tended to turn cloudy. In the transition to production, the show car's exterior door push-buttons were eliminated—which meant that the only way to open the door from outside was to reach inside for the release. To borrow a term from a later era, the first Corvette was a mixed bag indeed.

Though most 'Vette fans tend to assume otherwise, the decision to go with fiberglass body construction was made quite late in the game. GRP was expeditious for getting the Motorama show car ready on time, but Chevy seriously considered steel throughout most of the Corvette's harried gestation. Said engineer Ellis J. Premo at a meeting of the Society of Automotive Engineers: "At the time of the Waldorf show, we were actually concentrating on a steel body utilizing Kirksite tooling for the projected production of 10,000 units for the 1954 model year." Though a die made of Kirksite is faster and cheaper to create than a conventional die, its life is limited, and would have been unsuitable had that volume been achieved. The Kirksite dies were thus never cast.

The GRP used for the Motorama show car body was 2/10-inch thick and was hand-laid into a mold taken directly from the pre-production plaster styling model in Harley Earl's studio. GRP molding techniques were still not fully developed, and more experimentation would be needed before actual production could begin. Ultimately, improvements in process chemistry allowed the production body to be only 1/10-inch thick with no loss in surface quality or structural strength. Chevy would have to build several interim bodies as a trial, however, before it was convinced that fiberglass was feasible.

After months of frantic activity, Corvette production got underway in a small building adjacent to the Chevy plant in Flint, Michigan on the last day of June 1953. According to a much later press release, it was a day when the "division made automotive history. Amid shouted instructions and with flashbulbs popping to record the event, Tony Kleiber, a body assembler, drove a car off a Chevrolet assembly line." It was a grand accomplishment. Corvette had made the transition from dream car to road car with remarkably few alterations and in a remarkably short time. Chevy general manager Thomas Keating was on hand to emphasize the point: "This occasion is historic in the industry. The Corvette has been brought into production on schedule in less than 12 months from designer's dream to a reality tested on road and track."

Yet America's sports car was not quite "real" at this point, not quite ready for America's roads. As Keating continued: "The engineers want to keep on testing these first cars for a few thousand more miles. It may be important to Chevrolet's future plans to learn the amazing flexibility that is demonstrated

Another well-known GM Photographic scene lays out the early Corvette's major body sub-assemblies. Fiberglass was a time- and money-saver but it only complicated the hectic initial phases of production.

26

here in working out new design ideas in plastics." *Road & Track* was more succinct, noting in its August 1953 issue that "it is an open secret than the entire contemplated production is 'sold.'" That was a nice way of saying that Chevy didn't really intend to sell Corvettes, at least not just yet. Indeed, the division's General Office issued a dealer notice on July 10th listing the Corvette's wholesale net price at $2470, a delivery and handling charge of $248 and a suggested retail price of $3250. But, said the bulletin, "no dealer is in a position to accept firm orders for delivery of a Corvette in 1953."

Chevy was employing what we would now call a "controlled production start-up," and it made sense. Given the newness of fiberglass manufacturing techniques and Chevy's lack of experience, the quality of the finished product was very much in doubt. And, as always, GM was loathe to risk making a blunder in public should things not go according to plan— especially with a brand-new "image" car that had already attracted so much international interest.

Accordingly, the Corvette's initial production schedule was set at just 50 cars a month—a maximum of 300 units for the remainder of calendar 1953. All would be built the same way: Polo White exterior, Sportsman Red interior, radio, whitewall tires, black top. This way, workers would be able to concentrate on learning how to put the fiberglass bodies together without being rushed and without being distracted by trim and equipment variations. Much later, Pontiac would employ a similar go-slow approach with its mid-engine Fiero, like the first Corvette an innovative design concept with few manufacturing precedents.

Job One comes off the Flint mini-line on June 30, 1953. Shown with Tony Kleiber are Chevy assembly executive R.G. Ford and plant general manager F.J. Fessenden.

But quality was probably not Chevy's only concern. It's quite likely that, as production began, some managers may have had second thoughts about this newfangled sports car and decided it needed an extra dose of that magic elixir, publicity. Again quoting that press release on the car's history: "An estimated four million persons had seen the original Corvette at its Motorama appearances...In the fall of '53, Chevrolet sought to double this number by using the first production cars produced in Flint as dealer display attractions. Each of the eight Chevrolet wholesale regions was assigned a car to send from dealer to dealer for one- to three-day showings during the last three months of the year. In an effort to enhance the new Corvette's image as a prestige car, dealers restricted sales to VIPs in each community—mayors, celebrities, industrial leaders and favorite customers. This system continued into 1954 as Corvettes, now being built in St. Louis, began to come off the line at a faster rate."

Dealers had heard about the campaign back in July: "Only 300 of these cars can be built during the entire balance of 1953. Some of these, necessarily, will be used for further engineering and experimental purposes and many will be retained for display, publicity, and show purposes in connection with our regular regional trailer shows and exhibits around the country. In view of the fact that we have received urgent requests, both from dealers and directly from the public, totaling many times the few Corvettes available in 1953, we have not been in a position to accept from anyone or make any commitments as to delivery at retail to date."

It was probably just as well, because production problems surfaced quickly. Predictably enough, they involved the fiberglass body. Chevy described the Flint assembly line as a "miniature...its bins filled with all

the nuts and washers and trim pieces necessary for continuing production...only six chassis long but with every place... filled with additional chassis and component parts of the subsequent bodies needed to keep assembly rolling. However, the line is big enough for the initial rate of production which Chevrolet has established for pioneering in a new field of plastic bodies." Actually, the rate *had* to be slow. The body consisted of 46 separate pieces, supplied by the Molded Fiber Glass Company of Ashtabula, Ohio. To make each one, workers had to fit the various pieces into wooden jigs, then glue them up into larger subassemblies, all of which took time. Then, too, some pieces didn't fit very well together due to molding flaws, which necessitated more hand labor to correct. Not surprisingly, fit and finish

on the early Corvette bodies was quite variable, with judgments ranging from fair to excellent compared to steel construction.

Such teething problems are not uncommon in the first year of a new car design, especially if it's the first to employ some new material or engineering idea. The Corvette was no exception. And in view of the way things were going, Chevy must have been glad it had decided to use a proven chassis and running gear. Most of the body bugs would eventually be worked out, but those early months at Flint must have been a trial-and-error experience for Chevy, its workers, and its suppliers. This shows up in the makeshift use of certain minor components on the earliest production cars. For example, the first 26 rolled out the door with Bel Air wheel covers instead of the intended item,

a full disc with simulated knock-off centers. Also, a few cars lacked the Guide Y-50 left door mirror used in production through the early '60s. Meanwhile, permanent tooling was being completed in preparation for the move to Chevrolet's St. Louis facility, which would become the Corvette's home beginning with the 1954 models and running through the '81s.

Only two options were listed for '53, a recirculating hot-water heater and Delco signal-seeking AM radio. In the interest of simplicity, all the cars had them. Other standard equipment included the specified 6.70 x 15 whitewall tires, a clock, and a tachometer redlined at 5000 rpm. The latter had an accumulated engine revs counter, a feature that would be retained through 1959. The wire-mesh headlamp covers and rear li-

Opposite page: Corvette looked the same for '54, but wheel covers and other details were sorted out by now. Above: A turning point in 'Vette fortunes was the early 1954 showing of this wooden Ford Thunderbird mock-up. Left: The 1955 Mercedes-Benz 300SL, an upmarket rival.

this publicity had an unintended effect. With cars not yet genuinely available but with ads and countless stories about them appearing everywhere, some people began to get the idea that Chevy was pulling a fast one. Automotive flim-flams were nothing new, and the Tucker debacle was still fresh in the minds of many. Was this dream car still only a dream after all?

It wasn't, of course, but it would take a good many months for the Corvette to establish itself firmly in the market. In retrospect, Chevy's marketing plan backfired. It was all very well to favor VIPs and the "beautiful people" as opinion leaders. Trouble was, they didn't like the car as much as Chevy had hoped. And the growing suspicion during 1954 that the 'Vette was only a flash in the pan undoubtedly kept some buyers away, while others went searching for MGs, Jaguars, and Triumphs. The sales figures seem to bear this out. Coinciding with the transfer of Corvette production to the St. Louis plant,

cense plate cover were illegal in some states, but the owner's manual obligingly provided instructions on how to remove them.

Chevy's publicity machine worked hard to maintain the high initial interest in the Corvette during those first few difficult months after introduction. At first glance, this hardly seemed necessary—until you recall what the standard '53 Chevys looked like. The 'Vette was glamorous and exciting, and the division played it up for all it was worth. But coming right after the big pre-launch buildup,

Chevrolet announced that 1954 volume would be stepped up to 1000 units a month. However, the actual number built was only 3640—less than a third the projected total—and at year's end the division had a surplus of some 1500 cars. It wasn't long before rumors began drifting through GM corridors that the Corvette was on the verge of extinction.

It's interesting to note that the press was far kinder to the early Corvette than most of Chevy's selected opinion leaders. To be sure, both groups criticized many of the same things—the jet-age styling, crude side curtains, mongrel mechanicals, and high price were the main ones—and *Road & Track* capsulized the debate by asking, in its initial Corvette road test, "Is it really a sports car?"

But listen to what the editors had to say: "The Corvette makes a favorable impression immediately on the score of clean lines with a minimum of chrome trim. It looks like a sports car, a very modern one at that...The outstanding characteristic [is probably its] deceptive performance. Sports car enthusiasts who have ridden in or driven the car without benefit of stopwatch seem to have been unimpressed with the performance. This is an injustice, as the figures shown in our data panel prove." The key figures were 11.0 seconds in 0-60 mph acceleration, an 18.0-second average elapsed time in the quarter-mile, and a top speed just nudging 108 mph. That may sound tame by the standards of a later age, but it was hardly bad for 1954. Maurice Olley had been right.

Now for the eye-opener: "The second most outstanding characteristic of the Corvette is its really good combination of riding and handling qualities. The ride is so good that few American car owners would notice much difference from their own cars. Yet there is a feeling of firmness about the car, and none of the easy slow-motion effect of

our large, heavy sedans. The biggest surprise is the low roll angle—actually less than two of the most popular imported sports cars. The Corvette corners flat like a genuine sports car should." *R&T* also praised the easy-to-use folding top and its effectiveness in keeping out a Southern California downpour, along with the brakes and the roomy trunk.

R&T admitted that "Chevrolet may have committed some errors in presenting and merchandising a sports car," but said, "frankly, we liked the Corvette very much." *Motor Trend* was even more enthusiastic: "Chevrolet has produced a bucket-seat roadster that will hold its own with Europe's best, short of actual competition and a few imports that cost three times as much." With such favorable comments, it's amazing Chevy didn't make Corvettes available to the press sooner than it did.

Few significant changes were made on the '54s, but running changes took place throughout the model year. Tops and top irons were changed from black to tan, and gas and brake lines were relocated inboard of the righthand main frame rail. The engine carried a new-style rocker arm cover, the wiring harness was tidied up, and more plastic-insulated wire replaced the fabric variety. Engines, still built at Flint, were suffixed F54YG. The storage bag for carrying the side curtains in the trunk was changed mildly in shape and color-keyed to the interior.

This was also the first year a choice of colors was available. Pennant Blue accounted for about 16 percent of production and came with a tan interior. Sportsman Red, selling at about four percent, and Polo White, some 80 percent, were teamed with red interiors. A very small number of cars, as few as six, were painted black and also carried the red interior. Some '54 Corvette owners claim to have original factory paint in colors

other than these four, though they are not officially listed. However, paint bulletins are known listing a Metallic Green and a Metallic Bronze.

The 1953 Corvette had carried two short stainless-steel exhaust extensions that exited the body inboard of the rear fenders. It was discovered that air turbulence sucked exhaust fumes back against the car, soiling the lacquer. An attempted correction was to lengthen these and route them out below the body, but this didn't entirely solve the problem. (It would persist until the 1956 redesign, where Corvette chief engineer Zora Arkus-Duntov relocated the tips to the rear fender extremities.)

Some of the Corvette's initial inconveniences were remedied this year. For example, the original two-handle exterior hood latch was replaced by a more manageable single-handle mechanism after the first 300 or so '54s. The choke control was relocated from the right to the left

Left: The 1954 Corvette. Above: A subtle change for 1955 was the large "V" in the side script indicating Chevy's new V-8.

155 bhp—though this wasn't announced until the following year. Also, the three bullet-shaped air cleaners were ditched for a two-pot type after the first 1900 cars and through the balance of the model run. An unusual change concerned the rocker covers and ignition shielding. About 20 percent of '54 production had these pieces finished in chrome (serial numbers 1363 through 4381).

Another niggling problem concerned the top mechanism. On the early cars the main top irons had to poke through slots in the chrome moldings behind the seats and were capped with spring-loaded flippers. Beginning with serial number 3600, the top irons were redesigned with a dogleg shape that allowed them to slip between the body and the seatback. Unhappily, this led to another annoyance:

of the steering column, swapping places with the wiper switch. This eliminated the problem of having to reach across or through the steering wheel to operate the choke with the left hand while turning the ignition key with the right.

Moisture in the rear license plate recess caused its plastic cover to fog up, so Chevy threw in two little bags of a dessicant material to keep things dry.

Under the hood, a new camshaft boosted the Stovebolt's rated power output by 5 bhp—to

the top irons rubbed the upholstery. Because the preferred top-folding procedure was not that obvious, the factory took to sticking explanatory decals on the underside of the top cover.

The Corvette's price had been a sore point with critics and would-be customers. In a ploy to make the car appear more competitive, Chevy dropped the advertised base figure from $3498 to $2774 for '54. The catch was that the Powerglide automatic was now an option. Since a manual gearbox was not yet available—and since nobody wanted a transmissionless car—it's safe to assume all '54s had this $178.35 "mandatory option." However, even when all the legitimate options were added

The 1955 model in top-up configuration. Purists still chided certain Corvette features, but the lively new small-block V-8 earned critical plaudits.

in—directionals, heater, radio, whitewalls, parking brake alarm, courtesy lights, and windshield washer—the price was still about the same as before, precisely $3254.10. Unfortunately, this sleight of hand did nothing to spark sales.

The early Corvette may have had its faults, but reliability wasn't one of them. This was not a temperamental machine prone to breaking down like a Jaguar, nor did it demand the constant attention of, say, a Ferrari. Oh, there were a few quirks. The main ones were water leaks (mostly from around the top and side curtains, though the leading edges of the door openings were suspect on some cars) and synchronizing the triple carbs for smooth idle and throttle response. But these were hardly major, and Chevy issued service bulletins to cover them. The engine and running gear were

just as boringly reliable in the Corvette as they were in Chevy's everyday passenger models, which was expected but pleasant nonetheless.

By the end of 1954 the Corvette's future was looking grim. Underwhelming sales had cost it a good many supporters within GM—especially accounting types who viewed it as a white elephant and argued, no doubt persuasively, that it should be canned. The marketing was not on target so far, and neither was the car itself. Despite its description as a "sports car," it wasn't as sporty as it needed to be to appeal to buyers familiar with the performance and sophistication of European sports cars. Also, it was a specialty item and, as the days of the two-car family were yet to come, the Corvette found only a limited audience. Sports car devotees laughed at its American

eccentricities.

Things had become so bad, in fact, that MFG's Bob Morrison, who had built his business mainly on the basis of the Corvette body contract, worried he might go out of business soon. Fortunately for him, Chevy decided to use fiberglass for the bed of its 1955 Cameo Carrier pickup, which provided temporary relief.

The Corvette might have died right there had it not been for three key developments that would insure it a permanent place in the Chevy lineup. The first was introduction of Ford's new Thunderbird on September 23, 1954. Like Corvette it was a two-seater, but it was a "personal car," not a sports machine—a comfortable steel-bodied *boulevardier* with handsome lines, expected features like roll-up door glass, and a standard V-8 engine that made

it quite quick. Ed Cole was not unprepared, and his was the second key development: the brilliant new 265-cid Chevy small-block V-8.

The third stroke of luck for the 'Vette was the appearance of a 45-year-old German-trained enthusiast, race driver, designer and engineer named Zora Arkus-Duntov. Since joining the GM Research and Development Staff in 1953, Duntov had been "fiddling" with the Corvette in his spare time. He had done some racing, and knew what drivers of sporting cars demanded in their machines. He also knew how to make cars handle well, and he was appalled by the Corvette. In CONSUMER GUIDE® magazine's *Corvette: America's Only True Sports Car*, Duntov described the early model's handling problems: "The front end oversteered, the rear end understeered. I put two degrees of positive caster in the front suspension and relocated the rear spring bushing. Then it was fine; very neutral."

Those slight changes were typically Duntov. His seat-of-the-pants feel for what was right—and wrong—with the Corvette was to become legendary both inside and outside General Motors. In fact, his expertise became so respected that when it came to showdowns with management over his suggested changes, the white-haired wizard usually won. "Fiddling" with the Corvette would become Duntov's life's work for the next 20 years. Moreover, the Corvette had found another ally just when it needed all it could get.

Duntov also described what happened when the Thunderbird appeared: "There were conversations . . . about the Corvette being dropped. Then the Thunderbird came out and all of a sudden GM was keeping the Corvette. I think that Ford brought out the competitive spirit in Ed Cole." When it comes to corporate pride, nobody beats GM.

The Corvette's biggest booster

was still Harley Earl. For 1955 he had proposed a mild facelift, with a new wider eggcrate grille, similar to that on Chevy's all-new standard cars that year, plus a functional hood air scoop and dummy front fender vents. But with sales in the cellar and the high cost of tooling the '55 Chevys, there was simply no money. Lack of funds also precluded two other Earl ideas shown at the 1954 Motorama. One was a lift-off hardtop that made the 'Vette into a pretty, thin-pillar coupe. It was a natural, but it would have to wait until 1956. The other concept, a closed fastback coupe, wouldn't make production until much later with the advent of Bill Mitchell's Sting Ray generation for 1963. Interestingly, the show car was called "Corvair," a name that had been favored over Corvette at one time. It did, of course, resurface on Chevy's radical rear-engine compact of 1960. A third '54 Motorama concept was the handsome Corvette-based Nomad sports wagon. As everyone knows, this led directly to the production 1955 Nomad built on the standard passenger-car chassis. Though a few customizers would turn later Corvettes into wagons, there's no evidence GM ever seriously considered such a model for volume sale.

Though virtually unchanged externally, the 1955 Corvette was a much improved car in many respects. The improvement most welcome by car fans was Ed Cole's superb small-block V-8. It was identified discreetly enough on the outside—only an exaggerated gold "V" overlaid on the Chevrolet bodyside script. But on the road there was no mistaking a V-8 Corvette: it simply vanished—in a hurry. The 'Vette now had the power it had always needed to live up to its racy looks, and its performance became exhilarating instead of merely interesting. Everyone approved. In fact, the V-8 became so popular that probably no more than six or

seven of the '55s had the old Blue Flame six. Unfortunately, production bottomed out this year: only 674 units. But better times—much better times— were just around the corner.

The Corvette V-8 was basically the same as the passenger-car engine, sharing its block and 3.75-inch bore and 3.00-inch stroke. However, the 'Vette got a special camshaft that boosted output by 15 horsepower, to 195 bhp at 5000 rpm. Induction was by a single Rochester four-barrel carburetor. Final drive gearing with the still-standard Powerglide automatic remained at 3.55:1, though the V-8's rpm limit was higher and the tach was accordingly redlined at 6000 rpm. The V-8 took about 30 pounds off the front end compared to the six, so weight distribution improved slightly to 52/48 percent front/rear. Other changes adopted with the new engine were 12-volt (instead of six-volt) electrical system, automatic choke, and electric (instead of vacuum-operated) wipers. Foot-operated windshield

washers were reinstated as standard. As with other '55 Chevys, the transmission's vacuum modulator was eliminated so that kickdown was now governed solely by speed and throttle position. The V-8 was sold as a separate package priced at $2909, versus the six-cylinder car's $2799 suggested retail figure.

Another round of running changes occurred during the model year. Shortly after production began, the Pennant Blue color option was replaced by Harvest Gold teamed with contrasting green trim and dark green top. It proved a popular combination. Corvette Copper metallic was added to the chart, and Gypsy Red replaced the previous Sportsman Red. The latter came with white vinyl interior and red saddle stiching, tan carpet and top. The first cars off the line retained the frame mounting holes for the six-cylinder engine, though these were later plugged once engineers realized they'd probably never be needed again. The X-

brace for the underside of the hood was replaced by a lateral brace, necessary to clear the V-8 engine's air cleaner. Workmanship continued to improve. Despite their thinner section, the '55 bodies were smoother and tighter, and overall fit and finish was tidier.

Very late in the run a three-speed manual gearbox— Corvette's first shift-it-yourself transmission—appeared as an optional alternative to Powerglide. Only a small number of cars got it, making it a collector's find today. The shifter, a small chrome stick topped by a purposefully large white ball, sprouted from the floor, and was sealed with a vinyl boot surrounded by a bright rectangular plate that showed the shift pattern. It also held a small ashtray. Final drive gearing was shortened up to 3.70:1.

The new V-8 made a tremendous difference in the Corvette's performance. In its July 1954 test, *Road & Track* reported 0-60 mph acceleration of 8.7 seconds—2.3 seconds quicker

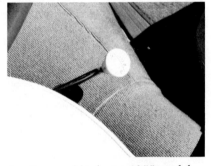

An all-around look at a 1955 model with the new three-speed manual gearbox added as a late season option. Restyle proposed for this year would have seen eggcrate grille insert and a raised trunklid lifted from the fastback "Corvair" experimental.

than its initial six-cylinder test car—a quarter-mile time of 16.5 seconds—1.5 seconds better—and a 119-mph top end—a 12-mph gain. And this with the higher-geared automatic. *R&T* also found improved fuel economy: 18-22.5 mpg, a 2-3 mpg benefit. The editors also commented on the V-8's greater smoothness and quietness, rated the brakes "more than adequate for ordinary usage" (but not for racing), and noted that "riding

qualities are excellent and directional stability at high speeds is near-perfect." Despite all this, they concluded that the Corvette "comes so close to being a really interesting, worthwhile, and genuine sports car—yet misses the mark almost entirely." Some people, it seemed, were simply embarrassed about liking the Corvette.

America's sports car had so far been a series of false starts. It had been launched with high

hopes—perhaps too high—and had attracted much attention. But its basic design was as debatable as Chevy's VIP-only approach to marketing it, and the Corvette had yet to attract a significant following. Nevertheless, the first-generation years were important if for no other reason than what they taught Chevy *not* to do. The lesson was blindingly simple: sports cars are a different breed, appealing to a different sort of buyer, and must be designed and sold accordingly.

Chevy learned quickly. The Corvette was about to be transformed.

Somewhere during 1953-55, the original idea for America's sports car got lost. Instead of a small, fun-to-drive car with a base price about the same as a Chevy sedan's, what emerged was a puffy, well-equipped showboat priced at close to $3500, about $1500 more than one of the low-priced three. Certainly the Corvette was not something many college kids could afford—unless they went to Yale and their name was Vanderbilt. And unfortunately, Chevrolet's initial VIPs-only marketing policy had not been the right one. Many doctors, lawyers, and other influential folk just didn't take to the car. It wasn't very comfortable, especially with those side curtains, and it wasn't very fast, either. It certainly wasn't like other American cars, but it wasn't exactly a European-style sportster. Like a lot of other cars that had come before it (and many that have disappeared since) the Corvette had found no real niche—and, so far, no real market.

Corvette had indeed come very close to extinction in 1954 because of GM management's reservations about the car's sales

1956-57: REPRIEVE AND RENAISSANCE

Corvette styling and performance took a giant stride with the totally redesigned second-generation 1956 model. Shown is an early fuel-injected 1957 example.

potential. The attempt had been made, the car had been built; why not let the Corvette rest in the history books? The reason: Thunderbird. Ford's two-seater arrived at the height of the perennial battle between the industry's two leading companies.

For 18 months after mid-1953, Ford had engaged in production warfare, and swamped its dealers with more cars than they could ordinarily sell. Ford was determined to become number one—even if it almost had to give cars away. GM naturally responded in kind, and the production blitz was on. Both corporations took to the media. Each claimed victory, made counterclaims, and then accused the other of fudging the statistics. Nobody really knew who came out on top for 1955, but the competition was enough to change GM's attitude toward the Corvette. The two-seater field would not be left to the Thunderbird, which Corvette advertising soon referred to as a "scaled-down convertible."

And America's sports car was about to grow up. Even as Corvette sales languished and dealer inventories mounted, Chevrolet was conjuring up an engi-

neering miracle that would forever alter the course of high-performance history. It was, of course, the 265-cid small-block V-8, today one of the most revered American engines ever built. It did for Chevy what the flathead V-8 had done for Ford two decades earlier, and together with Clare MacKichan's deft new styling created the first of what we now call the "classic" Chevys—fast, roadable, affordable machines of timeless appeal. It was a case of "power to the people," and it worked: the '55 Chevys were simply sensational and they sold like crazy. The small-block would also be instrumental to the Corvette's renaissance, which really began with the 1956 models.

The new V-8 was a huge step forward from the old "Stovebolt" six that had powered Chevys since the 1930s. It weighed 40 pounds less, but delivered 40 more horses in its initial form. Designed with modern combustion chambers and unique stamped-steel rocker arms, it would rev happily to 6000 rpm or more, and because of its eager character it was quickly dubbed the "rat motor" by its fans. As installed in the 1955 Corvette it had peak power output of 195 bhp at 5000 rpm, with maximum torque of 260 lbs/ft peaking at 2800 rpm. Further development would take those numbers far higher in just a few short years.

To alter Chevrolet's time-honored image as a builder of mundane people-movers to performance-car specialist, the division's new chief engineer, Ed Cole, knew he would need a V-8 engine. His predecessor, Ed Kelley, had toyed with a V-6 and

a 231-cid V-8, both of which Cole rejected. But he didn't have much time to consider alternatives. When all the development phases were accounted for, there would be just 15 weeks in which to design a new powerplant for the 1955 model line. With the help of Kelley and motor engineer Harry Barr, he made it.

"I had worked on V-8 engines all my professional life," Cole said later. "I had lived and breathed engines. Barr and I were always saying how we would do it if we could ever design a new engine. You just *know* you want five main bearings—there's no decision to make. We knew that a certain bore/stroke relationship was the most compact. We knew we'd like a displacement of 265 cubic inches, and that automatically established the bore and stroke.

Harley Earl's original proposal for '56 Corvette styling was approved quickly and with few changes. Front "face" was further emphasized and the elliptical "cove" indentations relieved the slab-sided look of the 1953-55 design.

And we never changed any of this. We released our engine for tooling direct from the drawing boards—that's how crazy and confident we were."

Of course, even a ground-up engine had to be designed within certain parameters. Since it was intended for Chevrolet, the new V-8 had to be relatively inexpensive to build and efficient in operation. It need not be a poor engine—and it was anything but—yet it had to be a model of simplicity and production economics, which it was.

One of the outstanding features that made the 265 such a watershed development was the lack of a common rocker shaft. Each rocker arm was entirely independent of the others, so that deflection of one had no effect on the others. Each was assembled over a valve stem and pushrod, retained by a fulcrum ball and lock nut. Regardless of whether mechanical or hydraulic valve lifters were used, the valves were lashed by turning the lock nut. In addition, this arrangement reduced reciprocating weight, which allowed higher rpm and cut down on raw materials. The intake manifold provided a common water outlet to both heads. The heads were die-cast with integral valve guides and were completely interchangeable. The valvetrain design was shared with that year's slightly larger Pontiac V-8, which was designed along the same lines.

A short stroke meant short connecting rods—just 5.7 inches center distance for a stroke ratio

41

of 1.9. Pressed-in piston pins eliminated the slitting of the rod and the need for a locking bolt. Five main bearings of equal diameter carried maximum loads in their lower halves. "By reducing the maximum oil film loads through omission of the oil groove in the lower half," noted the *SAE Journal*, "the capacity of the main bearings is increased approximately 100 percent, and wear is reduced." More weight was saved by circulating the oil through hollow pushrods, providing splash lube to the rockers and valve stems. This meant that separate and costly oil feeder lines were unnecessary.

Further details included "autothermic" pistons with three rings, slipper-type aluminum units with a circumferential ex-

Practical lift-off hardtop was a new-for-'56 option, and derived directly from a 1954 Motorama show car. Convertible top was reworked for a smoother appearance.

es allowed Chevrolet to reduce overall crank length. A chart of torsional vibration showed very low peaks without sharp points throughout most of the range; adding a harmonic balancer eliminated the vibration.

The exhaust manifolds were routed near the top of the cylinder heads, with exhaust passages pointing upward and out, and the entire length of the ports was water-jacketed. "This minimizes the transfer of distortion loads back to the valve seats," the *Journal* noted, "and dissipates heat uniformly from the valve area." Chevy switched to a 12-volt electrical system for the 265 that provided more efficient generator output, better starter-motor operation, and adequate voltage for the power-plant's higher compression.

Because the new engine had better heat rejection properties than the Blue Flame six, a smaller radiator could be used, which reduced frontal radiator

pander for the single oil ring providing axial and radial force to control oil burning. Instead of alloy iron, the crankshaft was made of pressed forged steel because of its higher specific gravity and modulus of elasticity. Newly developed forging process-

area. The lighter V-8 was in keeping with the concept of the '55 Chevy, which was, as Ed Cole said, "built around lighter components."

In 1974, *Special-Interest Autos* magazine asked Cole if there was any major breakthrough in the 265's design. Possibly, Cole said, it was "when we decided to make the precision cylinder blocks—the heart of the engine—by using an entirely different casting technique. We used the green-sand core for the valley between the bore. That is, for the 45-degree angle center, 90 degree total, we used a green-sand core to eliminate the dry-sand core, so that we could turn the block upside down. We cast it upside down, so the plate that holds the bore cores could be accurately located. This way, we could cast down to $5/32$nds jacketed walls."

In the same *SIA* article, Harry Barr pointed out certain advantages of the Chevy 265 over the '55 Pontiac V-8: "...Their design was heavier than ours. But they developed a sheet metal rocker arm that we thought had possibilities. It hadn't been decided yet, but we jumped into that, and gave it to our manufacturing group. They determined that they could make stamped rocker arms with no machining whatever—just a metal stamping.

"We also lubricated it differently from Pontiac...with the oil coming up through the tappet, up through the hollow pushrod into the rocker arms, then over to lubricate both the ball and the pallet of the rocker arm...These were all new ideas, and very good as far as automation was concerned. You never had to screw anything—just press these studs in."

Actually, the 265 was Chevy's second V-8, the first being the disastrous 1917 design. But this one was near-perfect. Overhead valves, high compression, light weight, and oversquare dimensions (3.75 x 3.00) made it efficient and powerful. Some 43 percent of 1955 Chevys were equipped with it—amazing for a make which hadn't offered a V-8 within recent memory. Horsepower for the 1955 passenger models was 162, or 180 with "Power Pack" (four-barrel Rochester carburetor and dual exhausts, available on all except wagons). In basic form, the 265 was both more potent and more economical than the rival Ford 272 or the Plymouth 260, and it outsold them easily. It had plenty of development room, too. For 1956, Chevrolet offered 205- and 225-bhp versions using four-barrel and dual four-barrel carbs, respectively.

The small-block V-8 was greeted with high enthusiasm, and its performance gain was as welcome in the Corvette as it was in the standard Chevys. Even so, the "buff" magazines weren't all that enthusiastic about the 1955 Corvette. *Road & Track* snidely suggested that the car might fill a need "for an open roadster the lady of the house can use as smart personal transport." Not exactly the macho image the Corvette would later embody. *R&T* did concede the V-8 car's much improved go, but there

were nagging complaints about lack of creature comforts, especially those pesky side curtains. Clearly what America's sports car needed was a more up-to-date body to match its hearty new small-block soul.

Harley Earl had been taking Corvette criticisms to heart—he did, no doubt, still consider it "his" car—and had been working on that very thing. On February 1, 1955, just as Ford's Thunderbird was beginning to be seen in serious numbers, Earl had all but finalized a new Corvette body design in a full-scale clay model. With some minor trim changes it was shown to GM management in mid-April and was approved on the spot.

The 1956 Corvette and the near-identical '57 model are considered by many today as the epitome of Corvette styling, at least before 1963. Even 30 years later this design looks fresh despite bearing a few typically Fifties cliches, and—the real test—it still draws admiring glances. It is one of those rare automobiles that looks good from any angle.

The new styling also looked very fresh in 1956, of course.

But it was, in essence, only an evolution of the original concept, with all the bad elements removed and the good ones emphasized. Perhaps the best thing about the 1953-55 Corvette was its definite "face." The "eyes" had been covered by wire screens, and surely "veils" wouldn't do on a "man's" car, so the headlamps were moved forward out of their little recesses and the mesh stone guards were thrown away. The "nose," essentially the large, round Corvette emblem, was given more prominence on the '56. The original "mouth" and its magnificent "teeth" were rightfully left alone.

The rear was just as tastefully revised. The jet-pod taillamps and the finny extended fenders were trimmed away, and new taillights were artfully "frenched" into the remaining sheetmetal. The license plate, which had occupied an indentation in the trunklid, was moved down between trim bumperettes. This left a smooth, gently curved deck, with the matching fenders protruding slightly, but only slightly, either side. Thankfully, Earl's staff resisted an impulse to have the

dual exhausts exit through the sides of the rear fenders, routing them instead through the rear bumper guards.

The 1956 Corvette was among the last GM production cars designed in Detroit before the design department was moved to the new Technical Center in Warren, Michigan. In a styling sense, the roots of the second-generation design were in three 1955 Motorama show cars, the Biscayne and two exercises dubbed LaSalle II. The Biscayne was a compact four-door hardtop painted light green, with a color-keyed interior. Appearance features included headlamps mounted inboard, parking lights placed in the fenders, and a grille made up of a series of vertical bars. Air scoops were positioned under the windshield on the cowl, and the passenger compartment floor was level with the bottom of the frame. The LaSalle II name appeared on a hardtop sedan and a roadster. Also carefully color-keyed, both had prominent vertical bar grilles and displayed a styling feature the '56 Corvette would inherit: a concave section on the bodysides. This swept back from the front wheel wells, imitating the "LeBaron sweep" of the classic period. The greenhouse used on the lift-off hardtop that would be a new option for '56 was taken directly from the show car prototype displayed at the 1954 Motorama.

The bodyside "coves," as they were nicknamed, gave the '56 Corvette a styling personality all its own. They also helped to relieve the slab-sided look that had led some people to refer to the 1953-55 design as the "plastic bathtub." Even surrounded by a narrow band of chrome—one of the few last-minute trim changes made to the production prototype—the sculptured bodysides were still extremely clean and attractive. The only gimmicky pieces on the entire '56 design were the small dummy scoops perched on the tops of the front fenders near the windshield. They were supposed to be functional (for cowl ventilation) but cost considerations ruled that out. The redesign also extended to a more integrated convertible top, tighter-looking and with a rounded curve at the rear that echoed the car's rear quarters. The new factory hardtop also had rounded contours, and its rear side windows afforded much better visibility compared to the soft top. The new-for-'56 wheel covers tried to simulate genuine knock-off hubs. They, too, looked a bit contrived, but they remained standard issue until 1963 and have become some of the best-known hubcaps in history.

Like many enduring designs, the '56 Corvette didn't just look better than its predecessor, it worked better, too. The fussy side curtains were gone forever, replaced by proper roll-up door glass. And power window lifts were available at extra cost, for heaven's sake. There were also genuine outside door handles for the first time, thus ending once and for all the hassle of reaching in through the side curtains on a rainy day. The interior was much as before, except for revised door panels to go with the wind-up windows. A waffle-pattern vinyl was used over a delicately sculptured armrest that blended into the door shape. A transistorized signal-seeking radio was another new feature, though it was not yet engraved with the words "Wonder Bar."

Under the hood there was more good news. The small-block V-8 returned not as an option but as standard. And it had even more muscle: 210 bhp at 5200 rpm with single four-barrel carburetor and higher 9.25:1 compression. That was 15 horsepower more than the '55 unit—and a big improvement over the 155-bhp Blue Flame six of just two years earlier. Special camshafts, a cast-aluminum intake manifold, and dual four-barrel carbs were available to up output to 225-240 bhp. Premium fuel was mandatory, of course. The special cam, developed by Zora Duntov, helped raise torque on the 225-bhp powerplant to an impressive 270 lbs/ft peaking at a highish 3600 rpm.

Running gear was beefed up

45

to handle the new Corvette's extra power. The standard gearbox was now the three-speed manual, and its clutch was strengthened with 12 heat-treated coil springs to replace the former diaphragm-type spring. Final drive with the manual was still 3.55:1, but a 3.27:1 cog was offered to improve off-the-line punch. Powerglide automatic now truly shifted to the options column, where it listed at $189.

With all this, the Corvette ceased to be an also-ran. It was now a genuine screamer with svelte styling and all the amenities any sporting motorist could ask for. Where the '54 car had made the 0-60 mph sprint in about 12 seconds, the '56 with manual gearbox and standard axle ratio could do it in 7.5 seconds and run the standing-start quarter-mile in 16 seconds at 90-plus mph. It was capable of near 120 mph right off the showroom floor. There was still some question about handling and stopping, however. Brakes—cast-iron drums with 158 square inches total lining area—were a weak point. They "faded into oblivion," as one tester said after a hard application. Handling was good, but understeer was ever-present. The steering, however, was quick: just 3.5 turns lock-to-lock. Weight distribution, at 52/48 percent front/rear, was nearly perfect for a sports machine. In all, road behavior was greatly improved on the '56 compared to earlier Corvettes. America's sports car had come of age.

Duntov believed that a race-winning image was vital to the Corvette's sales, and he would be proven correct. As Carroll Shelby, the man whose cars would become the Corvette's arch enemies in the Sixties, said later, "Racing was the thing that actually saved the Corvette." Duntov's high-lift cam had been developed specifically with an eye to competition. If the 'Vette could set a few speed records and win some races, Chevy advertising would do the rest.

Accordingly, the Duntov cam

was slipped into a modified '56 Corvette specially prepared at GM's Arizona proving grounds. The car was then shipped to Florida, where Betty Skelton and John Fitch would drive it at the Daytona Speed Weeks trials in January. The goal was 150 mph. Although beach conditions weren't favorable, the car managed an impressive two-way run of 150.583 mph with Duntov at the wheel.

Development work continued, and the addition of a new, high-compression head raised power output on the 265 V-8 to a claimed 255 bhp—nearly the magic one horsepower per cubic inch. In the actual Speed Weeks trials the 'Vette was beaten in the production standing-mile contest by a T-Bird driven by Chuck Daigh and prepared by ex-racer Pete DePaolo. However, the 'Vette was the fastest car in the modified class, and Fitch won it with a two-average of 145.543 mph.

By September, ads touting this feat had appeared in the "buff books," boasting that, "the 1956 Corvette is proving—in open competition—that it is America's only genuine production sports car," a swipe at the *boulevardier* Thunderbird. *Road & Track,* which had been generally favorable to the Corvette since its inception, described the '56 as "good to excellent compared to other dual-purpose sports cars."

Dual purpose? At long last, the critics seemed willing to admit the Corvette qualified as such. The new V-8 had made all the difference.

One person who agreed was Dr. Richard Thompson, a Washington, D.C. dentist. In the spring of 1956, he began campaigning a Corvette in the Sports Car Club of America's C-Production class. With the help of Duntov and others, he won the C/P championship that year. It was another boost to the "competition-proven" image that Duntov and Chevy managers were after, and the ads were quick to capitalize on it. One proclaimed "Bring on the hay bales!" Said the copy: "The new Corvette, piloted by Betty Skelton, has established a new record for American sports cars at Daytona Beach. But that's only the start. Corvette owners may enter other big racing tests in the months ahead—tests that may carry America's blue-and-white colors into several of the most important European competitions." And indeed they did. One modified Corvette made a decent showing at Sebring '56, finishing ninth in the grueling 12-hour run. And at Pebble Beach, a Corvette finished a strong second behind a Mercedes-Benz 300SL.

The new styling, greater power, and a modest but growing reputation as a track competitor to be reckoned with proved to be a winning formula. For the 1956 model year, Corvette production rose from 674 units to 3467, a nearly fivefold increase. Clearly America's sports car was, so to speak, on the right track. It's instructive to remember, though, that the Corvette was not making any money for Chevrolet at this point. It couldn't with that kind of volume, improved though it was. Of course, it was generating a great deal of favorable free publicity, and division managers undoubtedly knew that was

1956-57 Corvette two-toning involved the bodyside coves and was a popular option. Shown is the '57.

worth something, even if they were hard pressed to put a price on it. But Chevy could afford the losses. More importantly, management was willing to sustain them now that the Corvette had proven itself in the showrooms as well as on the circuits.

On the surface, the 1957 Corvette looked like the '56, but there were several significant under-the-skin changes. There was a larger V-8, a new four-speed gearbox introduced at mid-year, and—as Chevy boasted—up to one hp per cubic inch from the new "Ramjet" fuel injection system.

The larger V-8 was simply the Chevy small-block with a bore punched out by about 1/8-inch to 3.88 inches. Stroke was kept at 3.00 inches. The result: 283 cid. This engine was also offered in Chevy's facelifted 1957 passenger cars, where it produced 185 bhp at 4600 rpm in base form. For the Corvette, the standard engine was a four-barrel version rated at 220 bhp at 4800 rpm. Optional were two twin four-barrel setups offering 245 bhp at 5000 rpm and 270 bhp at 6000 rpm. All three of these ran 9.5:1 compression. So, too, did the lesser of the two "fuelie" engines, with 250 bhp at 5000 rpm. The top mill was a high-compression (10.5:1) unit with that rousing 283 bhp produced at 6200 rpm.

Fuel injection was certainly a concept alien to major U.S. automakers in the mid-Fifties, and the story of how this one came to be is an interesting one. Chevy had struck a blow with its small-block V-8 in 1955, but that was old news by 1957. Both Ford and Plymouth had fresh new models ready, while Chevy would have to field a facelifted version of its two-year-old passenger-car platform. As spring turned into summer during 1956, Chevy brass was concerned that its '57s would be overshadowed by the new competition. Since speed had already helped sales once, more of the same seemed in order.

This was the rationale behind

enlarging the V-8, of course. But what else could be done? More carburetion was clearly not the answer, what with dual quads already available. Supercharging? Possibly, but its high heat and extra internal stresses were considered undesirable for a make that had built its reputation on reliability. So, engineers took a page from the European performance book: fuel injection. With the '57 model year closing fast, a development team quickly got down to work. The key men involved were Ed Cole, who by this time had been promoted to Chevrolet general manager; Harry Barr, who succeeded Cole as Chevy chief engineer; John Dolza, head of the Engineering Staff's fuel injection project; and Zora Duntov.

Duntov had been working on the FI system since early 1956, and under difficult circumstances. In April he had taken a Corvette hardtop around the GM proving grounds for tests. The car had no seatbelts and was running with experimental disc brakes. At a good rate of speed, Duntov lost control, went off the track, and hit a drainage ditch. He was thrown upward into the roof, and the impact broke a vertebra in his back. For the following six months he worked standing up, confined by a body cast. He had to work in that condition because the fuel injection project was a top priority, and he knew the system would have to be ready in time for inclusion on the 1957 production cars.

With almost superhuman speed, the engineers put together a system that appeared to be relatively inexpensive to manufacture while still promising significant power gains. The only problem was, when the injected engine was dyno-tested it didn't produce any more power than the dual-carb engine. But Cole was a believer in fuel injection, and he wanted nothing less than to offer it across the entire '57 Chevy line. Higher stakes were involved here than

the relatively insignificant Corvette, for he saw the "fuelie" as the answer to winning in stock car racing. And as "Win on Sunday, Sell on Monday" was still a cherished marketing maxim in those days, Cole didn't intend for Chevy to come up short. So, it was back to the lab and more feverish sessions. Ultimately, Chevrolet and GM's Rochester carburetor division came up with a workable system that not only increased top-end output but also spread that power over a wider rpm range.

The 283 "fuelie" was carefully developed for good reliability. Mechanical valve lifters substituted for hydraulics when FI was specified. Longer-reach spark plugs with metal deflection shields were used to protect wiring and plug caps from manifold heat. The top of the block was a thicker casting to prevent cylinder wall distortion through over-tight hold-down bolts. Fuel passages were tapered, increasing in cross-sectional area toward the inlet ports and in the "ram's horn" exhaust manifold to provide better scavenging and increased volumetric efficiency. There was a new distributor, with breaker points directly above the shaft bearing to help reduce fluctuations in the gap setting. And the front and intermediate main bearings were 0.063-inch thicker.

Though made by GM's Rochester carburetor division, the Ramjet fuel injection system was designed almost entirely by the Engineering Staff, simplified for production by Barr and Duntov. It consisted of three main components: fuel meter, manifold assembly, and air meter, replacing intake manifold and carburetor. The unit took in air first, then injected fuel directly into each intake port for mixing. The amount of fuel used was very precisely controlled, again for better volumetric efficiency and mileage. Cold-weather starting and warmup were improved,

continued on p. 65

Corvette for 1955. Chevy's new small-block V-8 marked a turning point in 'Vette fortunes.

This page, top: GM publicity shot shows plain, domed disc wheel covers used on early-production 1953 Corvettes. Above: A head-on look at the Motorama show car. Nose script was deleted on production version. Right: The '54 roadster with the three Corvette show cars displayed at that year's Motorama. From top: the fastback "Corvair," the "Nomad" wagon, and the experimental hardtop. Opposite page, top: "Corvair" show car would have made a nice running mate for the roadster, but it was doomed by poor sales in the 'Vette's early years. Center: Corvette "parades" like this were staged in several cities during 1954 to convince people production was fully underway. Bottom left and right: '54 Motorama show car predicted optional lift-off hardtop that arrived in production for 1956.

Opposite page, top and center left: Colors other than Polo White became available on the 1954 models for the first time. Note spinner wheel discs, which had been standardized by now. Crude side curtains and make-shift folding top on the early 'Vettes didn't appeal to many buyers. Center right and bottom, this page left and below: Though outwardly very similar to the 1953-54 models, the '55 Corvette was the first available with Ed Cole's brilliant new 265-cid small-block V-8, which gave the car the performance to match its racy looks. All but a handful were so equipped, identified by the exaggerated "V" in the bodyside name script.

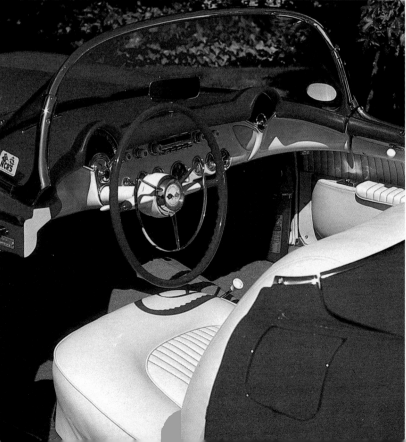

Both pages: A close-up look at a beautifully restored 1955 example shows the early Corvette's winning style, which still looks good 30 years later. Metal top boot (near left) was a Harley Earl show car idea. Cockpit was cozy but trunk surprisingly roomy for a sports car. Dash and instrument layout (above) was chided by purists, but high-winding small-block V-8 (left) was a revelation for 1955 in a car the Corvette's size.

Center spread: This Corvette cavalcade was staged in San Francisco to introduce the
1957 models. It's still a mouth-watering sight for high-performance lovers.
Above: A total restyle for 1956 completed the 'Vette's transformation from poseur to
powerhouse. Crossed-flag emblem in bodyside "coves" identified 283 "fuelie" V-8.

Both pages: Though typically
'50s in approach—two-toning
and more chrome—the Corvette's
1956-57 restyle was stunningly
effective and has stood the test
of time well. Highlights of
Harley Earl's work included
smoother rear fender shaping,
frenched-in taillights, bumperette-
mounted exhaust outlets, a
more rounded rear deck, and the
attractive bodyside indentations, called "coves" by 'Vette
fans. Roll-up door glass enhanced
interior comfort, as did the
newly optional lift-off hardtop.
Three-speed floorshift manual
gearbox was standard for '56,
and helped make the most of the
225-bhp V-8 with 9.25:1
compression.

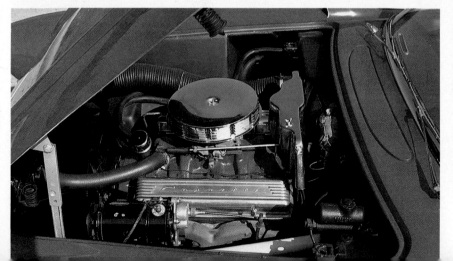

Both pages: The owner of this gorgeous '57 with the optional hardtop and potent fuel-injected 283 V-8 says it's definitely not for sale. This is one of only 240 cars equipped with the Ramjet injection out of total '57 production of 6339 units. Off-the-line go was electrifying, with 0-60 mph in 6.5 seconds.

Opposite page, top left: Twin chrome "backstraps" marked the heavier, more glittery 1958 Corvette, the only model so adorned. Opposite page, bottom, and this page: Chevy removed some of geegaws on the '59 edition, which continued into '60 with near-identical styling. Four-lamp front was retained, but the '58's washboard hood was planed smooth. Though more powerful, these 'Vettes weren't as agile as the 1956-57 models.

Above: Restyled "ducktail" rear gave the '61 Corvette a fresh look. Below: The 1960 model with optional hardtop.

continued from p. 48

and the unit by itself boosted output by about 5 bhp compared to the twin four-barrel carbureted engine. Chevrolet claimed that FI eliminated manifold icing, and reduced the tendency to stall when cornering hard.

A special two-piece aluminum manifold casting was used on 283 V-8s equipped with fuel injection. The upper casting contained air passages and air/fuel metering system bases, while the lower casting made up the ram tubes and covered the top center of the engine.

A major engineering development is never simple—or easy. And although the introduction of Ramjet injection was a milestone in Chevy's history, bugs were inevitable. At the Daytona Speed Weeks, for example, a fuel cut off problem was encountered in hard acceleration, creating a flat spot in response. Fuel nozzles, too, required attention. They were extended further into the air stream to prevent them from absorbing too much heat and causing rough idling.

Despite such problems, fuel injection gave Chevy the performance magic it needed. Ironically in view of all the advertising hoopla, the high-compression fuelie actually delivered somewhere around 290 horsepower, better than "1 h.p. per cu. in." This engine, which carried the code designation "EL," should not be confused with the "EN" version, which was strictly for racing and was sold as a package complete with column-mounted tachometer and a cold-air induction system. Chevrolet warned potential purchasers that the EN option was not for everyday driving. And to be sure they got the message, Chevy refused to supply EN-equipped Corvettes with heaters.

Perhaps more important than fuel injection, but certainly no less heralded, was the May 1957 arrival of a four-speed manual gearbox, Regular Production Option (RPO) 685, priced at $188.

It was essentially the three-speed Borg-Warner unit with reverse moved into the tailshaft housing to make room for a fourth forward speed. The ratios were close at 2.20:1, 1.66:1, 1.31:1, and 1.00:1. Positraction limited-slip differential was available with three different final drive ratios—3.70:1, 4.11:1, and a stump-pulling 4.56:1—to help you get the most out of the new engines and gearbox.

The experts still complained about handling and braking deficiencies, which Chevrolet solved with RPO 684. This was a $725 "heavy-duty racing suspension" package comprising heavy-duty springs, front anti-sway bar, Positraction, large-piston shock absorbers with firmer valving, a faster steering ratio that reduced turns lock to lock from 3.7 to 2.9, and ceramic-metallic brake linings with finned ventilated drums. This together with RPO 579E (the 283-bhp V-8) produced a race-ready car you could buy right off the showroom floor. And race it did. Two production examples finished 12th and 15th at Sebring 1957, the first GT-class cars across the line. The 12th place car, driven by Thompson and Gaston Audrey, ended up some 20 laps ahead of the nearest Mercedes-Benz 300SL. The larger engine bumped the 'Vette into SCCA's B-Production category, but it didn't matter: Dr. Thompson promptly took the championship.

In almost any form, the '57 Corvette had absolutely staggering performance. Walt Woron of *Motor Trend* tested the 250-bhp fuel-injected version and whizzed through the 0-60 mph sprint in just 7.2 seconds. The 283-bhp cars were even more incredible. *Road & Track's* four-speed example with 4.11:1 final drive clocked 5.7 seconds in the same test, breezed through the quarter-mile in 14.3 seconds at better than 90 mph, and sailed on to a top end of 132 mph. Another *MT* car with the 283-bhp engine, dual exhausts,

special cam, and solid lifters reached 134 mph, and Woron wasn't convinced that it was fully extended at that. *Sports Cars Illustrated* found its Corvette "the fastest accelerating genuine production car [this magazine] has ever tested." *R&T* headlined its test report quite simply: "Add fuel injection and get out of the way."

Corvette advertising continued to push the performance image, with headlines such as "Lesson from Lombard Street," and "FI=1 H.P. per CU. IN. x 283." The former showed a 'Vette winding down San Francisco's serpentine Lombard Street hill and stressed the car's handling abilities. The second ad with its cryptic headline referred to "the formula...for the most significant advance yet recorded in American sports cars. It means: The 1957 Corvette V-8 with fuel injection turns out one horsepower per cubic inch of displacement—and there are 283 cubic inches on tap!

"To anyone who knows cars," the ads continued, taking direct aim at sports car enthusiasts, "that fact alone is a warranty of significant engineering. But the driver who has whipped the Corvette through a series of S-turns really knows the facts of life: This sleek powerhouse handles! Matter of fact, you can forget the price tag and the proud names—no production sports car in Corvette's class can find a shorter way around the bends!"

Undoubtedly, 1957 marked the Corvette's arrival as a sports car respected as much by the cognoscenti as the kids on the street. One European writer said: "Before Sebring, where we actually saw it for ourselves, the Corvette was regarded as a plastic toy. After Sebring, even the most biased were forced to admit that the Americans had one of the world's finest sports cars—as capable on the track as it was on the road. Those who drove and understood the Corvette could not help but reach that conclusion."

There was now no question about Corvette's survival. Model year production rose to 6339 for '57. Of these, only 240 were equipped with fuel injection. Thunderbird's exit from the two-seater market for 1958 (which Chevrolet foresaw well in advance) brightened hopes that production would exceed 10,000. Despite a dreadful 12 months for the industry in general, that goal was nearly reached. The exact count was 9168.

But even with increasing sales, an action was taken which would have a serious impact on the Corvette, a decision that would turn the factory racing effort into a clandestine operation. That decision came on June 7, 1957 from the Automobile Man-

The 283-bhp 283-cid V-8 headlined the '57 Corvette engine chart, but only 240 fuel-injected examples were built.

ufacturers Association. The AMA's Board of Directors voted unanimously to adopt a two-point resolution which called on its members to cease immediately all sponsorship and assistance for race cars and race drivers. GM President Harlow Curtice was among those voting to adopt the measure, which effectively banned all factory-supported racing activities.

Racing, said the AMA, "over-sells speed and power and under-sells safety." The National Safety Council, which had been pushing for just such an edict, hailed it as a "big step toward a safer America." The AMA further urged drivers and buyers to "evaluate cars in terms of useful power and ability to afford safe, reliable, and comfortable transportation, rather than in terms of capacity for speed." References

were made to Detroit's performance-oriented ad campaigns, such as Chevy's "The Hot One's Hotter" and Ford's counterclaim "It Cools Off The Hot One." An unnamed industry executive was quoted as saying racing victories were costing the companies millions and "the whole thing got to be a monkey on everybody's back."

Reported the *New York Times:* "The last major race in which an American stock car participated was the Grand Prix of Endurance, held March 23 at Sebring. Two Corvette Supersport test cars were in the 5.2-mile race, which was won by a 4.5-liter Maserati. The Corvettes were the latest creation of the Chevrolet Division of General Motors. They were described as the first real threat to European sports car racing supremacy."

The AMA decision fell like an unsprung chassis on Corvette enthusiasts and Duntov, who said it was "a tremendous shock." Naturally, the ban put an end to official factory efforts to develop the experimental Sebring SS into a competitive sports racing car (see Chapter 12), but Duntov was caught holding the bag: he had already entered SS cars for Le Mans.

Among those who worked on Chevrolet's factory-supported racing efforts there was a period of stunned disbelief following the AMA edict. Like Duntov, they were in "shock." Yet in apparent defiance of the resolution, many continued to work directly with the racers. Duntov himself saw to it that anyone who wanted a racing Corvette could have one by checking the right options, and he began working on further refinements. And despite the ban, Duntov continued to appear "casually" at numerous races. Other GM executives could also be spotted in or near the pits at many events.

While the factory did downplay competition in keeping with the AMA edict, Duntov's enthusiasm for the Corvette continued to be quite evident. The decision would not diminish his desire to make the Corvette a winner, and it certainly would not disconnect his busy telephone, over which he reportedly dispensed priceless technical advice and (it is said with a chuckle) "back-door" parts to promising racers on occasion.

With the brilliant second generation, the Corvette became America's sports car in the true sense. It was now unquestionably a genuine race-and-ride machine in the time-honored tradition, yet it was also just as unmistakably an American machine in its styling, performance, and sheer visceral appeal. It had taken four long years, but the Corvette could no longer be accused of trying to imitate anything from Europe. And from here on, it would never be confused with anything from Europe.

1958~60: TURNING THE CORNER

Even as the 1956-57 Corvette was winning plaudits both on and off the track, Chevy was hard at work on a successor. In fact, at one point an entirely new closed coupe model was envisioned for 1958 introduction. This design was heavily influenced by the Mercedes-Benz 300SL Gullwing coupe that had drawn so many rave reviews from the motoring press. The major departure was unit body/chassis construction instead of the traditional separate body and frame. Styling highlights included pontoonlike fenders, four headlights and a fastback roofline. There were no gullwing doors as on the 300SL, but to ease entry/exit there were hinged roof sections that flipped up when a door was opened, harking back to several earlier Motorama cars. The front end featured two large air inlets which, in modified form, would later find their way into production.

The shift to unibody construction and the use of aluminum instead of fiberglass as a structural material involved more money than Chevrolet was willing to spend, however. Despite the fact that Corvette sales were up substantially for 1957, the overall market and the economy as a whole were down. Not only that, but fuel injection alone had not been able to stem the challenge from Ford, which had nipped Chevy in model year production. Management decided to expend more of its resources for a total remake of the standard Chevrolet for 1958 and, instead of a completely new Corvette, enthusiasts were left with what appeared to be a facelifted version of the second-generation design.

As Corvette facelifts go, this was not one of the most successful. Chevy stylists seemed to take some cues from the aborted unibody design and some from Harley Earl's SR-2 prototype racer. When it was all put together, though, the result was about as glitzy a Corvette as has ever borne the name. The extra-clean lines of 1956-57 were hoked up with a row of simulated louvers on the hood, fake air scoops outboard of the grille and in the side cove areas, and twin chrome bars running down the trunklid. Additionally, the '58 got quad headlights, quite the rage that year, surrounded by chrome bezels that met bright strip moldings atop the front fenders. Stylists considered replacing the distinctive grille teeth with a mesh insert, but that idea was abandoned. The Corvette did lose some of its teeth, however—

Though 1960 saw few changes, the year was notable because Corvette production exceeded 10,000 units for the first time.

69

now down to nine instead of the previous 13. Another external change was considerably more positive. The bumpers, which had previously been attached to the body, were now secured to the frame via long brackets, providing significantly greater protection for the already tough fiberglass body.

The Corvette also put on extra bulk for '58. For the first time the car tipped the scales at more than 3000 pounds (3085 to be exact), about 200 pounds more than the '57 model. The new body added almost 10 inches of overall length, and width was up by a little more than two inches. A final exterior change was a shift to acrylic lacquer paint.

The car was just as heavily revised inside, but here the revisions were far more successful. Stung by criticism of the original instrument panel layout, the interior designers made sure that every dial save the clock was placed right in front of the driver. Dominating the new board was a large semicircular 160-mph speedometer, and perched in front of it on the steering column was a round 6000-rpm tachometer. The customary four minor gauges were strung in a row either side of the tach. A vertical console dropped down from the dash center and housed the heater controls, clock and the "Wonder Bar" signal-seeking radio. A grab bar in front of a semicircular cutout made up the passenger's side of the dash. A locking glove compartment was installed between the seats just below the release button for the integral convertible top tonneau. The door panels were restyled, with reflectors added at armrest level for safety when opening the doors at night, and a "pebble-grain" upholstery fabric was used.

The Corvette was bulked up and hoked up for 1958, though its performance remained vivid and handling remained agile. Cockpit was revamped with a more orderly gauge layout and passenger "panic" handle.

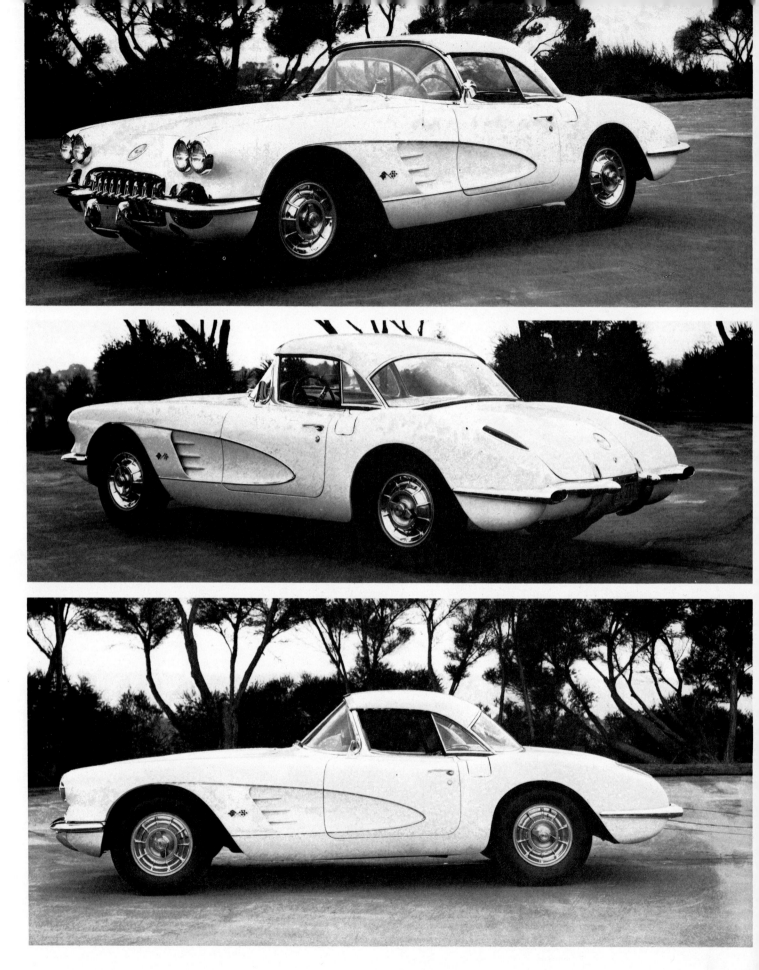

Left: Though it didn't appear so, the '58 Corvette body was completely different from the 1956-57 shell, being some 10 inches longer and 2.3 inches wider overall. Right: The '58 was unique in using these chrome decklid moldings.

All the new hoke and heft concealed an important fact about the '58: it had even more power and was still quite quick. The most potent engine in the lineup remained the high-compression fuelie 283 with Duntov camshaft and cool-air intake, advertised at 290 bhp at 6200 rpm, 7 bhp up on the '57 unit. A similar arrangement with dual carbs returned at 270 bhp, still on 9.5:1 compression. Still, the majority of buyers did not indulge themselves with such exotica. Nearly half of the more than 9000 cars sold were equipped with the base 230-bhp single-carb engine. Barely 1000 purchased the 290-bhp unit, and only about 500 bought the 250-bhp injected setup with the milder cam. Rounding out the choices was the 245-bhp version from '57, with four-barrel carb and mild 9.5:1 compression.

Speed freaks could still order a near race-ready Corvette straight from their local Chevy dealer. And the prices were certainly right. The hottest engine setup ($484.20), Positraction ($48.45), heavy-duty brakes and suspension ($425.05), four-speed trans ($188.30) and metallic brake linings ($26.90) added little more than a grand to the reasonable $3631 base price. With these goodies, the 'Vette was more than a match for Jaguars, Porsches, and other machines for supremacy in sports car performance, and even exotics like Ferraris were not out of reach.

The car magazines were mostly positive about this year's me-chanical changes. Stephen F. Wilder, writing for *Sports Cars Illustrated*, said, "We were able, in a very short time, to discover how the 1958 Corvette behaves in nearly every conceivable road situation. It may be summed up as 'very well indeed.'" The optional four-speed gearbox got special praise: "It is at least the equal of any box we've ever tried, not only with respect to the suitability of ratios to the engine performance, but the smoothness of the synchromesh brings to mind the old metaphor about a hot knife and butter." With the 250-bhp injected engine, *SCI* reported a 0-60 mph time of 7.6 seconds, and top speed was right around 125 mph.

Sam Hanks, writing for *Motor Trend,* tested four versions of the '58, and came up with some interesting comparative statistics (see below).

It would appear that for economy as well as speed, fuel injection was the way to go. It's doubtful that many buyers chose the FI engines for their fuel efficiency, though.

It was no secret that Hanks liked the 'Vettes: "Any way you look at it, I think the Chevrolet designers ought to be proud of the style of the Corvette and their engineers should be proud of a fine sports car. It's real great to have an American-built production car that's available to the public as a combination cross-country, city traffic, competition sports car. I'm impressed."

Despite the somewhat overblown styling, the '58 impressed the buying public, too. For the first time in its brief life the Corvette turned a profit for Chevrolet. Model year production was well up on 1957 levels, totaling precisely 9168 units. This

	230hp 4bbl.	245hp 2x4bbl.	250hp FI	290hp FI
0-60 mph (sec.)	9.2	7.6	7.6	6.9
¼-mile (sec.)	17.4	15.9	15.6	15.6
Top speed (mph)	103.1	112.0	113.6	118.7
Fuel consumption (mpg)	12.9	12.9	14.9	13.9

made the 'Vette one of the few domestic models to score a sales gain in that recession-ridden season, a fact usually ignored by automotive historians. (The only other '58 models registering gains instead of losses were the Rambler American and Ford's new four-seat Thunderbird.)

Critics have tended to scoff at the '58 Corvette, feeling that Chevy was beginning to move away from the race-and-ride concept as quickly as it had embraced it with the 1956-57 design. Yet the styling changes and the added bulk were appropriate for the late Fifties and, although they detracted some from the car's agility, they didn't do irreparable damage. As noted, the heavy-duty handling package was still available, and the 'Vette remained one of the quickest volume-production cars in the world.

Thanks to the efforts of Jim Jeffords and his "Purple People Eater," Corvette again won the SCCA's B-Production crown in 1958. Jim Rathmann and Dick Doane took the GT class at Sebring that year, and veteran Ak Miller won the sports car class at the Pike's Peak Hill Climb

with a time of 15 minutes, 23.7 seconds. But none of these triumphs were mentioned in Corvette advertising.

Chevy soft-pedaled performance in the wake of the AMA's "anti-racing" edict, with the emphasis on such things as the "silken cyclone of a V-8," the "beautifully compact body," and "a chassis that clings to the road like a stalking panther." Headlines asked "What's as effortless as a Corvette?" and "What happened to gravity?" (the latter a lead-in to a spiel about the car's handling virtues). A somewhat nationalistic tone was sounded in one ad titled "Corvette Does America Proud," in which a two-tone roadster was shown at the famous Pebble Beach, California Concours d'Elegance surrounded by an impressive array of vintage automobiles. Another pictured a roadster running at speed as a sailplane floated overhead, and made the obvious comparisons with florid phrases like this: ". . . acceleration as easy as a giant's stride, a liquid grace in motion, steering as sharp and precise as a scalpel. In plain truth, a Corvette travels in a way no other American car

can equal." Apparently it was okay to talk about performance as long as you didn't actually use the word—or publish race results.

The "cover-it-with-chrome" period in Corvette styling would prove to be mercifully brief. In fact, it is to Chevy's credit that it began cleaning things up on the mostly unchanged follow-up model. As *Road & Track* noted: "The appearance of the 1959 Corvette has been improved by the simple expedient of removing the phony hood louvers and the two useless chrome bars from the decklid." The editors also observed that "trim on Corvettes, like all GM cars, is extremely well executed whether it is functional or mere decoration." Interior alterations were equally minor, but just as welcome. They included repositioned armrests and door handles, reshaped seats providing better lateral location in cornering, and the addition of a shelf under the passenger grab bar for extra small-items stowage space. A new option was

Main external changes for '59 were no decklid "backstraps" or simulated hood louvers. New rear trailing arms helped control axle tramp.

first-time availability of sun-visors. Instruments were given concave rather than flat lenses to cut down on reflections, and a T-handle lockout was added to the manual transmission shifter to prevent accidental engagement of reverse.

A major mechanical change for 1959—the only one—was the addition of trailing radius rods from the frame to the rear axle. These helped to counteract rear axle windup brought on by the extra torque of the more powerful engines. Powertrain choices remained the same.

Despite its carryover design the 1959 Corvette was a very desirable car. The cleaner body and strong powerplants combined to make a very nice package that could blow the doors off most any machine around. Many examples could shoot through

the quarter-mile in less than 15 seconds and 0-60 mph times of less than eight seconds were typical. By now, "fast car" and "Corvette" had become synonymous.

Auto writer Ray Brock used

nothing but superlatives in his 1959 test report: "Handling and brakes are plenty good in stock trim. There is absolutely no need for any of the heavy-duty racing extras unless the car is intended for sports car racing."

Corvette powerteams for '59 were the same as for '58, with 245 up to 290 bhp on tap from five versions of the 283 small-block. List price shot up by over $200 this year to a suggested $3875 basic.

Road & Track's reaction was only slightly less exuberant: "Taking everything into consideration, the Corvette is a pretty good car. It probably has more performance per dollar than anything you could buy, and parts are obtainable without sending to Italy, Germany or England." The 290-bhp fuel-injected powerplant got the most praise from *R&T*. The magazine reported 6.6 seconds in the 0-60 mph dash, with the quarter-mile coming up in 14.5 seconds at 96 mph. Top speed was listed at 128 mph with 4.11:1 final drive.

In its April 1959 issue, *Motor Trend* compared a Porsche 356 Convertible D to a '59 'Vette, and came up with 0-60 mph figures of 7.8 seconds for the American machine and 15.2 seconds for the German one. The Corvette also beat the Porsche in the quarter-mile—by more than four seconds—and was also a big winner in the handling test. Only in fuel economy was the Porsche superior: 24.5 mpg to 14.3. Of course, this was something of an "apples and oranges" matchup, as *MT's* report concluded: "If getting performance from a precision-built, small-displacement engine is intriguing, then the Porsche is the answer. If you like the idea of having one of the world's fastest accelerating sports cars, then pick the Corvette. . . .The truth is that both are excellent buys. They're sturdy, reliable, comfortable and, above all, fun to drive. What more can you ask of a sports car?"

The *R&T* test had concluded with a broad hint that big changes were in store for the Corvette: "The changes. . .in the last six model years are not so great as we think will come about in 1960. We predict that this will be the year of the big changes for Corvette, and most of them for the better."

R&T was both right and wrong. Chevy had indeed been working on a new and far more radical concept for America's sports car. This was the so-called Q-model, a much smaller and lighter two-seater with very streamlined styling and an independent rear suspension likely derived from the transaxle being prepared for the rear-engine Corvair compact. How close the Q-car came to production is known (see Chapter 5), but it's quite possible this was nothing more than a smokescreen to divert attention from the Corvair project. In any case, Chevy's new small car arrived on cue for

1960, but a new Corvette didn't. The first real break with the original concept was still several years away.

Corvette sales scored only a fractional increase for model year 1959, rising to 9670 units. This was okay considering the economy had yet to recover fully from the recession, but it was hardly the sort of volume that would justify spending for anything more than a mild facelift—let alone a completely new design like the Q-model. Accordingly, the 1960 Corvette was almost indistinguishable from the '59. Sales, however, pushed past the 10,000 mark for the first time (by 261 units) on the strength of new options and even more horsepower.

The high-compression fuelie 283 still stood at the top of the engine chart, but an even tighter 11.0:1 squeeze and solid lifters boosted power output to 315 bhp, still at 6200 rpm. A second version with hydraulic lifters for easier maintenance produced 275 frisky ponies at 5200 rpm. Because of this gain, Powerglide automatic was no longer offered with this engine: it simply couldn't stand the extra torque. The carbureted engines remained much as before. The tamest was the 230-bhp V-8 with single four-barrel, followed by the dual-quad 245-bhp hydraulic-lifter version and the solid-lifter 270-bhp 4x2 unit.

Mechanical refinements for 1960 comprised new aluminum clutch housings on all manual-transmission cars for a savings of 18 pounds, and aluminum radiators were specified for cars running the Duntov cam. A power-saving thermostatically controlled cooling fan was a new option, as was a larger 24-gallon fuel tank ($161.40) for extended cruising range. Unfortunately, the RPO 684 heavy-duty suspension package disappeared, a victim of the AMA edict, but Chevy compensated both literally and figuratively by fitting a larger-diameter front anti-roll bar and a new rear bar as stan-

dard equipment. This, plus an extra inch of rear wheel rebound travel, provided a slightly smoother ride and more neutral handling response. Despite the shift in marketing emphasis toward smooth, no-fussing touring, there were still plenty of performance goodies available. The 315-bhp engine cost a formidable $484.20, but "Positraction" was a more palatable $43.05, the four-speed gearbox continued at $188.30, ceramic-metallic brake linings (RPO 687) were a steal at just $26.90 (sintered-iron linings were also offered as RPO 686), and 6.70 x 15 nylon tires (5.5 x 15s were standard) cost only $15.75.

Road & Track reported that the 1960 "high-performance engines (intended primarily for racing) are given very specialized treatment. In addition to customary inspection, many critical parts are now routed through a special department for a very painstaking examination of dimensions, flaws, finish and quality of materials. Included in this group are valves, rocker

arms, pushrods, pistons, connecting rods, and crankshafts. Just a few years ago, Chevrolet would have laughed at such a suggestion. This certainly shows how serious they are about the sports-car side of the business."

Another indication came in an interesting "experiment" that never quite got going. Early in the model year, Chevy offered cylinder heads cast from a high-silicon aluminum alloy as an option for the two fuel-injected engines. Based on the design first tried with the Corvette SS race car from Sebring '57, they had the stock 11.0:1 compression but featured improved intake and exhaust breathing. The high silicon content of these heads prefigured the block construction of the four-cylinder Vega engine of a decade later, which proved just as troublesome. The aluminum heads were fine in theory but tended to warp if the engine

Third generation soldiered on for 1960 with new 275- and 315-bhp "fuelie" V-8s. Radical Q-model envisioned for '60 was scratched.

overheated, and there were quality control problems with the castings. The option was quickly withdrawn, but Duntov and company were far from finished with aluminum-head engines.

By now, the Corvette's abilities on both road and track were widely acknowledged with all due respect. America's sports car reached a new competition pinnacle in 1960, when sportsman Briggs Cunningham entered a three-car team in the big-engine GT class at that year's 24 Hours of Le Mans. The lead Corvette, driven by Bob Grossman and John Fitch, scored a respectable eighth place overall finish. Karl Ludvigsen, writing in *Sports Car Illustrated*, commented on the revised chassis with this: "A tentative conclusion might be that the new setup will be good for all-around use and slower [race] courses..." but "many [owners] might usefully remove the rear anti-roll bar when trying for best results on fast tracks." Ludvigsen undoubtedly summed up the feelings of many by saying, "As before, the Corvette for 1960 is a formidable performer."

Even so,'Vette fans, perhaps more than any other group of enthusiasts, have always been interested in what's just around the corner. And it was in 1960 that rumors about an entirely new Corvette started circulating. Lending credence to this were the track appearances of a dramatic machine called the Stingray. It was being campaigned privately by GM stylist William L. Mitchell, and this plus the fact that Mitchell had just succeeded Harley Earl as head of GM design convinced many 'Vette watchers that here surely was the shape of things to come.

They would, of course, have to wait a while. The winds of change were definitely blowing, but there was still a lot of life left in the third generation.

The 1960 'Vette at what looks like a quiet lake. Photo was actually taken at the GM Tech Center in Warren, Michigan.

1961~62: CHANGING OF THE GUARD

There's an old saying in baseball that sometimes, the best trades are the ones you *don't* make. Perhaps the same can be said of automobile model changes. In the back rooms at Chevrolet during the late '50s and early '60s, there was certainly no shortage of ideas for new and different Corvettes. But, in the end, very few changes were made in the basic theme of the fiberglass sports car through its first 10 years of existence. One only has to look at the 1962 Corvette side-by-side with the '53 to see their close design similarity. But that is not to say that Chevrolet didn't at least consider making changes or that new model proposals were completely unappealing.

Perhaps one of the most appealing of the 'Vettes that never were was the so-called Q-model. Although the Corvette has always been a bona fide sports car and a unique entity in the Chevy line, it has always shared some parts with the division's higher-volume models—a practice that has enabled the Corvette to be one of the real values in its field. In this respect the Q-model would have been no different from the production 'Vettes that had gone before. The difference would have been in the parts the Q-car borrowed.

In the late 1950s, when planning for 1961-62 was underway, Chevrolet contemplated a radical

Bill Mitchell's "ducktail" for '61 mated well with Harley Earl's 1958-60 front. It was seen earlier on several show cars.

departure from its traditional design philosophy: a separate line of cars featuring a rear-mounted transaxle and all-independent suspension. The transaxle, an unusual piece of hardware in itself, sported integral inboard brakes. With it, engineer Zora Arkus-Duntov could at last realize his dream of a Corvette with fully independent rear suspension. Not only that, but the transaxle was slated to be made in both manual and automatic versions, some with an integral starter motor. Before anyone could say exoticar, Chevrolet engineers and stylists were drawing up Corvette proposals around this "Q" transaxle. One of the cleanest looked like a slimmed-down version of what would eventually become the 1963 Sting Ray. It too was a "split window" coupe, but in this case the split was at the front. Two pieces of glass were wrapped around from the sides to join at the car's longitudinal centerline, thus forming both windshield and the side windows. Other design aspects were just as radical: dry-sump lubrication, unit body/chassis construction, and pop-up hideaway headlights. The Q-model was quite light and, with its all-independent suspension, at least promised good handling.

But even as this new "European-inspired" Corvette was being developed, car sales as a whole remained in the doldrums brought on by the 1958 recession. With the market showing few signs of strong recovery—and with the compact rear-engine Corvair already a top priority—Chevy abruptly halted work on the Q-model. A similar transaxle setup with swing-arm rear suspension did appear in production for the 1961 Pontiac Tempest—which proved to be one of the most wicked-handling cars Detroit ever built. In retrospect, then, perhaps Corvette lovers can breathe a sigh of relief that the Q-model never materialized, innovative though it would have been.

That sigh of relief was entirely justified by what actually did emerge for 1961-62. As the final developments of the original 1953 concept, these were arguably the best Corvettes since the "classic" 1956-57 models. There was fresh new styling courtesy of a mild but effective facelift created by Bill Mitchell and a welcome change from the somewhat chrome-laden look of the 1958-60 period. Also, there were numerous mechanical modifications aimed at both better performance and improved running refinement. The result was a brace of Corvettes that almost qualified as all-new, which is why many enthusiasts tend to consider these cars as a distinct generation.

Externally, the most pronounced change for 1961 was a completely new rear-end treatment lifted virtually intact from Mitchell's Stingray racer and also seen on his XP-700 show car. The latter had a certifiably bizarre front end, with a large loop bumper/grille protruding well forward of the quad headlights set above it. But the rear portion on both cars had a very

The new rear-end contour visibly altered the '61 Corvette's profile. Other alterations included a mesh grille and the first use of four taillamps on a 'Vette. This would be the last year for the contrasting color insert on the bodyside coves and for the 283-cid version of Chevy's small-block V-8.

Chevy public relations issued
many rear-angle press photos
to emphasize the '61 model's
curvy new tail. Besides a
fresh new look, it gave the
car some 20 percent more
luggage space. Despite their
absence in these early press
pictures, sunvisors were now
standard equipment.

simple flowing shape that just happened to mate well with Harley Earl's production 1958 front-end design. A bonus of the new aft section, which was quickly dubbed the "ducktail," was that it increased luggage space by perhaps 20 percent. Highlighting it were twin taillights on either side of the central license plate recess and a modest longitudinal creaseline running down the trunklid through a large round Corvette medallion. Simple chrome bumperettes bracketed the license plate frame, and for the first time the Corvette's dual exhausts exited below the body, rather than through it or the bumper as in prior years. Up front, the basic four-lamp nose was retained but considerably cleaned up. The chrome headlight bezels were now body color, and the trademark vertical grille "teeth" were jettisoned in

favor of a fine, horizontal-mesh insert that had been under consideration for several years. The round medallion that had traditionally announced the 'Vette was replaced by a crossed-flags symbol and separate letters spelling out the car's name. The 1961 Corvette was also the last of the breed available with a contrasting color for the bodyside "cove" indentations and, at just $16.15 additional, most buyers ordered it.

Other options on the '61 included a heater, outrageously priced at $102.25 over the suggested $3934 base figure. Air conditioning, power steering and power brakes weren't available, but you could order a "Wonder Bar" signal-seeking AM radio, whitewall tires, Positraction limited-slip differential, and the all-important four-speed manual transmission. More than 7000 lusty souls, nearly three-fourths

of all Corvette customers for the year, paid the $188.30 asking price for the four-speed. Electric windows and a Rube Goldberg-like power top were offered, and the standard equipment list was bolstered by windshield washers, sunvisors, a temperature-controlled radiator fan, and a parking brake warning light.

Mechanically, the '61 'Vette retained the basic running gear used the year before, but there were a few fairly significant changes. One of the most important was substitution of an aluminum radiator for the previous copper-core unit. The new radiator offered not only 10 percent more cooling capacity but also weighed half as much as the 1960 assembly. Side-mount expansion tanks were added as a running change during the year. Engine choices were basically carryovers. Chevy's renowned 283 small-block V-8 was offered

in five versions ranging from the mild 230-horsepower, single-carburetor unit to the positively wild 315-bhp fuel-injected mill. In between were two four-barrel setups, one single and one dual, rated at 245 and 270 bhp, respectively. There was also a tamer version of the "fuelie" with 275 bhp. Again the standard gearbox was the familiar manual three-speed, now available with a wider choice of axle ratios. Powerglide automatic and the four-speed manual returned as extras. Powerglide was not listed with the three hottest engine choices and, as mentioned, most buyers opted for the four-speed over the base manual. That proved to be a good choice,

because the four-speed came encased in aluminum for the first time, effecting a weight saving of 15 pounds.

Inside, the '61 had no major changes except for a narrower transmission tunnel, which added much needed room in the close-coupled two-passenger cockpit. Four interior color schemes were available: black, red, fawn and blue.

Even with the mildest 283 and Powerglide, the 1961 Corvette was a fast little car by any standard. "Buff" magazine testers recorded 0-60 mph acceleration of just 7.7 seconds for this powerteam, better than that of a current Ferrari 308GTS (which, incidentally, goes out the door

for about $60,000). A fuel-injected/four-speed car knocked another two seconds off that time, making it one of the fastest cars in the history of street racing. Top speed with Powerglide was listed at 109 mph, limited mainly by transmission gearing. The close-ratio four-speed car lacked the long-legged overdrive ratio of most modern five-speed manuals but, even so, many of the fuel-injected and 4x2 carbureted models could see the far side of 130 mph.

Though Corvette still lacked an independent rear suspension like some of its more expensive European rivals, that didn't seem much of a factor on either street or track. Testers for the

and a single four-barrel carburetor. In fact, after 1961 the super-trick but troublesome twin four-barrel carburetion went out the window altogether, and a single four-barrel Carter instrument was used instead. In the 340-and 360-bhp engines, peak power speed was a screaming 6000 rpm, quite high for a pushrod mill, while in the 250- and 300-bhp versions it was 4400 and 5000 rpm, respectively. Powerglide automatic was available only with the latter two, and was treated to a significantly lighter aluminum housing this year.

The added go-power made more stopping power a virtual necessity. Accordingly, sintered-metallic brake linings appeared on the Corvette option list for the first time, and brought a notable improvement in fade resistance.

Though the '62 Corvette's engines were new, its styling wasn't. The quad-headlight body had been around since 1958 and was beginning to look a bit dated, even though Chevy stylists had by now removed most of the original design's worst excesses. In fact, quite a bit of brightwork disappeared on this final verison, making it the cleanest yet. One obvious alteration was removal of the chrome outline around the bodyside coves. The reverse front fender air scoops lost their triple chrome accent spears in favor of more conservative ribbed aluminum appliqués. And to emphasize this more cohesive look, the contrasting color insert for the coves vanished from the options sheet, so there were no factory two-tone '62s. Other styling elements were similarly updated. The chrome mesh grille introduced the previous year was painted black, the background of the trunklid medallion also went black, and the optional whitewalls were now significantly slimmer than the "wide whites" of yore. The only place where decoration was added was the rocker panels, now adorned with ribbed anodized-aluminum moldings.

The '62 Corvette marked the end of an era for America's sports car, a changing of the guard. Its design was finalized long before the car actually appeared because Chevy stylists and engineers were already hard at work on the completely re-engineered body and suspension ordained for '63. Yet the '62 did introduce the first of the new Sting Ray engines, the versatile 327, and thus bridged the gap between the old and the new. The fiberglass body panels and the X-braced frame both harked back to the first '53s, yet thanks to Duntov the car had long since shed its pedestrian origins. The '62 Corvette was faster, handled better, looked neater, and was significantly more modern than any of the earlier models, yet somehow managed to retain much of the charm of the original roadster concept. As an example of its transitional character, the '62 was the first Corvette with a heater as standard equipment and the last not available with factory air conditioning or power brakes even as options. It was also the last Corvette to have an external opening trunklid.

Whatever the '62 was or wasn't, it was certainly a star on the street, strip and track. The new power and torque of the bigger 327 engine resulted in truly ferocious 0-60 mph and quarter-mile acceleration. In fact, the car magazines routinely reeled off quarters in 15 seconds or less at trap speeds of about 100 mph or more. Equipped with the stiffer competition springs, it was an excellent production-class racer. The Sports Car Club of America's A-Production champion in 1962 was Dr. Dick Thompson, who would go on to greater glories with later versions of the plastic-bodied sports car. Even with only minor modifications the Corvette was a serious competitor. Don Yenko took SCCA's B-Production title that same year.

Meanwhile, Corvette was scoring in another kind of race more important to GM managers: the sales race. The company sold 14,531 of the '62s compared with 10,939 of the '61s. Corvette had turned the profit corner back with the 1958 model, but it was now beginning to show a sizable return on investment, no doubt to the relief of supporters like Duntov, Cole, and Mitchell, who kept the faith even before the car became profitable.

All in all, the 1961-62 Corvettes were a satisfying and successful conclusion to the first chapter of Chevy's great sports car experiment. Now it was time for a new chapter, the "all-new" Corvette that had been widely rumored for the previous two years. The Sting Ray was on its way, and the automotive world would never be the same again.

1963-67: THE SENSATIONAL STING RAY

In the May 1963 issue of *Motor Trend* magazine, staffer Jim Wright reported: "For the first time in its 10-year history the Corvette...is in such demand that the factory has had to put on a second shift and still can't begin to supply cars fast enough." He went on to state that customers were having to wait 60 days for dealers to fill orders and that no one would discount or even offer much of a trade-in allowance.

The object of all this interest? The 1963 Corvette Sting Ray. As the first completely new edition of America's sports car since the original, it was both a revolution and a revelation. In addition to the traditional roadster, Chevrolet fielded a beautiful new grand touring fastback coupe. Both not only looked sensational but had the speed and agility to match. To say the Sting Ray was an instant hit is an understatement: for the model year, Corvette production soared to 21,513 units, a striking 50 percent gain over the record-setting 1962 total. As the first of an entirely new line, the '63, especially the coupe, has since become the most coveted single Corvette model apart from the 1953 original. For 'Vette fans and many partisan critics, it remains a landmark in American automotive design.

The Sting Ray hit the market with a flying start and a look that seemed straight out of the future, but its basics had already been in place for several years. In fact, its origins probably go back as far as 1958, when William L. Mitchell took over as head of the GM Styling Staff on Harley Earl's retirement.

Like his predecessor, Mitchell considered the Corvette "his" car, his personal pet project. The 1960 model was his first challenge, and he got Bob McLean to assist him. McLean, remember, had been largely responsible for the original 1953 Motorama Corvette. Here he devised a fastback coupe with peaked fenders, a long nose, and a short, cropped tail. While the look met with general approval at GM, the chassis and drivetrains Zora Arkus-Duntov proposed for the new envelope were considered too expensive for the Corvette's

Below: The Sting Ray coupe for 1965. The emblem above the fender vents signifies fuel injection, the last time this item would appear in production until 1982. The fuelie small-block was rated at 375 bhp that year. Above: Hood vents on the first 1963 Sting Rays were imitations of the functional ones on the racing Stingray.

intended market. As noted in the previous chapter, a completely new design was put on the back burner, and the production 1960 Corvette emerged as simply a refined carryover of the 1958-59 package. But McLean's work would not be forgotten.

Much of the eventual production Sting Ray design came directly from Mitchell and one of the "bootleg" projects he carried on without GM's formal approval. The experimental Corvette SS that had made the assault on Sebring in 1957 had taught Duntov much about chassis design, and Mitchell had bought the "mule" development car from that effort. He wasn't about

Left and below: Building the '63 Sting Ray split-window coupe. Total production was 10,594. Below left: A Sting Ray clay model in Cal Tech wind tunnel testing.

to let this car die, and he spirited the chassis away to his "Studio X" special projects area. There he designed a brand-new body, put it on the mule chassis, and took it racing, ostensibly as a private entry.

Thus was born the "Sting Ray Special," as it was initially titled, financed by Mitchell with a little help from his friends. Though it never placed first, Dr. Dick Thompson, the "flying dentist," made a strong showing against many better-backed European competitors, placing high enough in the standings to win the SCCA's national C-Modified championship in 1959 and again in 1960. But it wasn't so much the Stingray's track performance as its beauty that earned widespread attention. It never ran as a "Corvette" or under the GM flag, of course. But it looked suspiciously like a GM product—

almost *too* complete for a racer. Some observers began wondering whether it wasn't really a sneak peek at the next Corvette. The basic shape made a favorable impression on the public— enough to provide strong impetus for the shape of the next-generation production model. Thus, the eventual 1963 styling was rendered more or less a *fait accompli* many months before the formal design program was started. By working outside the GM system, Mitchell accomplished what he probably could not have achieved by working within it.

Meanwhile, planning for future Corvettes was proceeding, and at least four different approaches were pursued during 1958-60. One was the so-called Q-Corvette, begun in 1957 as a spinoff from the radical rear-engine Q-series sedans proposed for 1960 (see Chapter 5). This program envisioned a smaller Corvette with independent rear suspension plus coupe bodywork with lines not unlike those of Mitchell's racer. The effort got as far as a steel-body prototype before the sedans were shelved. This rendered a separate Q-Corvette much too costly in view of projected sales, so it, too, was shelved. A second effort involved use of some Q-model componentry for a rear-engine 'Vette based on the powertrain of the Corvair compact. This progressed to a full-scale clay with taut, two-seat open bodywork featuring crisply creased bodysides leading into a beveled nose and tail. Two engines were proposed, the Corvair flat-six and the 'Vette's usual V-8. Duntov liked the idea, but costs again proved prohibitive.

A third idea was a major reskinning for the third-generation 1958-59 platform. Interestingly, this proposal, a possible 1962 development, featured Mitchell's Stingray-inspired "ducktail" rear end in virtually the same form as it actually appeared for 1961. The front end was something else: a low-set rectangular open-

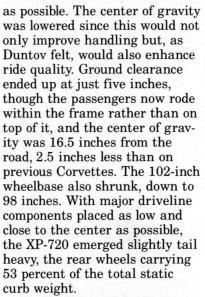

The '63 Sting Ray coupe's divided back-light was controversial, but it makes this a highly sought-after collectible today.

ing surmounted by bulging front fenders and flanked by quad headlights recessed under curious jutting "eyelids." All things considered, it's probably just as well this one didn't make it.

What did make it was the fourth effort, begun at Styling near the end of 1959. Given the experimental project number XP-720, it would lead directly to the production 1963 Sting Ray. According to Duntov, the overriding goals for this project were "better driver and passenger accomodations, better luggage space, better ride, better handling and higher performance." As was usually the case with Duntov's projects, the "higher performance" part had higher priority.

The chassis was entirely revamped and—shades of 1952—the passenger compartment was placed as far back

as possible. The center of gravity was lowered since this would not only improve handling but, as Duntov felt, would also enhance ride quality. Ground clearance ended up at just five inches, though the passengers now rode within the frame rather than on top of it, and the center of gravity was 16.5 inches from the road, 2.5 inches less than on previous Corvettes. The 102-inch wheelbase also shrunk, down to 98 inches. With major driveline components placed as low and close to the center as possible, the XP-720 emerged slightly tail heavy, the rear wheels carrying 53 percent of the total static curb weight.

The old X-braced frame went by the boards in favor of a ladder-type design with five crossmembers. This was chosen to ensure better torsional rigidity, an important consideration

because of the minimum 300 bhp initially envisioned for the XP-720. The independent suspension that Duntov insisted on would increase lateral stress on the frame in hard cornering, thus requiring the extra torsional strength. At one point, though, frame stiffness was found to be more than the engineers needed. While it might help roadholding, it would exact a penalty in ride harshness. A compromise was struck for production, providing more than adequate frame stiffness plus the desired ride characteristics. It was also less costly to build, no doubt an overriding concern given the expense involved in switching to an independent rear suspension.

In fact, cost was the reason GM management used in at-

continued on p. 113

The dramatic lines of the 1963 Sting Ray are evident even in this unusual overhead perspective.

This page and opposite page top: Arguably the nicest-looking of the "four-lamp" generation, the 1962 Corvette introduced the enlarged 327-cid version of the Chevy small-block that would be the basis for Corvette power over the next five years. It was initially offered in four versions with rated horsepower ranging from 250 to 360 bhp, the latter being the fuel-injected engine. Opposite page bottom: Built on the "mule" chassis left over from the 1957 Sebring car, Bill Mitchell's Stingray racer directly inspired 1963 production styling. It toured the show circuit in this form after its successful but brief competition career in 1959-60.

Both pages: Perhaps the single most collectible Corvette model ever produced—aside from the 1953 original—the dramatic 1963 Sting Ray "split-window" coupe remains a styling sensation even after 20 years. The divided backlight was dropped on the '64s.

Both pages: This "dynamic duo" for 1963 marked the first time Corvette buyers had a choice of body styles. Despite the arrival of the dramatic new coupe, the roadster would score more sales through the end of the Sting Ray generation. As before, a lift-off hardtop (shown immediately below) was an extra for the open model. Besides Bill Mitchell's curvaceous new styling, the 1963s carried a number of Corvette firsts, including independent rear suspension, curved door glass, and no external trunklid. Engine choices were a carryover from 1962, but improved front/rear weight distribution yielded better ride and handling. Handsome knock-off cast-aluminum wheels (shown opposite page top) are a collector's find today.

Opposite page and this page, top: Hard to believe, but 1963 Sting Ray roadsters like this restored specimen sold new for $4037 basic. Above: GM publicity shot emphasizes the futuristic lines of the '63 Sting Ray roadster.

This page: Vanity plate reflects the understandable pride of the owner in this mint 1963 Sting Ray roadster. Opposite page: The 1964 Sting Ray coupe was marked by distinctive wheel discs and one-piece backlight. Side exhausts are non-stock.

Center spread and above: The brutish Grand Sport was a short-lived attempt to make Corvette competitive in early-1960s road racing. Zora Duntov had hoped to build 125 examples, but only five were actually completed. Opposite page below: The Sting Ray coupe for '65, the last year for factory fuel injection. Below: The 1966 edition. Appearance changes were few.

Another mint '67 roadster, this time with the big-block 427 Mark IV engine rated at 400/435 bhp this year.

Sting Ray engines were carryovers initially, but twin-cowl cockpit was new and roomier than the old roadster's.

continued from p. 96

tempting to talk Duntov out of irs altogether. But Duntov would have it no other way, and to justify its expense he said it would help Chevrolet move 30,000 Corvettes a year.

While Duntov was earnestly seeking an innovative and ultimately produceable new chassis, the stylists had only to clean up and refine the basic Stingray shape that had been around for some three years. The earliest XP-720 mockups looked like nothing more than the racer with a fastback roof. Wind tunnel testing helped to refine the shape, as did more practical matters like interior space, windshield curvatures, and tooling limitations.

Both body styles were tested extensively in production-ready form at the Cal Tech wind tun-

nel, and body engineers spent a great deal of effort on the inner structure. Compared to the '62 Corvette, the Sting Ray had nearly twice as much steel support built into its central body structure, which resembled a racing-style "birdcage" frame. The extra steel was balanced by a reduction in fiberglass content, so that the finished product actually weighed a bit less than the '62 roadster. Despite the tighter wheelbase, interior room was as good as before and, thanks to the reinforcing steel "girder," the cockpit was stronger and safer.

The Sting Ray was far more than just a beautiful body. True, engines, transmissions and axle ratios were carryovers from 1962, and from the doorjambs back, the convertible version was quite similar in appearance to the 1961-62 models. But in near-

ly every other respect this was a totally new Corvette. The most dramatic evidence of that was the first production Corvette coupe. This futuristic fastback attracted even larger crowds than the roadster, partly because of one distinctive styling feature: a split rear window.

McLean's original design called for a one-piece backlight, and it was Mitchell who came up with the "backbone." The split-window configuration was not a unanimous decision. Duntov, for one, was opposed because it cluttered up the view to the rear. But purely practical arguments would not suffice for Mitchell, who insisted, "If you take that off, you might as well forget

Besides the two-seat '63 Sting Ray coupe (above) Chevy contemplated a four-seater on a stretched wheelbase (center spread and opposite page). Idea was quickly axed because of the more ungainly proportions.

the whole thing." His goal was a flowing "spine" from front to rear, beginning as a rise in the center of the hood (necessary to clear the plenum chamber on engines with fuel injection) and continuing as a creaseline over the roof, through the window and down the deck. Mitchell was the boss, so he got his way, and most Corvette fans today would vote with him on aesthetics. The split-window Sting Ray coupe remains one of the most stunning automobiles of all time. It certainly met one of Mitchell's prime criteria: it wouldn't be mistaken for anything else.

But the split backlight took a beating in the press. *Road & Track* disliked "that silly bar," and *Car and Driver* agreed, saying the "central window partition ruins our rear view." Sometimes it is difficult for the motoring press to see the styling forest for the tress, but many customers did. They loved this Corvette because it was a true go-fast machine that looked supersonic even just parked. Ultimately, Mitchell relented. He had his year of production, thus creating a car for future collectors. However, many split-window coupes were lost to cus-

tomizers, some of whom fitted one-piece Plexiglas windows as a substitute. Shortly after this became status quo for the '64 model, a one-piece glass backlight window became available as a replacement item through Chevy dealers. Undoubtedly, many more '63 Corvettes lost their value as collectibles—and their distinctive "split" personality.

The remainder of Mitchell's design was equally stunning. Quad headlamps were retained, but now they were hidden, mounted in pivoting sections that fit flush with and matched the front-end contours. This was the first car with hidden lights since the 1942 DeSoto. Another

DeSoto-type element, this time from 1955-56, was the "gull-wing" dash styling. "The dual cockpit was widely criticized at the time," one Corvette designer remembers, "but it was a very fresh approach to two-passenger styling."

Other interesting design elements included an attractive dip in the beltline at the trailing upper edge of the door, and the coupe's doors were cut into the roof, a feature now *de rigeur* at Ford. The interior received a few updates, such as cowl-top ventilation and an improved heater. Luggage space was also improved, though the Sting Ray was criticized for lack of an external trunklid (the only access

was through the passenger compartment). The spare tire was carried in a sealed fiberglass housing at the rear, hinged to drop to the ground when released. Styling critics chided the use of dummy vents in the hood and on the coupe's B-pillars. At one time these were intended to be functional, but the old cost gremlin again reared its ugly head. It didn't matter much anyway, for these wouldn't last.

Besides the roadster and the new coupe, Chevrolet also toyed with a four-place version of the Sting Ray design. The idea was suggested by Ed Cole, who felt that a back-seat model would give the Corvette broader market coverage, enabling it to compete directly with a number of upscale European 2+2s while appealing to those 'Vette fans who occasionally needed to carry more than one passenger. The plan got as far as a full-size mockup, photographed in the Design Staff auditorium in 1962 alongside a contemporary Ford Thunderbird, which was seen as its main domestic rival.

Based on the production-approved split-window coupe, the proposed four-seater had some 10 extra inches grafted in between the wheel centers, plus a higher roofline (to provide a semblance of rear seat headroom), revised rear fender contours, and a pair of fully engineered back seats with fold-down backrests. Unhappily, the resulting proportions were rather ungainly, which no doubt convinced some executives that the 2+2 might dilute the styling impact of the two-seat models. Chevy abandoned the idea, though it was basically a good one. As a matter of fact, Jaguar thought of the same thing, and a few years later released a stretched-wheelbase version of its slinky two-seat E-Type coupe with similarly awkward lines.

Though not as obvious as the styling, the new chassis was just as important to the Sting Ray's success. The solid rear axle of old was exchanged for the first independent rear suspension in 'Vette history. This consisted of a frame-mounted differential joined to each wheel by half-shafts, with U-joints at either end. The entire assembly was considerably lighter than the old solid axle and brought about a significant reduction in unsprung weight. The differential was mounted in rubber cushioned struts, which helped reduce ride harshness while improving tire adhesion, especially over rougher roads. A single transverse leaf spring was bolted to the rear of the differential case. Attached to either side of the case was a control arm (trailing arm) extending laterally to the hub carriers and slightly forward. A pair of trailing radius rods was fitted behind. Twin coil springs had been

115

Above and opposite page: The new Sting Ray coupe pushed 'Vette sales to new heights for '63, but the roadster remained more popular, if only by 300 units. Optional lift-off hardtop was continued from previous years. Right: '64 Sting Ray coupe emerged with fewer styling frills.

considered at one point, but they took up too much space in this smaller car. The halfshafts acted like upper control arms in this design, with the lower arms controlling vertical wheel motion. The trailing rods took care of fore and aft wheel motion while transferring braking torque to the frame. The shock absorbers were the conventional twin-tube type.

The new five-crossmember frame weighed about the same as the old X-brace chassis. With a curb weight of 3030 pounds, though, the base convertible came out about 100 pounds heavier than its 1962 counterpart. The frame rails were wider and boxed for stiffness, helping to provide 50 percent more torsional rigidity, meaning less twisting motion during cornering, especially over bumps.

Front suspension geometry was much as before, with unequal-length upper and lower arms and coil springs concentric with the tubular shocks. An anti-roll bar was standard.

Steering was conventional recirculating-ball with an overall ratio of 19.6:1. However, this could be easily changed to a much quicker 17.1:1 by disconnecting the tie rods and moving them to secondary mounting

116

to improve cooling and reduce unsprung weight. With that combination, brake fade from excessive heat was reduced considerably. Power assist was available with both standard and high-performance brake packages. Availability of power assist for both brakes and steering was a first for Corvette. Also new was an alternator instead of a generator. Other such evolutionary changes included positive crankcase ventilation, a smaller flywheel, and an aluminum clutch housing.

Sting Ray drivelines, as noted, were largely a carryover from '62. There was a choice of four engines, three transmissions and six axle ratios. The 327 V-8 was offered in carbureted form with 250, 300 or 340 bhp. The base and step-up versions used hydraulic lifters, a mild cam, a forged-steel crankshaft, 10.5:1 compression, a single-point distributor, and dual exhausts. The 300 produced its extra power with a larger four-barrel carburetor (Carter AFB instead of the 250's Carter WCFB), larger intake valves and a bigger exhaust manifold. By opting for fuel injection, the buyer paid $430.40 to get 360 ponies under the hood. As base prices were $4252 for the coupe and $4037 for the convertible, injection was looking quite pricey. A three-speed manual transmission was again standard, but neither that nor the optional Powerglide automatic was very popular. The preferred setup was the Borg-Warner four-speed. A wide-ratio box was available with the base or 300-bhp engines and close-ratio gearing (2.20:1 first gear) was listed for the top two engines. The standard axle ratio was 3.36:1 with the three-speed or Powerglide. The four-speeds came with a 3.70:1 final drive, with 3.08, 3.55, 4.11 and 4.56:1 available. The latter was quite rare in production, for obvious reasons.

If the Sting Ray's specifications sound like those of a well-developed, refined sports car,

holes in the steering arm. Bolted to the frame rail at one end and to the relay rod at the other was a steering damper (essentially a shock absorber), which helped soak up bumps before they reached the steering wheel. Power assist was optional and came with the faster ratio.

Maneuverability of the '63 Corvette was improved by the shorter wheelbase. Although this would ordinarily imply a choppier ride, the altered weight distribution partly compensated. Less weight on the front wheels also meant easier steering, and power steering wasn't often ordered. The additional 80 pounds over the rear wheels also improved traction and gave the Sting Ray a noticeable rear-end squat during hard acceleration.

Stopping power also improved. The four-wheel drum brakes had 11-inch-diameter drums, the same as before, but the linings were wider. Sintered-metallic linings, segmented for cooling, were again optional. Optional finned drums were made from aluminum rather than cast iron

117

you're right. This car seemed to have all the right stuff, and it proved a resounding success on the showroom floors, on the streets, among the automotive press, and on race tracks. *Road & Track* magazine had been appreciative of past Corvettes, especially from the standpoint of cost. It stated in 1960 that the Corvette was "unmatched for performance per dollar..." But its review of the Sting Ray was nearly ecstatic. A few excerpts: "In a word, the new Sting Ray sticks [with] great gripping gobs of traction...The S-bend was even more fun: every time through it we discovered we could have gone a little faster. We never did find the limit...As a purely sporting car, the new Corvette will know few peers on road or track...it ought to be nearly unbeatable."

That verdict was unanimous at all the magazines. In the May 1963 issue of *Motor Trend,* Jim Wright said: "It's far in advance, both in ride and handling, of anything now being built in the United States. It's completely comfortable without being mushy and it takes a large chuckhole to induce any degree of harshness into the ride. Sudden dips, when taken at speed, don't produce any unpleasant oscillations, and the front and rear suspension is very hard to bottom. There's very little pitch noticeable in the ride, even though the 'Vette is built on a fairly short wheelbase. At high cruising speeds—and even at maximum speeds—nothing but an all-out competition car will equal it in stability. We drove it under some pretty windy conditions and didn't notice any adverse effects from crosswind loading. We thought the old model cornered darn well, but there's no comparing it to this new one. It does take a little different technique, but once the driver gets into it, it's beautiful. Since the 49/51 percent front-to-rear weight distribution, plus the independent rear suspension, gives the Sting Ray an inherent amount of over-

steer, the driver will find that on fast corners the car will be doing most of the work through the corner instead of him powering it through." *Sports Car Graphic* was equally enthusiastic: "The ride and handling are great. We won't elaborate on how great: you've got to drive one to believe it." *Car and Driver* reported: "The Corvette is now second to no other production sports car in roadholding and is still the most powerful."

Even though the engines were unchanged, they seemed more powerful in this wondrous new machine. Wright tested a fuel-

injected version with 3.70:1 axle: "On a straight acceleration basis there's very little difference between last year's car and the new one. Our quarter-mile times are within fractions of what they were last year. The only real difference is that the new one doesn't have quite the wheelspin (with stock tires) that the old rigid-axle car had. The 0-30, 0-45, and 0-60 mph steps averaged 2.9, 4.2, and 5.8 seconds, while our average time through the quarter-mile traps was 102 mph, with a 14.5-second ET. Top speed was an honest 130 mph, with the tachometer reading

6000 rpm. A course longer than the Riverside Raceway backstretch would've produced something very close to the Sting Ray's theoretical top speed of 140-142 mph...because the engine was still winding when we had to back off."

Even some European journalists had to admit that the Americans had a potent piece of machinery. *Motor* magazine in England noted that its injected test car accelerated faster than anything else in the publication's test history. The Brits downgraded the Corvette for lack of refinement, though *Autocar*

noted surprise that its car didn't use any oil during the test period.

Most of the criticism leveled at the Sting Ray by American magazines concerned either the split rear window on the coupe or the cumbersome business of having to go over the seats to reach the luggage compartment. But the car's many creature comforts met with approval. The contoured bucket seats were judged comfortable, though some said they were too low. However, this was part of the low center of gravity that had been Duntov's goal. The seats did move fore

and aft, of course, and for the first time the steering wheel could be telescoped in and out allowing a variety of people to find a proper position at the helm. (The column adjustment required the use of a wrench on a collar under the hood.) Instrumentation was also improved and placed where it could be more easily viewed, though the attractive brushed-aluminum housings were shiny enough to make glare a problem in certain light conditions.

Several options reflected the desires of Mitchell, Duntov, and others for the new Corvette to be

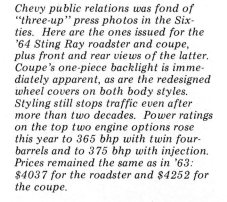

Chevy public relations was fond of "three-up" press photos in the Sixties. Here are the ones issued for the '64 Sting Ray roadster and coupe, plus front and rear views of the latter. Coupe's one-piece backlight is immediately apparent, as are the redesigned wheel covers on both body styles. Styling still stops traffic even after more than two decades. Power ratings on the top two engine options rose this year to 365 bhp with twin four-barrels and to 375 bhp with injection. Prices remained the same as in '63: $4037 for the roadster and $4252 for the coupe.

a serious and successful track competitor. Items such as the Al-Fin brake drums, the handsome (and now rare) aluminum knock-off wheels, stiffer anti-sway bars, metallic brake linings, dual master cylinder and a 36.5-gallon fuel tank all suggested this intent. Together, they made up the Z06 special performance equipment package, offered only on the coupe early in the model year. Four coupes so equipped (except for the knock-offs, which weren't yet ready) made their racing debut at the Los Angeles *Times* Three-Hour Invitational Race at Riverside on October 13, 1962. At the helm were Dave MacDonald, Bob Bondurant, Jerry Grant and Doug Hooper. This was also the debut of Carroll Shelby's Ford-powered Cobra. Though the Cobra would go on to savage the Corvette later, the Sting Ray was well up to the challenge of this Anglo-American hybrid. Three of the cars failed to finish, but the fourth took the checkered flag. Hooper drove the winner, a car owned by Mickey Thompson, who was reported to say, "I don't think it's ever been done before . . . a new production car winning the first time out!"

Sting Rays went on to other victories, but it would be the

Cobras that would dominate production-class racing in the Sixties. Many Corvette enthusiasts still fault the SCCA for certifying the Cobra as a production car, since it was mainly a low-volume special designed more for racing than road use. Still, Chevy's sports car managed some excellent showings, and its street manners were now so good that it didn't need a racing image to promote sales. Of course, Duntov still held out hopes for the creation of a full competition version, which led to the awesome Grand Sport (see Chapter 12).

Fuel consumption for the Sting Ray was fairly moderate considering the available horsepower, especially in the fuel-injected engines. The Rochester mechanical injection corrected mixture continuously for humidity, temperature and altitude changes, and *Motor Trend* stated: "This is one of the few high-output engines that can deliver decent gas mileage without being babied. Out on the highway, we averaged slightly better than 18 mpg for one trip where we didn't go above the legal speed limits. On another trip, where the speedometer stayed above 75 and 80 mph a good deal of the time, we saw 16.3

mpg. Whipping around town produced a 13.6 mpg average. For over 700 miles of all types of driving, the Sting Ray averaged 14.1 mpg." All that and 360 horsepower.

At a base price of $4393.75, the '63 split-window coupe was a relative bargain. *Motor Trend's* test car, with its top-line engine, would have marched from the showroom for $5322. The same machine in good condition would sell for about four times as much today, or about the same as an '84 Corvette.

When the last '63 rolled off the St. Louis assembly line, Sting Ray production totaled 21,513 units. This was split 49 percent coupes and 51 percent convertibles. More than half of the latter were ordered with the optional lift-off hardtop, continued from previous years. This would be the last time that coupes would be so close to the roadsters in sales until 1969. About 15 percent of 1963 production was equipped with power brakes. A slightly higher percentage had power windows. A slightly lower proportion got power steering. Factory air conditioning, a new option for the 'Vette and priced at $421, was specified by only 278 buyers. Saddle-color leather upholstery,

at $80.70, was found on only two percent of the '63s. This was also the first time the 'Vette could be had with genuine cast-aluminum knock-off wheels, Kelsey-Hayes 15 x 6-inchers costing $322.80 a set. Thus, the rarest and most collectible Sting Ray would be a split-window coupe with fuel injection, factory air, leather seats, finned aluminum brake drums, the knock-offs, and power brakes, steering, and windows. The aluminum wheels started off the year, by the way, with a two-prong hub, changed later to the more familiar three-prong design.

In looking at Corvette history, the 1963 Sting Ray has a unique distinction: it was the only all-new model (apart from engines, which were only a year old anyway) between the original Motorama car of 1953 and the 1984 generation. While the Sting Ray would undergo a very dramatic body revision just five years after it first hit the streets, the chassis would live on with only modest changes for a full two decades. That it did survive so long bespeaks the sophistication and foresight of its designers, especially Zora Arkus-Duntov.

Changes for '65 included front fender slots and no hood indentations. Car being painted carries the special hood used with the big-block V-8.

This page: Disc brakes appeared for '65 as a first-time 'Vette option, and were just in time to match the extra power of the burly new 396 big-block. All but 316 cars had them. Opposite page: Eggcrate grille, revised rocker moldings, and no B-pillar vents distinguished the 1966 Sting Ray coupe. Only 9958 were built.

With Corvette sales increasing some 50 percent in a single year, logic dictated that changes for the follow-up 1964 edition would be only evolutionary in nature. As noted, Bill Mitchell gave in to pressure and the coupe's split rear window became one-piece. The two fake air intakes on the hood, which had been inspired by the genuine article on Mitchell's racer, were eliminated, although the indentations remained. The simulated air exhaust vents on the coupe's B-pillars became functional, but only on the driver's side. The rocker panel trim lost some of its ribs, and the areas between the ribs were painted black. Wheel covers were simplified, and the fuel filler door gained concentric circles around its crossed-flags insignia. In the cockpit, the color-keyed steering wheel was replaced by one with a simulated walnut rim. Complaints about glare from the instrument bezels were acknowledged, and they were painted flat black on the '64.

An improved ride was among Duntov's original goals for the Sting Ray, and most reviewers judged him successful, especially compared to previous Corvettes. But as the cars rolled up miles, the shock absorbers weakened and owners began complaining about a deterioration in ride quality. Chevrolet attacked the problem with a few suspension refinements. The front coil springs were changed from constant-rate to progressive or variable-rate and were wound more tightly at the top. The leaf thickness in the rear transverse spring was varied from within. The idea was that small bumps would affect only the low-rate areas of the springs, while larger bumps would affect the high-rate areas. The result was to provide a softer ride without sacrificing handling. Shock absorbers were also redesigned toward this end. When subjected to frequent oscillations under near-full vertical wheel travel, such as on very rough roads, the standard '63 shocks tended to overheat, causing the hydraulic fluid to cav-

longer-duration camshaft to produce 365 bhp. This engine used a Holley four-barrel carburetor rather than the base engine's Carter instrument. The Holley could be more easily tailored to specific needs than the Carter because a large assortment of performance pieces were available for it. The 360-bhp injected unit also gained another 15 horsepower, to 375. But this option cost a whopping $538, a sum that fewer buyers were willing to spend. In the future, the route to 'Vette power would be through the time-honored expedient of more cubic inches, not injection.

If the magazine testers liked the first Sting Ray, they were thrilled with the '64. *Motor Trend's* report of September 1963 covered a fuel-injected coupe with four-speed, 4.11:1 rear axle, the knock-off wheels, sintered metallic brakes, and Positraction. (By adding AM/FM and tinted windows, these options would have pushed the $4394 base list price to $6367.) This Corvette ran the quarter-mile in 14.2 seconds at 100 mph, and notched a 0-60 mph time of just 5.6 seconds. "Acceleration in all speed ranges was, to say the least, fierce—of the 'smash-you-into-your-seat' variety. The engine proved willing, and pulled strongly right up to 6700 rpm and beyond in every gear."

Though transmission options remained ostensibly the same for '64, the two Borg-Warner T10s were replaced by four-speed units built by GM's Muncie, Indiana transmission facility. This was largely due to the wide use of these transmissions in other model lines, and it was thus easier and less expensive to use them in the 'Vette. The "Muncie" gearbox, originally a Chevy design, featured an aluminum case and had stronger synchronizers and wider ratios for better durability and driveability. The wide-ratio box was available only with the 250- and 300-bhp powerplants, with the gears set at 2.56, 1.91, 1.40 and 1:1. The

itate or bubble, losing effectiveness. The 1964 Corvette arrived with a new standard shock. Within the fluid reservoir was a small bag of freon gas that absorbed heat, thus preventing the fluid from bubbling.

The European press especially had marked down the '63 because of its relatively high interior noise. Accordingly, Chevy added more insulation and revised body mounts, plus a more flexible transmission mount, a new shift lever boot and additional bushings to quiet the

shift linkage. The result was a much more livable car for regular or long-distance transportation.

Again for '64 the Sting Ray was offered with a choice of four different versions of the 327 V-8, four different transmissions, and six axle ratios. The two least powerful engines were still rated at 250 and 300 bhp, both on 10.5:1 compression. The two high-performance mills received a few noteworthy improvements. The 340-bhp solid-lifter unit was massaged with a higher-lift,

Bored-out 427-cid Turbo Jet V-8 arrived for 1966, as shown on this roadster.

close-ratio version for the more potent mills had spacings of 2.20, 1.64, 1.28 and 1:1. Like the B-W units, the new four-speed also had a reverse lockout trigger, but with a thicker shifter.

Positraction was still a bargain option in '64 at only $43.05, and more than 80 percent of production had it. This clutch-type differential was designed to send engine torque to the tire with greater traction, as opposed to a standard open differential that transfers power to the tire with lesser traction. This worked quite well for getting good acceleration off the line and for get-

ting out of mud or snow. But on ice or really hard-packed snow, the torque transfer from one tire to the other caused the rear end to fishtail, somewhat unnerving in such a powerful automobile. Maintaining control on slippery surfaces required a deft foot.

A much costlier '64 option was the J56 sintered-metallic brake package. Priced at $629.50, this included not only the high-performance linings but the brakes that had been offered previously in the Z06 option. The J56 was really a competition option, and while not as easily modulated as the disc brakes yet to come, it certainly offered fade-free stopping power. The system was designed for harsh conditions, and while Duntov was bu-

sy looking at discs, he felt nothing else produced at the time was as good as these drums. Magazine testers agreed. *Car Life,* for example, noted: "The harder these brakes have to work, the better they are." But discs were coming into vogue at the time and, once Duntov found a set he liked, the Corvette would have them.

The Sting Ray was cleaned up and muscled up for 1965. The subtle styling alterations were confined to a smoothed-out hood (the old indentations were eliminated), a trio of functioning vertical exhaust vents in the front fenders (replacing the sculptured horizontal "speedlines"), restyled rocker panel moldings, and detail interior trim shuffling.

There were two big mechanical surprises this year. One was the advent of four-wheel disc brakes as a new option, accompanied by special hubcaps. These were a four-piston design with two-piece calipers and cooling fins for the rotors. The dual master cylinder had one fluid reservoir serving the front brake lines, another for the rear lines. The pads were in constant contact with the rotors even when the brakes were not applied. There was little drag, so fuel economy wasn't hurt, and the light touching helped to keep the rotors clean while not adversely affecting pad life. Pad life was, in fact, quite high: an expected 57,000 miles for the fronts, which took most of the braking force in all-out stops, and about twice that for the rears. Total swept area for the new system was 461 square inches, a notable advance on the 328 square inches for the previous all-drum brakes.

Road testers were amazed at the discs. Said *Sports Car Graphic* in October 1964: "After experience with the drum/sintered-lining setup—a previous HD option—we found this brake a distinct pleasure to operate, especially as the stopping potential is even greater. Repeated stops from 100 mph produced no deterioration in braking efficiency and over 20-foot decels could be made with hands off the wheel." The old drum brakes were still available for '65 as a $64.50 credit option, but only 316 of the 23,562 Corvettes built that year went without the full disc setup.

The Sting Ray hardly lacked for horsepower, but it seemed there were always a few customers craving as much as they could get. Chevrolet obliged them at mid-model year with a new optional V-8, the big-block Mark IV. This husky powerplant originated in early 1963 with the so-called "mystery" 427 racing engine that showed up for the Daytona 500. This unit was notable for its "porcupine" valve-gear, an idea of engine designer Robert P. Benzinger. The nickname referred to the way the pushrods poked through little openings at the oddest angles, the result of working "backwards" by starting with the ports and manifolds rather than the combustion chambers.

Intake valves were set at an angle of 26 degrees to the cylinder axis, and exhaust valves were tilted 17 degrees from the same axis. That wasn't all, for both intake and exhaust valve stems were also tilted in side view, one forwards and the other backwards, by 9 degrees. This lined them up with the pushrods to avoid setting up any rotation in the rocker arms. This basic cylinder-head configuration was then tested, fiddled with, honed, and polished until it provided optimal breathing. That part of the design was then frozen, and all other components were designed around it.

The 396 V-8 was just one member of a whole "Porcupine" family, officially titled Mark IV and marketed as the Turbo Jet. There were four in all: two high-performance car engines of 396 and 427 cid, a 366-cid heavy-duty truck unit, and a 427 heavy-duty marine version. The 396 was scheduled to replace the 409 in all its applications, even though that engine was hardly old. Why was it scrapped after barely five years' production? Aside from its basic design limitations, the type W had been tooled for relatively low production volume. To meet future demands, Chevy's Tonawanda, New York plant (near Niagara) would have to be retooled anyway. Semon E. "Bunkie" Knudsen, then division general manager, decided that only the most modern engine could justify such a major tooling reinvestment, so the "Porcupine" got the nod.

There was no thought of any carryover from the type W or 409 to the Mark IV. An all-new block with 4.84-inch spacing between bore centers was chosen, giving a bore of 4.094 inches. Stroke was 3.75 inches.

The 409 block had a deck angled at 33 degrees from horizontal to allow a wedge-shaped combustion chamber to be created with flat-faced heads. By contrast, the Mark IV block had the usual deck angle of 45 degrees to the cylinder axis. Main bearings were 2.75 inches in diameter, a quarter-inch larger than in the type W. Main-bearing width was also increased, adding two full inches to the cap-clamping surface. The forged-steel crankshaft was cross-drilled to deliver oil to the rod bearings through a full 360 degrees of rotation (a feature the W lacked), and crankpin journals were kept at 2.20-inch diameter.

The 396 was initially offered in two versions, both with four-barrel carburetors, 10.25:1 compression, and hydraulic lifters. One was rated at 325 bhp, the other at 360. Production began at mid-year 1965 at the Tonawanda plant, where all Mark IVs were built. For the Corvette, there was a 425-bhp version with 11.0:1 compression, impact-extruded alloy pistons with chrome-plated rings, solid lifters, bigger carburetors with twin-snorkel air cleaner, and enlarged oil pan capacity. This engine was in very short supply, but it wasn't short on performance. With it, a Sting Ray geared for a top speed of 140 mph could blast through the standing-start quarter-mile in 14 seconds flat at a terminal speed of 102-104 mph.

To handle such brute force, the Mark IV engine was accompanied by stiffer front springs, a tighter front sway bar, a new rear sway bar, heavier clutch, and a larger radiator and fan. Though the big-block weighed over 650 pounds, the Sting Ray's weight distribution remained fairly even at 51/49 percent. An aggressive-looking hood bulge and optional side-mounted exhaust pipes completed a very impressive package.

The Mark IV immediately replaced the 365-bhp small-block option on the 1965 chart. The reason displacement was limited to 396 cubes was a GM policy at the time that prohibited any car line smaller than intermediate size from having engines larger than 400 cid.

But that went by the boards the very next year, when the 427 bowed with a larger 4.25-inch bore. It headed a much revised Corvette engine lineup. Starting at the bottom, the 327s were slimmed down from five choices to two. On 10.5:1 compression the base unit was rated at 300 bhp at 5000 rpm, as in '65. The step-up option was again rated at 350 bhp at 5800 rpm on slightly higher 11.0:1 compression. The 250-bhp small-

block and the fuel-injected edition were both dropped. The 427 appeared in two forms. The lesser used 10.25:1 compression and packed 390 bhp at 5400 rpm. Higher (11:1) compression, larger intake valves, a bigger Holley four-pot carb on an aluminum manifold, mechanical instead of hydraulic valve lifters, and four-bolt instead of two-bolt main bearing caps helped produce 425 bhp at 6400 rpm on the upper engine. Though the latter had no more horsepower than the 396, it did have an extra 50 lbs/ft of torque—465 at 3600 rpm.

The 427 was available only with the Muncie close-ratio

(2.20:1 first gear) four-speed manual and Positraction. The 327 was available with either two-speed Powerglide, close- or wide-ratio four-speeds, or a brand-new three-speed.

Performance tests suggested the 427's power ratings were conservative in any case, and some estimated actual output of around 450 bhp. *Road & Track* ran a '65 convertible with the 396 and 3.70 axle ratio, and timed 0-60 mph in 5.7 seconds and the quarter-mile in 14.1 seconds at 103 mph. Three months later, *Car and Driver's* 427-equipped '66 with its higher 3.36 final drive hit 60 mph from rest in only 5.4 seconds and

went through the quarter-mile at 112 mph in only 12.8 seconds. With the 4.11:1 rear axle ratio, *Sports Car Graphic* managed 0-60 in a nearly unbelievable 4.8 seconds, 0-100 in 11.2, and a flat-out maximum of 140 mph. The only thing that could touch it was a 427 Cobra—but the latter was more of an out-and-out competition car, with none of the high-speed comfort qualities of the Sting Ray.

Big-inch 'Vettes for '66 received stiffer front and rear springs and a ⅞-inch anti-sway bar in front and a ¾-inch bar in back. Stronger halfshafts and U-joints and a larger capacity radiator and oil pan were also part of the package.

Appearance alterations on the '66 were minor. The roof-mounted extractor vents on the coupe had proved relatively inefficient, so they were erased. Both models got an eggcrate grille insert to replace the previous horizontal bars.

The 427 Sting Ray was never a match for the lighter and more powerful 427 Cobra on the track. But it was far superior as a street machine, and could be had with more horsepower than any reasonable driver could ever need. *Car and Driver* said: "It's the power more than the engine, that overwhelms every other sensation. There's power literally everywhere, great gobs of steam-locomotive, earth-moving torque." *Motor Trend* agreed: "The 427 has the kind of torque that made World War II fighter planes try to wrap themselves around their propeller on take-off."

Model year 1967 was supposed to see a brand-new Corvette. But the proposed styling turned out to have some undesirable aerodynamic characteristics, and Duntov insisted more time be spent in wind tunnel tests before it was approved for production. It seems no brand-new Corvette has ever made it into production on time.

There was little else to do but soldier on with the Sting Ray,

The Sting Ray coupe for 1967. This series would have ended a year earlier had body design problems not delayed its successor.

but the extra refinements made this perhaps the best of the breed. *Road & Track* said as much in February 1967: "The Sting Ray is in its fifth and probably last year with that name and body style, and it finally looks the way we thought it should have in the first place. All the funny business—the fake vents, extraneous emblems and simulated-something-or-other wheel covers—is gone, and though some consider the basic shape overstyled, it looks more like a finished product now."

Five smaller front fender vents replaced the three on the '66, less distracting flat-black and aluminum rocker panel moldings gave the car a lower, less chunky appearance. Unique to the '67 was a backup light above the license plate. Slotted six-inch-wide Rally wheels replaced the ornate wheel covers of earlier models, and were supplied with chrome beauty rings and lug nuts concealed behind small chrome caps. The cast-aluminum wheels were discontinued. Inside, upholstery pleating was again changed slightly, and the handbrake lever was redesigned and moved from beneath the dash to the more con-

venient spot between the seats. For the first time, the convertible's optional hardtop was offered with a black vinyl covering.

The two small-block V-8s continued unchanged. The base 427 big-block, still rated at 390 bhp, sat under a redesigned hood scoop. Two new big-block options appeared, though, with a choice of 400 or 435 bhp. Each had three two-barrel Holley carburetors. The 400 had the same specs and 10.25:1 compression as the 390, while the 435 came with solid lifters, 11:1 compression, and transistorized electronic ignition.

But the high-performance

highlight for '67 was undoubtedly the awesome L88. This was a 427 with aluminum heads, 12.5:1 compression ratio, no smog equipment, a radical high-lift cam, and 850-cfm Holley four-barrel carb on an aluminum manifold, plus a heavy-duty clutch. Rated at an incredible 560 bhp, it could push the 'Vette from 0 to 60 mph in less than five seconds and send it past the quarter-mile traps in just over 13 seconds. Only 20 of the L88s were produced. At last count, only three are known to survive.

By the end of the fourth-generation design America's sports car had reached a new pinnacle of acceptance and admiration. The Sting Ray captured the imaginations of car enthusiasts as no Corvette ever had before—and not just in its native land but around the world. America's sports car had become a truly international car for the first time—a high-style *gran turismo* that could easily be made into a fearsome dragstrip stormer by checking the right boxes on the order form. It's significant that sales rose steadily if slowly in each year of the Sting Ray era, except for a dip of about 5000 units for '67. The high came in 1966, when 27,720 cars were sold. That volume would have seemed unreachable 10 years earlier, and Chevy managers must have been gratified. The Corvette had indeed come a long way.

But it still had a long way to go. Government safety and emissions standards were on the horizon, new rivals were appearing from overseas—including some low-priced challengers from Japan, of all places—and GM was well along with a new Corvette generation. While much of the Sting Ray would survive in its replacement, the car itself would be missed. It may have been the shortest-lived Corvette series of all, but it was also the most fortuitous. And we can all take comfort in that.

1968~77: STAYING POWER

Rumors about new Corvettes are just like taxes: no matter how hard you try, you just can't seem to escape them. The prospect of a new 'Vette has always seemed just too tantalizing, so the car is wonderful grist for the automotive rumor mill. And if anything, the rumor mill was more active than usual in the mid-Sixties. The economy was going great guns—literally, in the Vietnam era—and Detroit automakers were locked in a performance race. One hot car after another vied for the public's attention: Cobra, Mustang, GTO, 4-4-2, Charger. But the leader of the pack—America's premier performance car—remained the Corvette.

As the decade wore on, though, one question continued to nag at Chevy managers and engineers: how to maintain the Corvette's prominent position? Should it simply evolve or should it be totally transformed? These questions were at the heart of every Corvette rumor, and for good reason. Other cars were appearing that were significantly more exotic than the Corvette

in both styling and mechanical layout. The race track was proving that the mid-engine configuration was best for pure handling capability, a confirmation of Zora Arkus-Duntov's long-held belief. Soon, cars like the Lamborghini Miura were offering mid-engine agility for street use, and the leading-edge mechanicals and attention-getting bodywork of this and other Italian exotics began to make the Sting Ray seem dated.

Meanwhile, at the other end of the spectrum, many sporting cars priced well below the Corvette were beginning to challenge it for performance, at least in a straight line. Within the Chevrolet lineup the Chevelle SS396, the turbocharged Corvair Corsa, and the new-for-'67 Camaro were all available, all good goers, all different answers to the same basic question. When the full-size Chevys began turning in 0-60 mph times that would have put the original 'Vette to shame, the engineering staff was forced to play a very serious game of "Can You Top This?"

Should the Corvette follow Italian exoticars by adopting the mid-engine layout? It was an intriguing question. After all, Chevrolet had had a rear-engine car since 1960, the much-maligned Corvair. By 1965, the original swing-axle rear suspension and its quirky handling were gone, and the Corvair was maturing into quite a nice small car. With its air-cooled powerplant, the similarity with Porsche was obvious. Perhaps a suitable Corvette could be designed around the 'Vair platform.

It seemed logical to experiment in that area, but marketing considerations also dictated a herd of horsepower. The race to see who could pack in the most ponies was definitely on, and Corvette engineers could scarcely allow their car to give any ground in the acceleration derby. So a V-8, rather than the Corvair's flat-six, was wedged in back as a trial. Predictably, the V-8 made for a car that was too tail heavy. One preliminary design had a huge bulge necessary to clear the engine, and thus did without a rear window, sub-

A brace of 'Vettes come into a turn on the high-speed loop at GM's Milford, Michigan proving grounds during Chevy's 1973-model long-lead press preview.

stituting a periscope instead. Sensing correctly that the public wanted to drive cars and not tanks, Chevy consigned a rear-engine 'Vette to File 13. Other proposals used Q-Corvette themes, with a split front windscreen and storage space provided behind the engine assembly. But no matter how hard they tried, the stylists couldn't seem to find the right look.

Perhaps the search had been in vain from the beginning, because a rear- or mid-engine 'Vette would have required mechanical components that just didn't exist in the Chevrolet parts bin. GM had yet to produce a suitable transaxle, and the design and tooling costs for one that would only be used on a low-volume model like the Corvette would have sent prices out of sight.

But Bill Mitchell and his staff had just what they needed to make their baby considerably more exotic at the relatively low price of a new fiberglass skin. They'd prepared it in 1965, one of the most famous show cars of all time.

The Mako Shark II is treated elsewhere in this book. Suffice it to say here that this car was immediately set apart from anything else on four wheels by its styling. Love it or hate it, there was no doubt that the Mako Shark had presence and pizzazz. People say you can literally feel it when a famous star is in the room, and the Mako had just that kind of star quality. And it looked like it was born to run.

The Mako Shark II was not merely a showcase for GM Design's latest ideas: it was mainly a trial balloon for the next-generation Corvette. The Motorama shows were a thing of the past by now, but GM was still gauging public reaction to its near-term model plans by displaying them in slightly exaggerated show car guise. In this case, the development program had been started in early 1964, more than a year before the Mako Shark II appeared. The major goal was to come up with a radically different body design compatible with the existing Sting Ray chassis. Underneath, the forthcoming new production

model would not really be *that* new, but Chevy was betting that a new body and high-power engines would be enough to keep America's sports car on its upward sales course.

In profile and in the nose and fender shapes, the production prototype bore a very strong resemblance to the Mako II. It was only in the roof and rear window treatment that the two differed markedly. The show car had a tapered roof in plan view and carried jazzy backlight louvers. On the 1968 prototype, this treatment was replaced by "flying buttress" sail panels flanking an upright flat rear window. This configuration was favored for the successor to the Sting Ray coupe, and from the beginning it was intended that the backlight as well as that portion of the roof above the seats be removable. Though a convertible would also be offered, it was felt that this arrangement combined the open-air appeal of the traditional Corvette roadster with the better weather protection and structural rigidity associated with closed body types. Porsche

131

Corvette lost the Sting Ray name for '68 but gained dramatic new styling inspired by the dazzling Mako Shark II show car. New body was 7 inches longer and concealed carryover chassis, drivetrains.

had engineered its Targa convertible much the same way.

The styling work did not go as smoothly as expected. One problem was that the new body turned out to have excessive front-end lift at high speeds, which seriously compromised handling. A rear spoiler was added, which held down the tail but also contributed to even greater front lift. Duntov had already been through this battle with the Sting Ray, and he was intent upon licking it before this new design went into production. More time in the wind tunnel led to the use of functional front fender louvers and a front spoiler. It also led to a one-year production delay, so the new Corvette planned as a 1967 entry didn't emerge until model year 1968.

Another problem was the Targa-style roof. Throughout the design phase the removable section had been conceived as a single piece of fiberglass. However, engineers found they could not make the body-and-frame combination stiff enough to prevent creaks and groans, so they added a longitudinal member

between the windshield header and the fixed rear roof section—the birth of the T-top. This solution came so late that it didn't appear in some early publicity photos of the '68 coupe.

One feature from the Mako II that survived to production virtually intact was a vacuum-operated panel that concealed the windshield wipers. It was a great idea for a showmobile, flashy and attention-getting, but in ice and snow it proved about as practical as glass tennis shoes. A great deal of development time went into perfecting this idea for production, but the finished product was

none too reliable.

Perhaps the most important problem with the Mako-inspired styling was inadequate cooling for the big-block engines that would be carried over from the Sting Ray. With the narrow engine bay and shallow grille opening proposed for the new model, radiator air flow was found to be marginal in hot weather and when the air conditioning was switched on. Duntov did what he could by cutting down the size of the front spoiler (the original had actually impeded air flow) and cutting in front fender exhaust slots, but the cooling system was still

problematic, especially with the more powerful engines, when the 1968 model was officially introduced.

The styling of the Mako Shark II may have been great for a show car, but it proved controversial in production form. "If there's such a thing as a psychedelic car, the 1968 Corvette is it," said *Road & Track* magazine in its initial test. It doesn't seem all that radical now, so it's hard to imagine what all the uproar was about. The lines were definitely distinctive—exotic, really, compared to most other cars on the road at the time. Even so, the '68 Corvette drew a decidedly mixed reaction. To many, the styling was wretchedly excessive. "We wish we could express more enthusiasm for the new model," said *Road & Track*, "but we feel that the general direction of the changes is away from

Sports Car and toward Image and Gadget Car."

The magazine had particular complaints about the interior layout, expressing the opinion that comfort and ergonomic logic had been sacrificed to styling. It praised the driver/steering wheel relationship, but deplored the difficulty of getting in and out and complained about the location of the secondary gauges in the center of the dash, away from the driver's direct line of sight. Inadequate interior ventilation was also cited despite the incorporation of windows-up "Astro Ventilation" with dash-mounted vents. The *R&T* testers found not enough air was getting through the ducts to keep things cool. Luckily, factory air was available and was ordered by more than 5000 customers, who must have agreed with *R&T*.

On the other hand, motor

noters had more than a few good words for the engines, all carry-overs from the previous year. While many thought the big 435-bhp 427 was simply too brutish, the 300- and 350-bhp small-blocks were judged quite favorably, as were the Muncie four-speed manual transmission and the new three-speed Turbo-Hydramatic.

As for handling, the press seemed to like the skidpad and slalom numbers they got, but didn't really like the way the car felt. There were several complaints about a hard ride. Nobody liked the power steering and brakes much, either, *Road & Track* labelling them imprecise and suggesting potential customers skip them entirely.

But the *R&T* review was downright benign compared with Steve Smith's "non-review" in *Car and Driver*. He slammed just about everything from the windshield wipers to the ashtray. His biggest beef was the new model's fit and finish—or, more precisely, the lack of it: "Few of the body panels butted against each other in the alignment that was intended," he wrote. "Sometimes the pieces chafed against each other, sometimes they left wide gaps, sometimes they were just plain crooked." He also complained about a chronic water leak from the T-top and claimed that one of the door locks was so stiff it bent the key. He termed all this "a shocking lack of quality control" and declared the car "unfit to road test."

Unhappily, this state of affairs was not confined to the *C/D* test car. The 1968 model is generally considered to be the low point for 'Vette workmanship, with bad paint, knobs that fell off, cooling bothers, and other problems. The feeling in many quarters is that Chevrolet tried too many new ideas that were not adequately sorted out and put too big a rush on production.

Certainly the 'Vette was now a far more complicated car than it had been just six years earlier. The new model came in two body styles: the familiar roadster, available with optional lift-off hardtop, and the totally new T-top Sport Coupe. On the 1962 Corvette you couldn't get power steering, power brakes, or air conditioning. All these were available on the '68, plus rear window defogger, three different four-speed manual transmissions, a new automatic transmission, telescoping steering column, speed warning indicator, AM/FM stereo radio, and a futuristic fiber-optic light monitoring system—not to mention the disappearing headlights and the trouble-prone hidden wiper panel. Very simply, there were now a lot more gadgets, and that usually means more things to go wrong.

On the other hand, when everything was working right, the '68 could be quite satisfying to drive. It had plenty of power

on tap even with the small-block engines, the all-independent suspension was more than adequate if not exactly state of the art and, cooling problems aside, none of the glitches that cropped up were in the basic mechanicals. The gadget problems were irritating, but in the overall scheme of things they weren't major flaws.

And the car could go. Ron Wakefield tested a 350-bhp 327 roadster with four-speed and the 3.70:1 final drive and came up with some pretty impresive numbers. Top speed was 128 mph, the quarter-mile time was 15.6 seconds at 92 mph through the traps, and 0-60 mph acceleration was 7.7 seconds. This was nothing to sneeze at, and the big-block versions were faster still, if not nearly as streetable.

In any form the new car was quite thirsty. In those pre-EPA days *R&T* estimated its 327 car's mileage at 11-15 mpg, a figure that gave a cruising range of 220-300 miles on its 20-gallon fuel tank. Of course, short trips were the order of the day since there was only 6.7 cubic feet of trunk space. Further, that space was again accessible only from inside the cramped cabin: there was still no external opening. Speaking of the cabin, the seats were narrower and the backs raked much more steeply than

before to accommodate the two-inch lower roofline. The resulting laid-back posture and the high dash with its huge tach and 160-mph speedometer gave one the impression of being locked in a cave. With the long, low nose disappearing from sight somewhere near the horizon, the driving position definitely left something to be desired. Handling, though, was improved by the addition of wider, seven-inch-wide wheels. This plus the special Goodyear bias-ply tires (radials were abandoned in pre-production) provided taut cornering at the expense of harshness over rough roads.

Overall, the press was luke-warm about the new '68—certainly not as laudatory as Chevy had come to expect. And the division was particularly stung by *Car and Driver*'s scathing criti-

The '69 edition was marked by the return of the Stingray name plus chrome-framed fender vents and a new dashboard pouch.

cism. Ron Wakefield, who owned a Sting Ray at the time, had a more even-handed assessment: "The Corvette 327 remains a comfortable, fast, safe, and reliable automobile. For those who like their cars big, flashy, and full of blinking lights and trap doors it's a winner. The connoisseur who values finesse, efficiency, and the latest chassis design will have to look, unfortunately, to Europe." Yet despite all the problems and press carping, more people than ever looked to the 'Vette. Model year sales set a new record at 28,566 units, some 5000 cars better than the year before, though only fractionally ahead of the previous all-time best year, 1966.

If 1968 had been the year of the Big Switch, then 1969 was the year of the Little Fixes. Duntov and his team went to work, making as many detail changes as they could in the basic design to remedy the problems noted by owners and the press.

The reworking began with the cockpit. The fifth-generation body was seven inches longer overall than the Sting Ray, most of it in front overhang, even though the wheelbase remained unchanged at 98 inches. However, the pinched-waist styling and the lower roofline made the interior more cramped, another sore point with the typewriter jockeys. Accordingly, one lap-saving inch was carved from the steering wheel diameter, and Duntov pushed through a $120,000 tooling change for the inner door panels to open up a half-inch per side in extra shoulder width.

Thanks in part to Mr. Nader, door handles were revamped so as to be more "occupant friendly," and the dash knobs got rubberized covers for the same reason. The dash-mounted ignition switch was moved to the steering column where it was combined with the mandated locking column for additional security,

and a warning light was added to tell the driver that the headlights weren't completely open. Attempts were also made to improve flow volume on the Astro Ventilation system, but *Road & Track* reported things were no better than on the '68.

Exterior changes on the '69 were minimal. The most noticeable perhaps was the return of the "Stingray" designation— now spelled as one word—over the front fender louvers. It makes you wonder whether Chevy needed to differentiate the '69 or whether the castings for the side IDs simply weren't ready in time for the '68. Another change involved the door handles. Originally, these were covered slots, with the covers releasing the door latches. But the idea ran into production delays, so the '68s had used a chrome-covered handgrip with a thumb-operated external pushbutton. The original handles finally made it on the '69s—to the gratitude of thumbs everywhere. A new headlight washer system arrived, as did a revised version of the already over-engineered windshield wipers, which *Road & Track* thought was "amusing." The new system retained the hidden wipers and added washers relocated to the wiper arms and override switches so that the panel could be left up (no doubt it often froze shut in cold climes) and the wipers stopped for blade-changing. At the rear, the separate backup lights were incorporated into the inboard taillamps.

More interesting news awaited under the hood. The famed Chevy small-block was stroked about a quarter-inch, to 3.48 inches, boosting displacement from 327 to 350 cid on the same 4.00-inch bore. Two versions were offered for '69, with the same 300- and 350-bhp ratings as their '68 equivalents but with compression dropped a quarter-point in each case (10.25 and 11.0:1, respectively). Significantly, peak power engine speed was also lower (by 200 rpm), now

4800 and 5600 rpm, respectively, in this second year of federally mandated—and still relatively uncomplicated—emissions controls. The trio of 427 big-blocks returned unchanged and a fourth version rated at 430 bhp at 5200 rpm on a high 12.5:1 squeeze was added, though not many were built. Axle ratios ranged from a super-low 4.56:1 to a long-striding 2.75:1. Frames on all cars were stiffened up to reduce body shake, and wheel-rim width went up by one inch for improved handling.

A mechanical-lifter small-block, derived from Chevy's earlier 377-cid racing engine and known as the LT-1, was promised for 1969, then delayed. But fans of unusual street engines had nothing to worry about, because there were two new mills that were simply outrageous: the L88 and the ZL-1.

The L88 was the 435-bhp aluminum-head 427 Mark IV that had been introduced late in the '68 model run. Despite its

size it weighed just 60 pounds more than its small-block brothers, not much of a penalty for an extra 85 horses. The claimed horsepower was reputed to be low, and some experts have suggested a healthy L88 would easily churn out 500 ponies. Its performance—and a formidable $1032 price—were not for the faint-hearted, though. The ZL-1 was even wilder: a 427 with aluminum-alloy heads *and* block derived from the engine Bruce McLaren was running in his championship-winning Can-Am racers. The ZL-1 weighed 100 pounds *less* than the L88 and produced just as much conservatively rated horsepower. Both engines boasted stronger bolts and connecting rods, a new camshaft, and cylinder heads with better breathing.

Most testers found both these powerhouses ridiculous for the street. They were built with just one thing in mind: acceleration, as in quarter-mile, as in drag racing. They accomplished that

with ease—to the detriment of virtually everything else. With their wild cams, they burped and shuddered like a colicky baby. And the ZL-1 could not be ordered with a heater, to discourage its use on public roads—as if the $3000 price wasn't discouragement enough. But it was a tremendous racing machine. A typical example set up for a road course could do sub-13-second quarter-miles and hit 115 mph through the traps. Top end was reputed to be around 170 mph—amazing for a car you could theoretically buy off the floor at your local Chevy dealer.

The L88 and ZL-1 were the ultimate '69 Corvettes, but they were predictably few and far between. Division records show that only 116 L88s and just two ZL-1s were completed during the year. On the other hand, thousands were delivered with the small-blocks, both very docile engines with more than enough pep.

This was supposed to be the year that Chevy tightened up on the 'Vette's quality control, but there's evidence the effort was only partially successful at best. *Road & Track*, in its test of a 435-bhp big-block car, remarked that fit and finish was worse than on its '68. Again, it was mainly minor maladies like squeaks, rattles and knobs falling off rather than major mechanical ills. But testers expected much more from Chevy's highest-priced car.

The editors summed it up thusly: "The Corvette 427 is an entertainment machine, and compared to some of the more exotic entertainment machines we drive from time to time, it's a rather crude one. But it's cheap when you compare it to other sports cars that offer performance anywhere near its own, so we shouldn't expect a great deal of refinement."

In its June 1969 issue, *R&T* published a four-way test matching a Corvette with the base 350 and Turbo-Hydramatic, an automatic Mercedes 280SL, and a manual-shift Jaguar E-Type and Porsche 911T. The "comparo" showed the 'Vette still bothered the press: "In purely objective terms, the Stingray was the biggest, heaviest, most powerful, fastest, thirstiest and cheapest of the four GTs included in this test." And none of the four testers chose the 'Vette as his personal favorite. One picked the SL and, to Chevy's likely consternation, the other three picked the Porsche with its rear-mounted flat-six. The SL was the most expensive of this foursome at $7833. The E-Type was next at $6495, followed closely by the Porsche at $6418. The 'Vette was the least expensive, with an as-tested price of $6392 including automatic, stereo and A/C. In the eyes of some, the Corvette was no longer at the top of the sports car price/value heap.

R&T attempted to sum up the style and character of each car, and its description of the 'Vette

was telling: "The word that comes to mind is 'Plastic.' The image, like the styling, is flashy, with lots of deliberately eye-catching angles and gimmicks that aren't strictly necessary. Lacks finesse; like using a five-pound axe when a rapier, properly designed, could do as well. And with more grace. The personality we associate with the Stingray is the Animal, one who prefers to attain the goal with brute strength and bared chest rather than art and fast footwork." This was far from complimentary, especially next to the comments on the Porsche: "The word is serious. The driver will take himself and his driving

seriously. Damned serious in fact. Almost certain to have no more than a limited sense of humor, especially concerning Porsches...A car for the technician rather than the engineer, if you get the distinction."

Even if you don't get the distinction, it was becoming obvious that the fifth-generation design was far from perfected. Nevertheless, sales took a vertical leap, rising by over 10,000 units to 38,762—a record that wouldn't be broken until 1976. Evidently, there were at least a few sports car buyers who disagreed with *Road & Track*'s conclusion about the 'Vette's value for money.

Corvette's 1970 styling changes, though minor, were obviously last-minute, as the early factory photo above suggests.

Chevrolet seemed to get it all together for 1970. Due to a strike, the '69 model run was extended two months longer than usual, which may have been the time Chevy needed to make good with the '70. The strike was no doubt a factor in the '69 production record, but it also delayed the '70s from reaching dealer showrooms until February, and that sent Corvette production plummeting to just 17,316, its lowest point since 1962.

Once again the major news was under the hood. The LT-1 solid-lifter small-block appeared at last, boasting 370 bhp at 6000 rpm and a hefty $447.50 price. It differed from the lesser small-blocks in having more radical cam timing and valve lift, larger-diameter exhaust system, and the carburetor from the big-block engines, along with special cold-air hood intake. The lesser 350 V-8s returned, unchanged from their '69 specs. Reflecting the increasing stranglehold of

emissions requirements, Chevy stroked the big-block to a full 4.00 inches for 454 cid. Output was 390 bhp at 4800 rpm on 10.25 compression. Also listed was the LS-7, a 465-bhp behemoth running 12.25:1 compression. It was ostensibly available to anyone, but it was really a competition engine and none were installed in regular production. *Sports Car Graphic* did manage to get its hands on one, though, and recorded a quarter-mile time of a bit under 14 seconds and a terminal speed of near 110 mph. As with the small-block the year before, the enlarged big-block produced less power per unit of displacement than its predecessor and its peak power speed was lower. Conversely, it was somewhat torquier and thus more flexible at low rpm.

Corvette cosmetics were again altered only in detail for 1970. The extreme bodyside tuck-under on the 1968-69 models was found to be susceptible to stone damage, so Chevy flared the aft portions of each wheel opening, which was some help. The grille—actually false as the radiator air intake was on the

car's underside—was changed from horizontal bars to an egg-crate pattern, and the parking lamps changed from small round units to clear-lens, amber-bulb rectangular fixtures. The grille pattern was repeated on the front fender vents, replacing the four "gills" used before. The dual exhaust outlets also shifted from round to rectangular.

Inside, the seats were re-shaped to provide better lateral support, more headroom, and easier access to the still-lidless cargo bay. The shoulder belts, separate from the lap belts, got inertia storage reels, thus ending some cockpit clutter. Carried over from 1969 was a three-pocket map pouch on the starboard side of the dash, which provided more convenient small-items stowage than the hard-to-reach twin lidded behind-the-seats bins. A deluxe interior group was added to the options list, consisting of full cut-pile carpeting and ersatz wood trim on the console and doors. Some people liked it, but the snap-brim-cap crowd said the fake bark made the Corvette seem too much like a Monte Carlo.

Road & Track, which seemed

to test 'Vettes more frequently than most other "buff books," tried a 1970 example with the "stock" 454 and automatic. It recorded 7.0 seconds in the 0-60 mph run, a 15.0-second quarter-mile at 93 mph, and a top speed of 144 mph. Though the editors described this as "one of the better Corvettes we've driven lately," they found the ride suffered from "lack of suspension travel [that] decrees too much damping in the up direction and too little in the down; the result is considerable harshness over sharp bumps but a distinct 'floatiness' over gentle undulations at speed. On bad roads the Corvette simply loses its cool, rattling, shaking and squeaking in a scandalous manner." The brakes got only "fair" marks as they "faded more than in any recent Corvette we've tried; the extreme weight of the car [4070 pounds as tested] with the heavy engine and air conditioning, etc., are responsible."

But the days of the big-inch, big-power Corvettes were already numbered. Horsepower and displacement would both fall as the '70s wore on. As they did, America's sports car would become a more balanced package of the sort *R&T* could endorse.

The future arrived with a thud for 1971 as GM ordered an across-the-board compression drop so all its engines could run on low- or no-lead fuel. The 'Vette didn't escape, and the results were dramatic. The base small-block V-8 now ran a mild 8.5:1 squeeze and packed only 270 bhp at 4800 rpm. Compression on the LT-1 sighed to 9.0:1, and rated output sank to 330 bhp at 5600 rpm. These same compression numbers were applied to a brace of big-blocks, the LS-5 rated at 365 bhp at 4800 rpm, and the LS-6 with 425 bhp at 5600 rpm.

None of these engines were weaklings exactly. If they seemed to be at the time, it was only in relation to the prodigious power we had grown used to in the muscle car era, and Corvettes remained exceptionally strong performers next to most other cars on the road. Predictably, the aluminum-head LS-6 was the top dog, capable of pushing from 0 to 60 mph in less than 5.5 seconds, with the quarter-mile shooting by in just under 14 seconds at 105 mph. Top speed was claimed to be in excess of 150 mph. The somewhat milder LS-5 was good for quarters in the low 14s with automatic, and was only marginally slower in the 0-60 mph test.

There were virtually no styling changes on the '71s and for at least three reasons. One, the 1970 run had started late. Two, the engineers were up to their ears in meeting emissions limits. And three, the car still looked good, so why fool around?

Significant for engineering, though not numbers, was the ZR-1 option, a racing package that was ostensibly offered this year. It comprised the LT-1 small-block, heavy-duty four-speed transmission and power brakes, aluminum radiator, and a revised suspension with special springs, shocks, stabilizer bar, and spindle strut shafts. Since it was a competition option, it could not be ordered with power windows, power steering, air conditioning, rear window defroster, wheel covers or radio. Only eight examples went out the door.

After the previous year's abrupt downturn, Corvette sales made a satisfying recovery for '71, with 21,801 units delivered for the model year. The coupe had taken the sales lead over the roadster beginning in 1969, perhaps reflecting the T-top model's greater all-weather versatility. By this time the gap had

Below: No, it's really a '71. Opposite page: Styling remained the same again for '72, but engine power took a beating.

widened to a ratio of about 5 to 3. Convertible popularity was on the wane throughout the industry, and the government seemed ready to enact a safety standard for rollover protection in a crash that would have effectively made sale of fully open cars illegal in this country after 1975. All these factors conspired against the romantic 'Vette roadster, which had only a couple of years left to run.

Corvette mainly marked time for 1972, but engines now bore the full brunt of emissions tuning and both horsepower and performance were further deemphasized. The big-block LS-6 option was cancelled, leaving the 365-bhp LS-5 the most potent engine in the lineup. Otherwise, changes were few. The fiber-optic light monitors were scratched, which cleaned up the center console considerably, and the anti-theft alarm system previously offered at extra cost was made standard, a belated recognition of the 'Vette's high "thieveability." This would also be the last year for the coupe's removable backlight (it would be

fixed from here on). Sales inched upward for '72, scoring a gain of nearly 5200 units to reach 26,994 cars for the model year.

The LT-1 small-block was also in its last year, but for the first time it could be combined with air conditioning. Chevy engineers had been reluctant to offer this combination, fearing the solid-lifter unit's higher revving ability would pull the A/C belts off their pulleys. To forestall this possibility, tachometers on cars so equipped were redlined at 5600 rpm rather than the normal 6500.

The first major styling change

in the fifth generation arrived for 1973. It was a new "soft" body-color nose designed to meet the government's 5-mph front-impact protection rule that took effect this year. The new system—actually a steel bumper covered by deformable urethane plastic—added but 2.2 inches to the Corvette's overall length and only 35 pounds to the curb weight, and it looked quite nice. Another piece of mandated safety equipment was steel reinforcement beams in the doors to protect against side impact intrusion.

Another kind of safety equip-

ment change was the substitution of radial tires for the former bias-belted covers. *Road & Track*'s 1973 test made much of this. The change was significant, but the much-touted radials actually delivered poorer performance than the old belted tires. *R&T*'s results showed longer braking distances and lower "g" figures on the skidpad. Worse, the new tires were rated only to 120 instead of 140 mph. This was an improvement?

Maybe not, but it was symptomatic of what was happening to most performance cars this year. In the 'Vette's case, the

mechanical-lifter engines were now a thing of the past—the first time this had happened since 1956. Engine options were two SAE net-rated choices: a 350 V-8 dubbed L82 with 250 bhp at 5200 rpm, and the big-block LS-4 advertised at 270 bhp at 4400 rpm. Neither was a screamer, although the 'Vette was still quicker than most of its competition, which was being bogged down by smog and safety hardware, too.

Apparently, Chevy had decided that if the Corvette couldn't be the all-out terror it once was then it had better be a more pleasant and practical car to live with. Thus, an attempt was made to reduce engine roar by adding sound deadener at various points in the body and a deadening pad under the hood. New chassis mounts made of a rubber and steel combination for flexibility and strength were specified to help eliminate all but good vibrations. The problem-prone trap door for the concealed wipers was junked for a simple rear hood extension. Nobody was too sorry to see it go, but there was some objection to the permanently fixed rear window on the coupe. However,

this added a couple of inches to the small cargo compartment, since the window stowage receptacle went away as well. A new option serving both form and function was a handsome set of aluminum wheels. The only problem was that some structural problems were found in the first 800 sets, and they had to be recalled. Rumors are that some remain in service. (Later 'Vette aluminum wheels used very similar styling.)

Road & Track magazine, which tested a four-speed L82 with 3.70:1 final drive, generally liked the changes for '73. The latest Corvette wasn't as fast as previous models and it didn't handle quite as well either, but it was a more civilized machine for long-distance touring or an afternoon's run in the hills: "For all its age, size and compromises, if the Corvette is equipped with the right options it is a pleasant and rewarding car to drive, and this 1973 example was one of the best Corvettes we've ever driven." Even considering its faults, the '73 was a heck of a buy for performance compared to all but the really low-buck sports cars of the day. Despite less power the 'Vette could still run the quarter in the mid-15s, virtually the same as a Porsche 911E or De-Tomaso Pantera, but it listed at $5635 while the Porsche sold in the U.S. for $10,025 at the time and the Pantera retailed at around $10,000 even. The Datsun 240Z, introduced for 1970, wasn't even in the same ball-park with its 17.7 quarter-mile, though it did sport a more attractive $4600 price tag.

The *R&T* test also showed that rumors about a new Corvette still made good copy: "The '73 Corvette is not the exciting new Corvette, not the mid-engine car promised to us (and by us to you) for this year. That

Corvette tail was reworked for '74 to match the new '73 front and to meet the year's tougher bumper rules. Cockpit was more luxurious than ever but just as tight.

is still most definitely on the way, however." The men from Newport Beach predicted that the mid-engine Corvette was about three years off. As we now know, a decade would pass before a really new design of any kind would appear. Yet despite the now six-year-old styling and body engineering, the Corvette continued to find a steady supply of customers. Chevrolet retailed a healthy 34,464 units for 1973, an increase of about 8000 over the previous year.

Model year 1974 is not remembered very fondly by performance fans. It was the year of the Arab oil embargo, which prompted the nation's first energy crisis with rising gas prices, rationing, and long lines at the pumps. Suddenly, the big, heavy, thirsty Corvette looked woefully anachronistic, but there was little Chevy could do but carry on with it and hope for the best. The major change for the year was a body-color rear-end treatment to match the new '73 front. Again urethane plastic was used, and the new ensemble tapered downward instead of upward as on the original Kamm-style tail. The 1974 back bumper was a two-piece affair with a seam in the middle. In later years it would be a one-piece unit. The '74 model marked a couple of "lasts." Among these were the last genuine dual exhausts, which henceforth would be routed into catalytic converters and then to separate pipes and mufflers. The '74 was also the last 'Vette able to run on leaded gas, the unleaded requirement coming, of course, with the switch to the "cat con." And, this was the last Corvette available with a big-block V-8, in this case the 270-bhp LS-4 version of the 454.

continued on p. 161

Corvette was all-new again for '68.
Shown is that year's new T-top coupe.

Both pages: 1968 Corvette body design was predicted by the more extreme Mako Shark II show car of 1965. New model was slated for 1967 release, but was delayed due to Zora Arkus-Duntov's insistence on wind tunnel tests, which helped hone the final shape. Sexy new styling concealed carryover chassis and drivetrains.

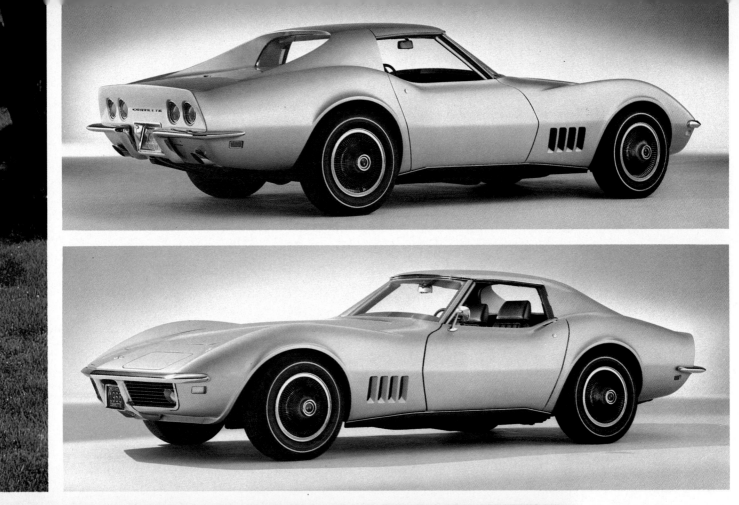

Both pages: Corvette roadster proved more popular for '68 than the new T-top coupe shown here, but this situation would be permanently reversed the following year. With its twin lift-off roof panels and removeable backlight, the coupe offered much of the ragtop's open-air allure plus greater comfort and quietness when buttoned up. Slinky body stretched seven inches longer overall than the 1963-67 Sting Ray's, and was the most extreme expression of GM's "coke-bottle" look in the late '60s. Besides hidden headlights, the '68s featured wipers concealed under an electrically operated cowl panel, plus "hidden" door handles with slot grips.

Above: The 1968 Corvette coupe. Compare the standard hood here with the bulging affair fitted with the big-block V-8s as shown on the previous pages. Top and opposite page: Changes for '69 were subtle but welcome. They included reviving the Sting Ray name—but as one word—plus tidying up some exterior details and a bit more cabin width.

Both pages: Model year 1970 saw more refinements to the '68 Corvette design, including a newly enlarged big-block V-8 packing 390 bhp (SAE gross). A planned 465-bhp version never materialized. The LT-1 solid-lifter 350-cid small-block offered 370 bhp with 11.0:1 compression. Sales were down sharply from '69 levels.

Top: Last of the true high-performance 'Vettes were the '71s. Top 454 V-8 was rated that year at 425 bhp. Above and

opposite page: Power ratings tumbled for '72, a sign of the stiffer emissions limits then in effect.

Center spread and top and center: With the advent of 5-mph bumpers for '73, the Corvette got a new nose with a body-color plastic grille surround. Also new that year was a domed hood with automatic air induction. Coupe's roof panels were fixed this year only. Above: Rear end was similarly redone for '74, visibly altering the profile.

This page and opposite page top: Big-block V-8 vanished for 1975, which would see the end of the true Corvette roadster. Buyer demand stayed strong despite the deemphasis on performance in the early '70s. The sole engine was now the 350-cid small-block, rated at 165 or 205 bhp (SAE net) depending on compression. Opposite page bottom: Changes were almost non-existent on the '76 models, but the 'Vette had become a tauter, better-handling machine, particularly when equipped with the optional Gymkhana suspension. Aluminum wheels were a new factory extra.

The 1975 Corvette roadster is a sure-fire collectible today. Will this body style be revived in the '80s?

continued from p. 144

The base and extra-cost small-block V-8s were still available and unaltered in output from 1973.

Other changes were extremely minor. The move to "performance" automatic transmissions was seen in availability of the new M40 three-speed unit. Shoulder and lap belts were combined into a single three-point harness and the inertia-reel setup was changed somewhat. The rearview mirror got wider. Radiator efficiency was improved. The burglar alarm switch was moved from the rear of the car to the left front fender. The power steering pump was altered for greater durability. And so it went.

One of the all-time bargain Corvette performance packages appeared this year. This was the "gymkhana suspension" option, code FE7, costing a mere seven bucks. Though it was little more than the tried-and-true formula of higher-rate springs and firmer, specially calibrated shocks, it yielded a handling improvement all out of proportion to its paltry price. In a way, this reflected the tenor of the times. Mammoth engines and pavement-peeling acceleration had been rendered obsolete by inflation, high insurance rates, and the sky-rocketing price of fuel. Then too, buyers were becoming more sophisticated, beginning to demand more well-rounded cars.

Thus, the Corvette's character had changed by the mid-Seventies, and Chevy's marketing approach changed with it.

Small bumper pads front and rear helped distinguish the 1975 'Vette (below) from the similar-looking '74 (bottom).

161

The '74 was not nearly as hairy-chested as the 'Vettes of four years earlier. Nor was it as light and nimble as the small-block Sting Rays. Even so, it was satisfyingly quick. With the 250-bhp small-block it could scamper from 0 to 60 mph in about 7.5 seconds and top out at around 125 mph. And it could return about 14-15 miles per gallon which, considering the go-power, wasn't at all bad. It was also the most luxurious 'Vette yet—still a bit noisy, perhaps, but a capable and refined grand tourer with plenty of creature comforts and far greater re-

liability than most of its high-buck European competitors.

Enthusiasts were about to learn that the fifth generation had staying power in more ways than one. With the appearance of the '74 model, some pundits began wondering whether Corvette development had not been frozen. It had not, of course, and rumors continued to fly about the all-new mid-engine 'Vette that was presumably just around the corner. But what most failed to notice was that the fifth generation defied industry sales trends, selling at or near its best-ever levels at a time when it should have done anything but that. The model year total for '74 was 37,502, quite close to the record figure of 1969, a year when the economy and the energy picture were both considerably brighter. Understandably, Chevy saw no compelling need for a new Corvette design. And apparently, neither did the buyers.

Model year 1975 saw no obvious physical changes in America's sports car, but it would mark a milestone of sorts. This would be the last year for the genuine Corvette roadster. Since the 1953 original, this body style had been a big part of the Corvette tradition, but GM was up against declining interest in convertibles generally and a rising chorus of safety-firsters. The last of 4629 ragtops came off the line in July, the end of an era.

At least the convertible was available throughout the year. The big-block V-8, which had been first wedged into a Corvette for 1965, was dropped altogether, a casualty of the oil wars. The only optional engine was now the L82 small-block, rated at 205 bhp (SAE net), and the base 350 was detuned to a measly 165 bhp. Helping to keep the power ratings from being even more anemic was the switch to catalytic converters, a move made by most automakers this year. A positive note was the advent of breakerless electronic ignition, accompanied by an electronic (instead of mechanical) tachometer drive. Outside, small extrusions with black

Corvette horsepower sank to its lowest point yet for 1975, 165 bhp standard or 205 bhp optional, both SAE net. Despite this, demand remained strong and model year production totalled a healthy 38,465 units.

pads were added to the front and rear bumpers. A headlamps-on warning buzzer was added per Washington's dictates. Sales hit 38,465.

Such was the Corvette's hold on the public that it set a record the following year even though the '76 version was mostly a holdover. Despite the convertible's demise, 46,558 coupes were sold before dealers closed their books, a reflection of the recovering market and lack of any real price/performance competition. There were few changes in the engine room, and the bogus air extractor vents vanished from the rear deck and rear bumper trim was slightly altered. A sport steering wheel was offered, but 'Vette fanatics got their dander up because it was the same wheel found on the lowly Vega. To increase rigidity and keep out some of the heat from the hotter-running engines, a steel subsection was added to the forward part of the body structure. Induction was modi-

fied so that instead of air coming in from the cowl area near the windshield, it entered from up front above the radiator. This change was made to remedy a noise problem caused by having the air flow close to the passenger compartment.

Like the watch on the TV commercial, the fifth generation could take a licking and keep on ticking, and it did so again for 1977. Once more the mechanicals were left alone, and most of this year's efforts were aimed at boulevard cruising refinement. Naturally, the most visible ones were inside. The console was redesigned to accept a larger array of Delco music-makers, including an AM/FM stereo radio with integral tape deck, a first-time option. Also new were a revised sport steering wheel with leather-wrapped rim, and a steering column stalk control for headlamp dimmer switch and windshield wipe/wash. The steering column itself was redesigned to allow would-be John

Power was up for '77, as was production, which sailed past 49,000. The T-top panels could now be carried on the luggage rack.

Greenwoods to drive with their arms extended; this also made it easier to get into and out of the car. A related modification lengthened the manual transmission lever for easier use of the handbrake. Leather upholstery was now standard, and cloth seats with hide bolsters were a new extra-cost item. Power steering and brakes were both standardized this year as well. The alarm switch was relocated again, this time incorporated with the left door lock button. Rear view mirror position and sunvisors were revamped, and the console gauges and heater controls were restyled for a more contemporary look.

Outside, the optional rear deck luggage carrier was reworked so that the twin lift-off panels could be carried there instead of

in the luggage compartment, where they were less convenient to stow. Glass roof panels were listed as a new option at the start of the model year, but GM cancelled it in a reputed dispute with the supplier over sales rights. The vendor eventually marketed them himself—and Chevy promptly went to another source for '78. One final exterior change would be noted instantly by car spotters: the Stingray nameplate came off the front fenders, replaced by the traditional crossed-flags insignia, and the car was simply a Corvette.

Sales continued to climb, with 46,558 units retailed for the model year. This was great going for a design that had been in production for 10 seasons—the longest run of any Corvette generation to date and eloquent testimony to its near-universal appeal. It also said a great deal about GM's knack for being able to update a design successfully in light of new federal requirements without any major alterations and without detracting from aesthetics or performance.

This was as much a factor in the resurgence of the Chevrolet Camaro and Pontiac Firebird pony-cars as it was with maintaining the popularity of this Corvette.

The fifth generation had done exceptionally well indeed, prospering during one of the most difficult periods in the history of the U.S. industry. But it was far from finished. It was about to be rejuvenated with some special revisions for a very special year. America's sports car was about to celebrate its Silver Anniversary.

1978~82: MORE AND LESS OF EVERYTHING

America's sports car passed an important milestone in 1977. On March 15th at precisely 2:01 p.m., Robert D. Lund, then Chevrolet Division general manager, drove the half-millionth production Corvette off the St. Louis assembly line. It was an historic occasion to rival that day in late June nearly a quarter-century before, when Job 1 rolled out the door of that small plant in Flint. It was a time for looking back and looking ahead. Yet even as this feat was being recorded for posterity, the Corvette's future was being decided. This was not immediately evident, though, and the fifth-generation design would simply carry on for the next five years with more and less of everything that Corvette lovers expected.

Several developments in the early Seventies combined to shape the Corvette's destiny in the Eighties. The signs of change had been visible in the car itself since about 1973. Perhaps the most important factor was the Arab oil embargo of 1973-74, which would trigger a whole series of events with enormous impact on the entire U.S. auto industry. Its immediate effects were to stunt sales of Detroit's big cars while causing all car owners a lot of extra grief and expense at every fillup. But it had a more vital, long-term consequence as well: it made the nation energy-conscious in a way it had never been before. In particular, it highlighted the need for smaller, more economical cars in all size and price ranges, the kind of cars America would need to produce for the uncertain times that seemed to lay ahead.

Car buyers got the message and, for a time, flocked to Detroit's compacts and the smaller, high-mileage imports in record numbers. The big sales winners were the various Japanese makes, which up to this time had made only a fairly small dent in the U.S. market. Toyota and Datsun did especially well. Within a few months the oil started flowing again, gasoline supplies eased, many buyers forgot all about the shortages, and big-car sales bounced back. But

Corvette for 1981. Model year production totalled 45,631 units.

the damage had been done. Japanese models continued to sell well, though the reason now was not so much their fuel efficiency as their Americanized styling and creature comforts and—most of all—their superior workmanship and value-for-money.

None of this affected the Corvette much. In fact, America's sports car defied the market by setting new sales records. Recalled Zora Arkus-Duntov in a 1977 interview with *Road & Track* magazine's John Lamm: "In 1970, production in the St. Louis Corvette plant reached 32,000 and they said no more, that is the utmost capacity. Then came the energy crunch and we were forced to let people go from

our plants in St. Louis. But the Corvette was not affected by the oil crisis and that plant tried to find work for the furloughed employees. With the same facility and same floor space, we ended up eventually producing 44,000 Corvettes."

Still, this was only a drop in the bucket for mighty General Motors, which was understandably more concerned about its volume-car business in the wake of the energy crisis. The grim new realities were that natural

resources are finite and that the nation's economy—indeed, the American way of life—could be severely disrupted by the actions of other countries in an interdependent global economy. Other fuel shortages could occur just as easily—and suddenly—as this first one, and some experts were predicting more. Meanwhile, much higher energy prices were creating an inflationary spiral that was pushing interest rates and the prices of all consumer goods to unprecedented highs.

167

This made new-car ownership increasingly difficult for a growing number of Americans, and more and more people found they could no longer afford to change cars every two or three years like they used to.

GM evaluated all this with a critical eye. It concluded that it needed more timely products as soon as possible. But there were already a number of good economy cars around, so these new models would have to offer more than just good mileage. The keys to future sales success would be quality and durability, factors that had already emerged as the critical ones in the high acceptance of Japanese models.

While Ford and Chrysler went back to business as usual, GM embarked on a massive, long-term program to revamp its entire fleet. Its future cars would be smaller, lighter and more economical, and some would employ the space-saving front-wheel drive layout to provide about as much interior room as its older

cars within a smaller exterior package. The first of the new downsized breed appeared for 1977, the smaller B- and C-body full-size cars that are with us yet. Then came similarly reworked intermediates for '78, followed by the front-drive X-body compacts two years later and the subcompact J-cars for 1982.

With all this, it would be easy to assume GM had forgotten the Corvette. But it hadn't. This was still an important car: the line leader for the firm's largest-volume division. Even so, there was no rush put out an all-new model. As John Lamm observed in 1977: "There's been little point in spending the money on a new car when the old one is selling out year after year. Yet there has always been an alternative waiting for a quieting of Corvette sales—a mid-engine alternative. It was first meant, according to Duntov, as a possible counter for the mid-engine Ford Mach I program, but when that

died, so did the new Corvette. On two other occasions the car was so close to production that actual production techniques had been developed—once with 350 and 427 engine choices, once as a rotary—but the folks just keep buying the old ones."

Lamm refers to XP-882, an experimental program begun in the late Sixties which fueled persistent widespread speculation that the next Corvette would be a mid-engine design. The original full-scale running prototype surfaced in late 1969 as a curvy, low-slung coupe with mechanicals borrowed from the front-drive Oldsmobile Toronado, modified by Duntov for a midships production installation. By mid-1970 this car was slathered all over "buff books" like *Road & Track*, which said in its July issue: "We'll stake our repu-

tation on this being the Corvette of the future—but don't expect it until 1972 at the earliest." A January 1971 story forecasting a 1973 announcement would prove equally misguided, though the car now bore Corvette script and looked close to production-ready.

But GM had something else in mind. At the enthusiastic urging of then-president Ed Cole, the company was busy developing a rotary engine patterned after Felix Wankel's pioneering design in Germany. Originally, it was intended as an option for Chevy's subcompact Vega to provide a domestic alternative to the rotary NSU and Mazda models then arriving in the U.S. With its light weight and compact size, the Wankel was also deemed ideal for a new sports car. With this in mind, Cole ordered up two prototypes based on the XP-882 chassis. One used the basic two-rotor unit being readied for the Vega, and had a sleek body styled and built by Pininfarina in Italy. Sometimes called the "two-rotor" car, it carried the XP-987GT project designation. The other car was an arresting gullwing coupe created by Bill Mitchell and powered by a pair of two-rotor engines bolted together and producing some 420 bhp. Both these cars toured the show circuit and got wide press coverage. Again, everyone assumed that here was tomorrow's Corvette. But then the energy crisis hit—and revealed the Wankel's comparatively poor fuel economy. Mazda sales took a nosedive, and GM abruptly stopped further work on its own rotary—and the mid-engine Corvette designed around it.

But Bill Mitchell was nothing if not persistent. At his behest a 400-cid small-block V-8 was slipped into the four-rotor coupe and the car retitled "Aerovette." It again went on tour, and again the rumors started flying. Mitchell began lobbying at Chevrolet for this car's production. As usual, if he wanted something badly enough, he usually got it, and then-GM-chairman Thomas

Murphy actually approved the Aerovette for the 1980 program. By the end of 1977, clay models were complete and tooling orders were about to be placed. So, for a moment, the Aerovette was the next Corvette.

But it was not to be. The project lost its most influential supporter when Mitchell retired in 1977. Duntov also supported it, but he had retired at the end of '74. And, by this time, Cole was gone, too. A further blow came from Duntov's successor, David R. McLellan, who preferred the "front mid-engine" concept, inaugurated with the 1963 Sting Ray, over a pure midships layout for reasons of packaging, manufacturing, and performance. Also, Chevy looked at some of the Aerovette's design elements —especially the radically vee'd windshield and the gullwing doors as well as the mid-engine mechanicals—and concluded the whole thing would be simply too expensive given the Corvette's

sales volume. And, while manufacturers like Porsche and Lotus had offered mid-engine production models, none had sold really well. Meanwhile, Datsun couldn't build enough of its front-engine (and admittedly less costly) 240Z. The pundits had predicted the mid-engine layout was the wave of the future for road-going sports cars, but it wasn't working out that way. Porsche only confirmed that with its next new model, the front-engine 924 of 1976.

As these events unfolded, Chevy faced the more immediate problem of what to do about the 1978 Corvette. It would be the 25th edition and the division wanted something dramatic, yet there was no replacement in the works for the aging fifth-generation design. As usual, the stylists had the answer. Chevrolet's public relations staff described it this way: "The biggest change in the 1978 Corvette is the new fastback roofline [cre-

ated by the] wide expanse of glass [that] wraps around to the sides of the car, which improves rear-quarter visibility while contributing to a feeling of greater interior roominess. Also new for 1978 are front and rear emblems to commemorate the 25th anniversary model. The luggage area, now larger and more utilitarian...is more accessible as well." It would have been even more accessible had the big backlight not been fixed. It looked like it should swing up hatch-fashion but, though Chevrolet considered this, it was rejected on cost grounds. "Because the storage area is clearly visible through the large glass area, new standard equipment on all 1978 Corvettes includes a package security shade mounted at the rear of the compartment on a spring-loaded roller."

The press release went on to describe 1978 as a year of "both major and minor changes for the Corvette." Among the latter were new squared-up housings for the speedometer and tachometer to match the restyled center console gauges from '77. The interior door panels were redesigned with a new armrest and integral door pull. A glove compartment with a real door, a sorely needed item, was added to the dash. A retrograde step was moving the wipe/wash controls from the directionals stalk back to the instrument panel. Fuel tank capacity was increased from 17 to 24 gallons for greater cruising range, and the standard anti-theft system was now wired into the lift-off roof panels, which had an unfortunate habit of disappearing. The glass panels finally arrived on the options slate. Like the steel ones, they were modified to provide a bit more headroom and had a one-handle instead of two-handle locking mechanism. The three-point seatbelts were given a single inertia reel, and belt guides were eliminated. For the first time, 60-series tires were available (with some inner fender shearing) "to put the most aggressive tire on the car as possible," said Chevy. These HR60s (225R/60-15s in metric measure) were an option to the standard GR70s. The FE7 gymkhana suspension package was still the bargain extra, though its price had risen quite a bit in the last few years, now at $41.

The possible historical interest in the '78 Corvette wasn't lost on Chevrolet management. The di-

The 1979 edition saw only detail revisions. Horsepower was up a bit on both versions of the Corvette V-8. Production leaped past 50,000 units for the first time in the history of America's sports car.

Model year 1980 saw integration of the former added-on front and rear spoilers plus a raked-back nose. Production fell to nearly 41,000 units for the model year.

vision capitalized on it with not one, but two limited editions, both highly sought-after today. One, appropriately named the Silver Anniversary model, featured two-tone paint (silver over a grey lower body with separating pinstripe) plus nice-looking alloy wheels carrying the fat Goodyear GT raised-white-letter radials. The tinted-glass roof panels were standard along with a color-keyed silver interior. Aside from these differences, the Silver Anniversary Corvette— actually a package option—was depressingly stock for a celebration car.

The other '78 special was a facsimile of the Corvette pace car used for the 62nd Indianapolis 500. This, too, was a package option, RPO Z78, and brought the base model's $9322 price up to $13,653. It was decked out with a black upper body and silver-metallic lower body, plus the alloy wheels and wide tires. It also carried prominent front and rear spoilers, which some viewed as ruining the car's basic shape. A novel touch was inclusion of a package of identifying "Pace Car" decals for the owner to apply if desired to complete the effect (most owners didn't bother). Upholstery was your choice of full silver leather or the same with grey cloth inserts, and carpeting was color-keyed to match. Other standard features included power windows, rear window defroster, air conditioning, dual sport door mirrors, tilt steering wheel, power door locks, and AM/FM stereo radio.

The Pace Car replica was announced in October 1977 with a planned production run of 2500 units, 100 for each year of Corvette production. Rumor had it that Goodyear would issue special tires with white letters spelling out C-O-R-V-E-T-T-E, but this didn't materialize. Also, Turbo-Hydramatic was supposedly the only transmission available, but a four-speed manual showed up on quite a few examples. In the end, Chevy decided to up the run to 6200 cars, one for each of the division's dealers, which represented about 15 percent of total Corvette

output—not really all that "limited" when you think about it.

Despite its formidable price, demand for the Pace Car was high—so much so that a few bogus ones appeared. At the time, the "real" replicas fetched at least $15,000, many dealers were asking $22,000-$28,000, and some people were even willing to pay $75,000 for what was viewed as a surefire collector's item. All this tempted some owners of standard 'Vettes to try to pass them off as factory Pace Cars—at the same high prices, of course. It was easy enough to do: all you needed was a black or silver car with the right options, a spray gun, the two fiberglass spoilers, and the silver cabin trim available through a friendly parts man. What many counterfeiters forgot was the seats: a new thin-shell plastic design scheduled for the '79s but issued only for the Pace Car models in '78. Naturally, all this created anguish for dealers and buyers alike. In fact, it still does. Chevrolet would remember this pain-

ful experience when it came time to create another limited-edition 'Vette in a few years.

If performance seemed to get lost in such goings on, there was a reason: not much changed. The now-familiar 350 V-8 returned in two forms with marginally revised power ratings. The base L48 unit was now listed at 185 bhp, up 5 bhp from 1977, while the California version came in at 175 bhp. The latter also pulled a shorter 3.55:1 final drive for a bit better dig off the line. The optional L82 engine, priced at $525, received a dual-snorkel air intake for better breathing and a revamped exhaust system aft of the catalytic converter to reduce back pressure. Power output was 220 bhp advertised, quite healthy for the time.

Despite inflation and soaring prices, car sales had long recovered from the effects of the energy crisis and were perking along well for the '78 model year. Corvette was no exception, although total production dipped slightly (by about 2500 units) to 46,776.

With Dave McLellan now in charge of Corvette engineering, work began on a replacement for the fifth generation, which by 1979 was looking quite long in the tooth. Though changes were few in this year's 'Vette, sales swelled beyond the 50,000 mark for the first time. It was a generally good year for the industry as a whole, and Chevy undoubtedly saw no need to rush a successor.

Alterations on the 26th edition were minor. The new lightweight bucket seats from the '78 Pace Car appeared on cue. They also acquired an extra inch of rearward travel plus more convenient inertia seatback locks. The passenger's seatback could also be folded forward to create a longer ledge for awkward cargo, but reclining seatbacks—something the purists had long demanded—weren't available at any price. All engines got the L82-type twin-snorkel air clean-

er, and the base L48 engine gained an extra 10 horses. Shock absorber valving was standardized (previously the rates had been different depending on whether manual or automatic transmission was ordered), and the final drive ratio with automatic was lowered from 3.08 to 3.55:1 for all 50 states. Per federal requirement, a smaller fuel filler neck was fitted so only unleaded gas could be pumped in. Pace Car-style front and rear spoilers were added to the options list, along with an illuminated visor vanity mirror. Tungsten-halogen high-beam headlamps were phased in, and the base AM/FM radio option was also made standard. One final touch was the return of the crossed-flags insignia to the nose and bodysides.

One interesting development during the year came from drag racer Doug Nash, who developed a new five-speed manual transmission for the 'Vette as an aftermarket item. Road & Track's John Dinkel reported it was "designed strictly for competition and features a lightweight magnesium-alloy case that splits like a clamshell to facilitate gear changes and servicing, straight-cut spur gears offering higher strength and lower friction than conventional helical gears and a choice of 17 different ratios." Called the "4+1 Quick Change," it was available in both street and racing versions, priced at $995 and $1100, respectively. The fifth gear was not the overdrive ratio coming into vogue at the time but rather a direct 1.00:1. Dinkel said "the combination of a low numerical axle ratio and high numerical transmission gearing will live longer than the reverse combination, because as the final drive ratio increases numerically the size of the pinion gear decreases and the number of pinion teeth increases . . . .And because most of today's cars are being built with low numerical axle ratios for reasons of improved fuel economy and

173

lower emissions, it means no change in final drive ratio is necessary to take advantage of the Nash 5-speed." *R&T* found the new gearbox raised the 'Vette's top end from 116 to 139 mph compared with the factory four-speed. Though there was no difference in quarter-mile performance, there was a gain of about 1.5 mpg in fuel economy, plus reduced noise levels. The interesting thing about this transmission is that it forecast a radically new manual gearbox being developed for the still-distant sixth-generation Corvette.

Also that year, *R&T* matched the 'Vette in a comparison test against the Mazda RX-7, Datsun 280-ZX, and Porsche 924. The American sports car came in last overall, and the editors jumped all over its harsh ride, buried driving position, minimal cargo space, and indifferent

workmanship. But in summing up they said: "Much loved and still very desirable, it's quick, has excellent brakes, a superb automatic transmission, and is filled with many appreciated amenities...all of which make it an excellent value."

With the advent of the government's corporate average fuel economy (CAFE) standards for 1978, Chevy decided the 'Vette needed to go on a diet. The first evidence of this showed up on the 1980 models. Curb weight was pared by about 250 pounds by using aluminum instead of steel for the front frame cross-member and differential housing, plus greater use of plastics. The aluminum intake manifold previously used on the L82 engine was extended to the base L48, though in federal trim this powerplant lost 5 bhp to emissions tuning (190 bhp at 4400 rpm and 280 lbs/ft torque at

2400 rpm). The L82 returned with five more horses (230 bhp). Californians had to settle for a special 180-bhp 305-cid small-block, available only with automatic.

Also in the interest of better mileage, the previously optional front and rear spoilers were made integral with the surrounding bodywork, and the grille was raked back slightly. The result was a drop in the coefficient of drag (Cd) from 0.503 to a more respectable 0.443—not great, but a welcome improvement all the same. Air conditioning and tilt/telescope steering wheel were now standard, the power door lock button was relocated, and the two storage compartments behind the seats were combined (the battery remained in a separate cubbyhole behind the driver). A depressing sign of the times: the speedometer now read to only 85

Greater use of plastics and lightweight metals trimmed 250 pounds from the '81 Corvette's curb weight. Sales recovered this year, pushing past 45,000 units. Glass roof panels, offered since 1979, were popular with buyers.

mph, in line with another government mandate.

There was indeed another fuel crunch, and it hit in early 1979. In the ensuing economic chaos, the bottom fell out of the U.S. car market. Yet the Corvette sailed on. Though volume was down by some 20 percent, the model year total of 40,614 units was still quite respectable for a heavy, thirsty specialty car that had become almost too expensive (about $13,140 basic) for those most likely to buy it.

For 1981, weight was reduced even further through some clever materials substitutions. Heading the list was a new transverse monoleaf rear spring made of reinforced plastic—just like the body—instead of steel. It pared 33 pounds off those cars equipped with automatic. Other weight-saving engineering measures included use of thinner

glass for the doors and roof panels and a stainless-steel (instead of cast-iron) exhaust manifold. There was now but a single engine, a reworked version of the familiar 350, called L81. It featured magnesium rocker covers and an auxiliary electric cooling fan to supplement the regular engine-driven fan. In line with other 1981 GM cars, the 'Vette gained the firm's new Computer Command Control electronic emissions control system. This provided more precise fuel metering, and also governed the lockup of the automatic transmission's new torque converter clutch, adopted as a fuel-saving measure. The interior was spiffed up with a six-way power driver's seat and quartz clock as standard, and all factory radios acquired electronic instead of manual tuning. Prices, which inflation had been pushing inexorably upward, rose again, the base list now at a bit over $15,000. Despite a generally dismal sales year for the industry as a whole, Corvette once again proved the oddsmakers wrong by moving up smartly to

45,631 units.

Perhaps the biggest Corvette news this year was the transfer of production from the old St. Louis plant to a brand-new high-tech facility in Bowling Green, Kentucky. Many of the loyal workers from Missouri were relocated to the sleepy college community that would be the 'Vette's new home. An interesting historical footnote is that for two months during the summer of '81 the cars were built simultaneously in both places. A key advantage of the new plant was its more advanced paint shop. St. Louis had used lacquer exclusively, but Bowling Green would apply more durable enamels and clear topcoats, emulating European and Japanese practice. The new factory also had much more automated manufacturing hardware in the quest for tighter quality control. It was expensive, but Chevy evidently considered the Corvette worthy of the investment. How things had changed!

With the opening of Bowling Green, some observers concluded that Chevy was preparing for the arrival of an all-new Corvette. And they were right. The existence of a new design was more or less an open secret by this time. Said *Road & Track* in November 1982: "...after all these years of rumors, conjecture, glimpses of exotic mid-engine project cars, hearsay, and slightly blurred photos shot through knotholes in the Milford Proving Ground fence, we can swear with confidence...that there really is an all-new 1983 Corvette in the wings." But it made more sense to test new machinery and work out new assembly procedures with a familiar design rather than a new one, so the fifth generation would put in one final appearance.

It also made sense to use the existing platform to gain field experience with the new model's drivetrain, so the 1982 Corvette was, as *R&T* put it: "...truly the last of its series...a transi-

tion car [with the] new drivetrain in the old body." The engine was still the time-proven 350 V-8 but with a newly developed twin throttle-body fuel injection system, called Cross-Fire injection, instead of a carburetor. It was the first time injection had appeared on a production 'Vette since 1965. The system consisted of an injector unit for each cylinder bank plus cross-over intake manifolding to speed up the velocity of the fuel/air mixture. Computer Command Control electronics governed duration of injector opening in response to signals from various engine-mounted sensors. This revised power unit, intriguingly dubbed L83, was rated at 200 bhp at 4200 rpm, with peak torque of 285 lbs/ft developed at 2800 rpm. For the first time since 1955 there was no manual gearbox available. The standard transmission was a new four-speed automatic with torque converter lockup, effective on all forward gears except first and still governed by the engine's electronic control unit. Also new

Above: The experimental Turbo 'Vette 3 of 1980 boasted 7-psi boost. Horsepower was not disclosed. Opposite page: The 1982 Corvette, priced at $18,290.

were an in-tank electric fuel pump and a solenoid-operated trap door in the hood that opened at full throttle. The air filter, which had previously contained charcoal, reverted to paper. The exhaust system was extensively redesigned around a significantly smaller and lighter catalytic converter, dictated mainly by emissions standards.

To commemorate the last of the "big" 'Vettes, Chevrolet issued a special Collector Edition model for '82. However, recalling its experience with those bogus '78 Pace Car replicas, the division handled this one differently. It was built only as needed to satisfy customer orders, not as a fixed proportion of scheduled production. To prevent someone from turning a standard car into a Collector Edition, Chevy also fitted special vehicle identification number plates.

In many ways, the Collector

Edition was the best of the fifth generation. Setting it apart were cloisonné emblems on hood, rear deck, and steering wheel; a unique silver-beige metallic

paint scheme; graduated "shadow" contrasting paint stripes on hood and bodysides; bronze-tinted glass roof panels; and finned, cast-aluminum wheels styled like the ones first seen on the '63 Sting Ray. Inside were special silver-beige cloth upholstery, leather door trim, leather-wrapped steering wheel, and luxury carpeting. The most obvious external difference was the Collector's frameless lift-up glass hatch, postponed from the '78 restyle (and, incidentally, not in-

cluded on base models).

With 10 more horsepower than the previous L81 engine, the new injected L83 showed a definite performance gain despite its automatic transmission. *Road & Track,* comparing the

'82 with its '81 four-speed car, said "...the power shows in quicker dragstrip numbers. The new car ran the quarter-mile in 16.1 seconds at 84.5 mph and accelerated from 0-60 in 7.9 seconds. The pre-wundermotor did

it in 17.0 at 82 mph and 9.2 seconds. At last relief from years of backsliding. And throttle response is excellent. In the 1983 Corvette, predicted to be at least 500 pounds lighter than this year's 3425-pound car, it should

Left: The special Collector Edition '82 offered lift-up hatch and unique trim for $22,538. This page, top: Corvette for '81. Above: The standard '82 model.

be a very nice engine." The injection also improved economy a little, and it certainly deterred owners from anything remotely like "hot rod" modifications.

A lot had happened to the long-running fifth generation. The Collector Edition earned the dubious distinction of being the first Corvette to break the $20,000 price barrier (base list was $22,538), a far cry from the $4663 it took to buy a nicely equipped '68. Besides escalating prices, the intervening 15 years

had seen two restyles, the demise of the big-block engines, big performance losses and slight performance gains, and the addition of more and more creature comforts. Yet for all that, the essential character of America's sports car had survived. Said *R&T*: "No matter how much luxury...you pack into a Corvette, the basic honesty of the car rises above its own image. It tells you this is an uncompromised two-seater with a big engine and that it's made to go around corners and come out of them fast. The car has its own particular flavor and appeal, and the automotive world would lose a great deal if the

Corvette were to become too much like other automobiles."

Chevy was not about to let that happen, of course, but the time for change was definitely at hand. Perhaps because of the faltering economy, perhaps because a new model was known to be close, Corvette production fell to its lowest point since 1967, a disheartening 25,407 units. Of these, only 6759 were the Collector Edition, and for this reason every one of them seems destined to live up to that name in the very near future.

It was the end of a remarkable motorcar and a remarkable era. Now a new Corvette was ready. The long wait was over.

1984 AND BEYOND: A NEW ERA BEGINS

Few cars have been more eagerly anticipated than the 1984 Corvette. After all, this was not just another new model but the latest expression of what had become an automotive institution. It would be the first really new version of America's sports car in 15 years. As such, it couldn't help but generate intense scrutiny and widespread debate among enthusiasts and members of the automotive press even before it appeared.

It had indeed been a long time coming, this new Corvette, and, because of this, great things were expected of it. The automotive world had changed a great deal since the last generation was born. Fuel economy standards were now a fact of life—and law. Everything had become more expensive. America's sports car had long since ceased being the ultimate wheeled possession for many people. Cars like the Datsun Zs, the Mazda RX-7, and the Porsche 924 and 928 had raised considerably the standards by which sports cars are judged. How would the new Corvette compare against such respected rivals? Equally important in the minds of many was how the new car would compare with its illustrious predecessors. Would the sixth generation be worthy of the hallowed tradition it inherited? And would it be able to maintain that tradition in the brave new world of the Eighties?

After several delays, which only served to heighten the anticipation, the new Corvette was at last publicly unveiled in the early spring of 1983. The reaction was generally a mixture of relief and unrestrained excitement. The sixth generation was, thank goodness, still a Corvette in appearance and mechanical layout. Yet it was startlingly and entirely new, completely up to date and oozing high technology

A pre-production 1984 Corvette on test near the GM Desert Proving Grounds in Arizona.

from every pore of its fiberglass being. In some ways it was not exactly the car some people had predicted, but it was obviously a car to be respected.

The press was quick to give the '84 its due. Said *Car and Driver* in March 1983: "You have waited long enough. So let's get it over with: the new Corvette is a truly stout automobile. It is all that the fevered acolytes so desperately wanted their fiberglass fossil to be—a true-born, world-class sports car loaded with technical sophistication...The roadholding on this new machine is so advanced that we recorded the highest skidpad lateral acceleration—0.90g—ever observed with a conventional automobile by this staff. That figure practically trivializes the previous high-water marks... generated by such exotics as the Porsche 928 and assorted Ferraris...It is the hands-down fastest American automobile, capable of 140-mph top speeds, 0-60 mph times under seven seconds, and 15.2-second quarter-mile forays...one of the half-dozen fastest production automobiles in the entire world."

That same month, *Motor Trend* echoed: "All the qualities it needed to have, it has in great abundance. Stylish appearance? Obviously. Fresh engineering? Just look. Proper comfort? But of course. Formidable performance? Stand back. There may be no better way to see the USA. Mission accomplished."

Said *Road & Track:* "There's a great deal of thoughtful design evident in this new Corvette, quite enough to bring it to the attention of those who felt the previous versions had become increasingly tacky. Is it now the best exotic car in the world? The best exotic car value? Its performance levels...stack up very well with those of the Ferrari 308GTSi or Porsche 928. Or should we measure the tremendous market pressure the Corvette puts on less expensive high-performance cars... Resolution of these questions

awaits proper comparative testing, but three things are clear: the new Corvette is abundantly more than an updated clunker to any of us, the questions posed are far from trivial, and the car's enthusiast appeal is immensely broad."

The development program for the '84 design began in earnest in mid-1978. This was shortly after GM management cancelled plans for a productionized version of the mid-engine Aerovette (see previous chapter). This new effort involved the closest collaboration between the Engineering and Design Staffs yet seen at GM. In this case the chief collaborators were Corvette engineering head David R. McLellan and designer Jerry Palmer, head of Chevrolet Studio Three. This close liaison was vital if the new Corvette were to be built with a high level of quality, important as the new model would sell for considerably more than the last of the fifth-generation cars.

According to Palmer, the keynote for the new 'Vette was "form follows function." While many automakers have paid only lip service to that well-known dictum over the years, both he and McLellan deemed following it essential for the new Corvette to be competitive with more recently designed sports cars. Specifically, the task was to eliminate the deficiencies for which the fifth generation had been criticized while at the same time maintaining the traditional Corvette look and driving feel. And, the new car had to have superior aerodynamics, more passenger room and—most importantly for a driver's car— even better handling than earlier models.

Accordingly, the sixth generation was engineered literally from the ground up. Both design groups began with the so-called "T-point," which defines the position of the seated driver's hip joint relative to the interior and the rest of the car. For the new model, the T-point was raised

Though retaining a recognizably Corvette face, the '84 model was all-new, boasting low-drag styling, a space-age cockpit, and a beautiful, very accessible underhood layout. The long-lead press preview (right) was held at Riverside Raceway in late 1983.

about an inch and moved an inch or so rearward compared to the previous Corvette. This opened up more legroom and also put the driver higher in relation to the road for better visibility. Further, it enabled the chassis to sit higher than before for more ground clearance, though the choice of 16-inch rather than 15-inch-diameter wheels and tires also played a part.

Handling was a major consideration, of course, so the chassis was engineered around Pirelli's then-state-of-the-art P7 radials. However, the '84 emerged on Goodyear covers called Eagle VR50. This was a new tire developed specifically for this car and sized at P255/50VR16. The "VR" refers to speed rating, which was in excess of 130 mph. Mounted on

cast-alloy wheels of 8.5-inch width front and 9.5-inch width rear, these tires were notable for their "gatorback" tread design, said to shed water more effectively to resist hydroplaning in wet weather. The wheels would be unidirectional owing to the

shape of their radial cooling fins, meaning specific left and right/front and rear wheels that weren't interchangeable.

Complementing the new wheels and tires was a considerably revised chassis. The old perimeter-type ladder frame

body panels. Completing this basic assembly were an aluminized bolt-on front suspension carrier and a bolt-on extension for the back bumper.

This more rigid platform allowed McLellan's staff to rework the suspension. The front end retained the familiar unequal-length upper and lower A-arm arrangement of previous years but with a new twist. Instead of a coil spring on each side, the '84 emerged with a single reinforced-fiberglass leaf spring mounted transversely between the two lower arms. A 20mm anti-roll bar would be standard, while a 25mm bar would be included with an optional handling package, RPO Z51. The big change occurred at the rear. Zora Duntov's old three-link geometry was replaced by a newly designed five-link setup consisting of upper and lower longitudinal links mounted between the hub carriers and the body, twin lateral strut rods connecting the differential with the hub carriers, another transverse plastic leaf spring (as used since '81), plus U-jointed halfshafts and rear-mounted tie rods. Steering was changed from GM's usual recirculating-ball mechanism to rack-and-pinion. This featured a forward-mounted rack for greater precision and a standard high-effort power assist for better control at high speeds. The normal steering ratio was set at a constant 15.5:1, quite fast for a U.S. car. It was raised to 13:1 for the Z51 package. A tilt-and-telescope steering wheel would be standard.

As before, stopping power would be supplied by big vented disc brakes at each wheel, hydraulically assisted. The brakes themselves were a new design created by Girlock, an American offshoot of the British Girling company. Making extensive use of aluminum, they had 11.5-inch rotors and featured quick-change (via a single bolt) semi-metallic pads with audible wear indicators.

was abandoned for a new steel backbone design not unlike that pioneered by Lotus of England. In the Corvette, the "spine" took the form of a C-section beam carrying the propshaft and rigidly connected to the differential. The benefits of this were less weight and more cockpit room through elimination of the transmission and differential crossmembers. It also allowed the exhaust system to run under the propshaft instead of alongside it. Welded to this frame was what Chevy called an "integral perimeter-birdcage unitized structure"—"uniframe" for short—making this the first Corvette to employ unit construction instead of body-on-frame. The "birdcage" formed the windshield and door frames, lower A-pillar extensions, rocker panels, rear cockpit wall, and front subframe. It also included the "hoop" at the rear of the cockpit that acted as the attachment point for a new lift-up rear window. The entire structure would be galvanized inside and out for corrosion resistance. In effect, it was a "skeleton" for hanging the major fiberglass

McLellan claimed that "even in base suspension configuration, the new Corvette...is absolutely superior to any production vehicle in its part of the market." An extra margin of superiority was the rationale behind the Z51 option, a $51 bargain. This comprises the Eagle VR50 tires plus heavy-duty shocks front and rear (RPO F51) and the FE7 Sport Suspension with heavy-duty lower control arm bushings, uprated front and rear springs and stabilizer bars, plus the faster-ratio steering. The Z51 package also included a shorter 3.31:1 rear axle ratio.

More evidence of Design and Engineering teamwork was found under the new Corvette's "clamshell" hood, a part of the design concept from the beginning. The hood includes the tops of the front fenders and lifts to near vertical to facilitate service access. What you found under there was a familiar friend in somewhat different dress. It was the trusty 5.7-liter/350-cid V-8 as

A stunning car from any angle, the 1984 Corvette will look good for years to come. Drag coefficient is a low 0.34.

used for 1982—and still called L83—with twin throttle-body electronic fuel injection, the "Cross-Fire" induction system with dual ram-air intakes. Rated output was boosted by 5 bhp and 5 lbs/ft of torque, reflecting the adoption of a less power-robbing radiator fan and accessory drive. The underhood area was dominated by a new flat-top silver-finish air cleaner created by Palmer's crew and

made of die-cast magnesium. This has separate vacuum-modulated doors that regulate air flow from ducts molded in on the underside of the hood. The ducts connect to the air cleaner when the hood is closed. A single air intake under the nose (actually below the bumper, making this car a "bottom breather") feeds outside air to the underhood ducts. The entire engine compartment is now color-

coordinated in silver and black. Palmer even persuaded GM's AC-Delco Division to come up with a matching battery.

For the first time since 1981 the Corvette's standard transmission was a four-speed manual unit, but it was nothing like any previous gearbox. Basically, it was a normal unit with a second planetary gearset attached, actuated by the engine's Computer Command Control electronics. The auxiliary gearset sits at the rear of the transmission, and engages in all ratios except first through a hydraulic clutch. The effect is to provide a stepdown or "overdrive" reduction of 0.67:1 in each of the top three cogs to improve part-throttle fuel economy. At wide throttle openings the overdrive is automatically locked out. It could also be disengaged via an override switch on the center console. Standard final drive is 3.07:1, with 3.31:1 gearing

available for better standing-start performance. Returning from '82, but now as an option, was the four-speed overdrive automatic, the GM 700-R4 unit with lockup torque converter clutch effective in all ratios except first.

Production delays forced postponement of the "4+3 Overdrive" manual until early 1984, so the first of the new 'Vettes were equipped only with the automatic. Dennis Simanaitis, engineering editor for *Road & Track,* called this "a gearbox smarter than your average driver," and liked the way it worked. But he noted that "even with all [its computerized] wizardry, [fuel economy] is little different from that with the automatic. We recorded 15.0 mpg versus 15.5 for the car with the Turbo Hydramatic, and that sounds like a wash." Originally, the OD override switch was reserved for a special export ver-

sion of the new model owing to vagaries of the EPA's fuel economy test procedure. Had the car been tested without the automatic OD engagement, there was a real possibility that it would have come under the dreaded "gas guzzler" tax mandated by CAFE. McLellan stated that the OD lockout was intended for U.S. sale all along, even though the first manual cars shown to the press didn't have it. Still, all this brings up a telling point: despite Chevy's considerable effort to keep weight as low as possible, the new 'Vette emerged heavier than most expected—by a good 300 pounds.

Nevertheless, the new car did emerge 250 pounds lighter than a comparably equipped '82, a worthwhile gain. This was largely the result of numerous, subtle weight-saving tricks. We've already mentioned a few, but there were others, some industry firsts in the use of lightweight materials. One of these is a propshaft and supporting yokes made of forged aluminum, welded together. Another was a radiator support made of plastic sheet molding compund (SMC). The reinforced-fiberglass transverse springs weighed half as much as four steel coil springs of comparable size. They were also claimed to be more durable (5 million full cycles versus about 75,000). The new cooling system has twin expansion tanks made of plastic, as are the radiator fan and shroud. Aluminum figures extensively throughout. The front suspension control arms and knuckles and the rear suspension's lateral arms are all aluminum forgings. So is the chassis "spine." The automatic transmission's torque converter housing is formed from aluminum sheet. The brakes' splash shields are aluminum, not the usual steel, and the calipers are an iron-aluminum alloy for greater strength with less weight.

While McLellan's engineers busied themselves with technical

Main '84 body features included hatch rear window and massive "clamshell" hood.

intricacies, Palmer's staff was shaping the new model in Production Studio Three. This program moved along quite rapidly once the designers shifted their efforts back to a front-engine configuration. A full-scale "theme" clay based on a Palmer sketch was completed in September 1978. By mid-November of the following year—a scant 14 months later—the new design was more or less final except for taillamps, front fender trim, and the shape of the nose. Though the wheels and tires were the dominant design element in all the various sketches and clay models, Palmer's staff wrestled with the overall proportions as much as with surface detailing. As Palmer told *Car and Driver's* Jean Lindamood: "The evolution ...was a very slow, methodical one. It wasn't bangety-bangety-bang. We made incremental changes—very slight. I'm talking about one-eighth-inch movements, just enough to change the accent of a form or the loading of a line."

The design brief was a tall one. First and foremost was the demand that the new car must look like a Corvette. In other words, it couldn't break with traditional 'Vette appearance "cues." Drivelines would be carried over, and though the new car could be a bit smaller outside it had to have more room inside. Other goals were improved visibility and less aerodynamic drag. A key change affecting room, drag, and visibility came when Engineering relocated the steering linkage further forward than originally envisioned. This allowed the small-block V-8 to be lowered in the chassis, thus achieving a lower hoodline for better forward vision and reduced frontal area, the latter a big factor in reducing air drag.

What emerged was a car recognizably new but still very much a Corvette. Said Palmer: "I really believe we've designed a car without compromises, but we've managed to retain the Corvette identity. The car still, for example, has folding headlamps. It has a Corvette 'face,' even though there are foglamps and turn lamps where air intakes used to be. The front fender vents are still there, as is the large backlight and the functional rear spoiler. The first time people see this car, they're going to know what it is...[Yet] the new car's massive surfaces, such as the hood, are deceiving. On first glance you probably wouldn't believe it is smaller than the previous year's model in every dimension except width."

Though some of the dimensional changes in the '84 weren't that large, the new car's proportions were definitely fresh. Overall length was down a significant 8.8 inches despite only a two-inch cut in wheelbase (from 98 to 96 inches) and a mere 1.7-inch reduction in front overhang. The secret was a 5.2-inch chop in rear overhang, which gave the effect of a longer hood even though it's actually shorter. Contributing to sleekness is a very "fast" 64-degree windshield angle (as measured from the vertical)—the steepest of any American production car in history. Compared to the fifth generation, the base of the windshield sits 1.5 inches lower and a bit further forward. In turn, this allowed the beltline to be dropped, giving the '84 a "glassier" appearance.

As Palmer suggests, the real change in the new car's looks comes from that increase in width. The old pinched-waist midsection is gone, along with the bulged front and rear fenderlines. In their place is a smoother, more "organic" contour, especially when viewed from the front or rear three-quarter angle. The new car retains its predecessor's flared wheel arches, which combine with the fat tires to accentuate the hunkered-down look. There is no more conflict between the fenders and the beltline, which now rises uninterrupted from the windshield toward the near-vertical Kamm-style tail with the traditional quartet of lights. In profile, there's a discernible wedge shape that's pleasing and functional in the GM idiom.

One styling element new to the Corvette is a perimeter rub strip that completely encircles the car, and serves visually to link the tops of the front and rear bumpers. It also conceals the shutlines for the new "clam-shell" hood along the bodysides.

After 15 years of Corvettes with T-tops the '84 could hardly have reverted to a fixed roof, and it didn't. But the T-bar is gone, replaced by a one-piece removable panel with four attachment points (two on the windshield header, two on the roof "hoop"). Unlike some recent 'Vettes where the twin panels had to ride on the rear deck, this new one stows its panel in special slots built into the top of the luggage bay. For added protection against vandals, the top can be removed only with a special wrench. Buyers have a choice of either a solid body-color panel or a tinted transparent top made of scratch-resistant acrylic, the latter an option delayed until well after introduction. Either type is far lighter and easier to wield than the awkward glass panes of old.

Chevy boasts that the '84 Cor-

vette's shape was partly refined in the wind tunnel. One new wrinkle in this car's development was use of a sensor to compare pressure differences at various points on the car as it sat in a moving airstream versus pressure in other parts of the tunnel. This technique yielded a detailed picture of the "actual pressure variants and vortices created by passage of the vehicle. Such an image is far more useful than is a picture of surface flow only, and Corvette is believed to be the first sports car ever designed with the assistance of such a tool." While the resulting drag coefficient was only average by today's standards—0.34—the reduced frontal area made the new Corvette much slipperier than that often-misleading value suggested. And it represented a useful 23.7 percent drag reduction compared with the 1982 Corvette's 0.44 Cd.

With its striking exterior, the new Corvette needed an equally striking cockpit, and this it has. The creation of GM's Interior Design group directed by Pat Furey, it's dominated by a very space-age instrument panel and the usual tall center tunnel/console. Occupants sit a bit lower in the '84, but the cockpit looks more spacious and open than in the fifth generation. Appearances are not deceiving. Despite the shorter wheelbase and a 1.1-inch reduction in overall height, the new model offers fractional gains in head and leg room and a whopping 6.5-inch increase in total shoulder room, an area where the old car was decidedly lacking. Cargo room is also greater, by a useful—and welcome—8 cubic feet or so. And, as mentioned, it's much more accessible thanks to that new lift-up hatch window.

All instrumentation is now directly ahead of the driver—no more minor dials in the center of the dash. In fact, there are no dials at all: the new Corvette uses an all-electronic display supplied by GM's AC Division.

This features digital and analog graphic displays for speedometer and tachometer, plus numerical engine function readouts in a smaller panel flanked by the two main displays. A switch panel in the vertical portion of the center console allows the driver to select which functions will be monitored. These include instantaneous and average miles per gallon, trip odometer, and fuel range, as well as engine temperature, oil pressure and temperature, and electrical system voltage. The console also houses the sound system (the much acclaimed GM-Delco/Bose unit is an $895 option), and the heat/vent/AC controls.

Standard seats in the '84 are newly designed high-back buckets with prominent bolsters on both cushion and backrest, manual fore/aft adjustment and —at long last—reclining backrests. Full cloth trim is standard, with leather upholstery optional. Also offered at extra cost is the latest in "super seats," supplied by Lear-Siegler. These provide electric adjustment for backrest angle and cushion bolster in/out, plus a powered three-stage lumbar support adjuster using inflatable bladders that can be individually air-bled to achieve the proper contour.

Shortly after the '84 went on sale a couple of running changes were announced. An oil cooler became standard equipment, and the base 15-inch wheel/tire package was deleted (thus making the 16-inchers a mandatory option with the base suspension). Meanwhile, motor noters were subjecting the new models to their first full road tests and, as a result, the initial enthusiasm of some scribes cooled. *Car and Driver* was the most critical, though there's some reason to think its reviewers weren't completely objective. Most everyone described the ride as harsh, but the Z51 package earned special scorn from technical editor Don Sherman: "The problem...is that it's a balls-out calibration that ruins the car for day-to-day use...Really bad pavement sent its wheels bounding, and even minor bumps or irregularities threw the car off on a momentary tangent...In exchange for these hardships you get lightning reflexes...and imperceptible body roll." *Motor Trend's* Ron Grable was more charitable. He praised the quick acceleration and phenomenal handling of his manual-transmission example, then noted: "This level of cornering performance does not come totally without cost, however, and the Corvette can be a harsh environment at times, on certain surfaces. For instance, you definitely want to stay out of the far right lane on freeways that have seen lots of heavy 18-wheeler traffic. The 'Vette will jiggle your eyeballs on any surface the big rigs have roughed up."

CONSUMER GUIDE® magazine's testers also criticized the "tough" ride. Though our car had the softer base suspension, we felt even this was too stiff and jarring most of the time on patched city streets. We also found "exhaust and road noise are loud at anything above idle speed, though the exhaust settles down when cruising in OD. The automatic transmission is sensitive to throttle changes in city driving, so it seems to be changing gears almost constantly. It's also slow to come out of higher gears unless you really pour on the throttle."

Most colleagues shared our initial dislike for the flashy instrumentation. *C/D's* Sherman described it as "purposely too futuristic to be appreciated by anyone mired in the twentieth century," while his fellow staffer Pat Bedard quipped that "everything about the cockpit is so George Lucas, from the glow-winkie dash to the g-couch seats." Our view was that "the instrumentation is complete and entertaining, but the bar graphs are just for color; they're too hard to read to be useful... The test car's panel was dimly lit on one side, and the entire display is hard to read in sunlight."

Despite such carpings, the press had nothing but good things to say about the new 'Vette's acceleration and road-holding. Most reports showed 0-60 mph available from rest in around 7 seconds and handling numbers that were nearly untouchable by any other series-production automobile. Our overall verdict: "More sophisticated and technically up to date than its predecessor, and a world-class sports car with few rivals in performance. You have to live with a bump-and-grind ride and plenty of noise to enjoy it, but it provides motoring thrills in potent doses." Said *MT's* Grable: "The '84 Corvette is...taut, responsive, predictable, and desirable. The running changes...have addressed —and improved—a couple weak areas, areas that had been uniformly criticized. Does this mean Chevrolet is listening? We certainly would like to think so, because that bodes well for the future of this outstanding American representative in the GT arena."

The future does indeed look bright for America's sports car. The '84 went on sale in California on March 24, 1983, mostly to placate dealers in the Corvette's most important market; April 21st was the introduction date for the other 49 states. Through the end of November, sales totalled 20,610, satisfying if not anywhere near the record-setting 1979 pace. Of course, the market right now is not what it used to be, but the new 'Vette's much higher price has probably been something of a sales barrier. At this writing, the base list price is $23,360 (up from the announced $21,800 and reflecting the usual price rise at the start of the formal model year plus standard equipment

changes), and most examples go out the door for $25,000 with just a few options. There's little doubt prices will continue to escalate in the years ahead.

Chevy's buyer profile indicates the new car is so far appealing to a slightly older, more monied clientele, which was all part of the marketing plan. Median income of the '84 Corvette owner is $67,200, a 34 percent increase over buyers of the '82, and at least 40 percent have household incomes exceeding $75,000 annually. Also, median age of the '84 buyer is 40, five years higher than before. Chevy notes that about a third of the cars go to executives, salesmen, and managers, while lawyers and judges account for another 12 percent. If the Corvette has moved up-market, at least it is giving some foreign marques a good run for the money. Chevy proudly points out that foreign trade-ins— including a number of high-buck "exotic" sports cars—are running at three times the rate of

Perimeter rub strip conceals body joins on the '84. Note massive wheels and tires.

the '82 model.

As for what lies ahead, it seems clear that the '84 design will carry on comfortably into the next decade, maybe even into the next millenium. It will take another six to 10 years for GM to complete current plans for overhauling its volume models, and it would likely not consider budgeting for another all-new Corvette before then.

In the meantime, the sixth generation will be progressively honed and refined. The exact nature of these changes and when or if they appear will depend on many factors, of course, not the least of which are fuel prices and the success of new competitors from overseas. In general, though, we can say that the modifications will be aimed at improved aerodynamics and weight reduction through more extensive use of lighter materials, both in the interest of better fuel economy. A turbocharged V-6 engine may be in the offing as well. It's a familiar quantity

within GM and could be prepared rapidly if the need arises. However, the small-block V-8 appears to have a lot of life left in it yet, though its construction is likely to become more exotic as time goes by.

We can report that the 1985 model will definitely have port fuel injection. It's a more efficient but more costly system than the stopgap throttle-body type, but it is the approach that is now nevertheless favored by GM engineers. We'd estimate a 10-15 horsepower gain, with a similar improvement in rated torque. Spring and shock calibrations may come in for some minor adjustments to improve the ride, though McLellan is adamant that handling and roadholding will not be compromised. It's doubtful the svelte styling will change at all, at least for the next few years. At most, expect a mildly reshaped tail in the interest of cutting a few hundredths off the drag coefficient.

In the modern new sixth-generation design Corvette lovers again have a car they can be excited about. It is the latest in a long proud line, with a heritage of innovation and performance 30 years deep. It will no doubt be as revered as much as its splendid forebears and as much a "dream machine" for countless enthusiasts not yet born when we thrilled to the spirited 1956-57s and the sensational Sting Rays.

The 1984 model is very up-to-date, though it's hardly the last word in efficiency. It has a number of advanced features, though many of these are found on other cars. It is most definitely a high-performance machine in the Corvette tradition, yet it does not stand as far above its rivals as Corvettes of the past. But, in the end, the '84 excels and excites because it is a Corvette, America's sports car. And that is enough to ensure it a secure place in the hearts of car fans everywhere.

CORVETTE PEOPLE

From its inception, the Corvette has never been a car for the masses. So it's no surprise that those responsible for its design and engineering over the years have never been the sort inclined to follow the crowd. They were—and still are, we're happy to say—individuals, creative and talented professionals for whom the Corvette is a labor of love and not just a job. And though each Corvette generation has, to some extent, reflected the personalities of its principal creators, the basic character of the car has remained remarkably consistent. That such a highly specialized product continues to be sustained by one of the world's largest manufacturers of mass-produced goods is even more remarkable.

Of course, the truly great cars have never been conceived by committees, where excellence is almost inevitably sacrificed on the altar of compromise. Nor are they the product of corporate accountants and financial advisors, who care mostly about profitability and know little about roadability. As we've seen, it took some time before the Corvette even began to make money. The people who challenged GM to build its first enthusiast's car had to be enthusiasts themselves, people who could relate to the concept of a uniquely American sports car and to the people who would come to love it. And it is a credit to them and those who followed in their footsteps that the Corvette has not only survived for more than 30 years but flourished, against all odds.

For many GM designers and engineers the chance to be involved with any aspect in the development of this one model represents a "dream" assignment—perhaps the highlight of one's career. Fortunately for 'Vette fans—and indeed anyone who considers automobiles more than just "wheels"—some very able and enthusiastic people have been given that chance, and this must be a key factor in the Corvette's consistent success over so many years. It's probably fair to say that the car's guiding lights have always been more devoted to and passionate about their tasks than any other single group of people in Detroit, a fact that has become part of its undeniable mystique. Yet all this is only logical. If the Corvette has always been a very special car, it is precisely because of the very special personalities and talents that have gone into it.

There are thousands of people who have made their own unique contributions to the Corvette's growth and evolution over the years and, in so doing,

Zora Arkus-Duntov in a show version of the 1957 Sebring SS racer with special bubble canopy envisioned for long-distance events.

created an automotive legend. They're found within the vast GM organization, in the world of motorsports, and in the hundreds of aftermarket companies that serve 'Vette owners. In this chapter we introduce you to the figures who loom largest in the legend.

191

Harley Earl

It is generally agreed that the impetus for the first Corvette came from Harley Earl, pioneering automotive stylist and founder of GM's Art & Colour Section. For this reason some consider him to be more the "father" of the Corvette than engineer Zora-Arkus Duntov. Regardless, it's doubtful the fiberglass-bodied two-seater could have progressed from Motorama dream car to production reality without Earl's backing. He fought for the Corvette from the very first, against some fairly stiff odds, and for a reason: it was just his sort of car. Of course, Earl carried considerable clout with GM management, the kind that comes from a swift, sure rise to fame and a winning track record.

Harley Earl was almost born to be a stylist. His father had designed horse-drawn carriages in Los Angeles, and by the time young Harley had graduated from Stanford he was a genuine car "buff." In the early 1920s he secured a post designing dashing custom bodywork for Don Lee, that doyen among coachbuilders catering to the Hollywood elite. While at the Lee studios he was "discovered" by Lawrence P. Fisher, then general manager of Cadillac, who hired the 32-year-old as a consultant. One of Earl's first assignments was body design for the 1927 LaSalle, the first edition of Cadillac's "companion" make. This would be the first mass-produced car to be "styled" in the modern sense. Its lines were gracefully handsome and reminiscent of the contemporary Hispano-Suiza—no surprise, really, since Earl was quite familiar with European design trends of the day.

That first LaSalle proved an instant hit, and many attributed that to its styling. The connection wasn't lost on GM's astute managers, and Earl was soon invited by president Alfred P. Sloan Jr. to work for the company full time, with the specific task of setting up an in-house styling department. This was duly organized as the Art & Colour Section (the English spelling for "color" being Earl's way of denoting prestige). It was an industry first, and after 1927 the professional hand of the stylist would be increasingly evident in American automotive design.

Sloan and Fisher had been impressed by Earl's total approach to his work. For example, he pioneered the use of modeling clay to evolve the forms of various body components, and in those days clay was considered a highly unusual material for this purpose. Earl also created *complete* automobiles. The main body, hood, fenders, lights, and other parts were conceived in relation to each other so as to blend into a harmonious whole. This contrasted with most custom bodybuilders, who usually worked from the cowl back, leaving a car's "stock" hood, radiator, and headlamps pretty much intact.

Earl realized that one person couldn't hope to carry the styling workload at GM singlehandedly, so he surrounded himself with talent. Many of these designers would owe him their careers. Virgil Exner, who would later win fame with the "Forward Look" at Chrysler in the mid-'50s, trained under Earl and

continued on p. 209

LeSabre experimental of 1951 was a direct precursor of the original Corvette.

The slick 1984 Corvette (foreground)
with two illustrious forebears, the
1966 and 1963 Sting Ray coupes.

This page: Corvette sales remained brisk in the '70s, so Chevy was understandably reluctant to tamper with a winning formula. This '76 is one of the 46,558 sold for the model year. Opposite page: Changes were again minor for the 1977 edition, which would be the last to carry the Stingray nameplate.

Center spread and opposite page below: Corvette marked its 25th birthday for 1978, and was chosen pace car for the 62nd annual Indy 500. Chevy issued facsimiles, which quickly became instant collector's items selling way above the suggested price. This led to a good deal of counterfeiting that caused many headaches for dealers and customers alike. Below: Silver Anniversary model was 1978's other limited edition, and featured the distinctive paint scheme seen here. Above: All '78s had special birthday badges.

This page, top: Huge fast-back rear window completely altered the Corvette's profile for '78. Shown is the standard coupe. The backlight was intended to open hatch-style, but costs and engineering considerations forced postponement to 1982. Left and below: Little changed for '79, nor was much needed. Production rose to 53,807 units for the model year. Opposite page: Photographed at the 1979-model long-lead press preview, this car carries a non-standard rear spoiler. L-82 small-block delivered 225 bhp (SAE net).

Opposite page, bottom: Another facelift for 1980 brought the fifth-generation design up to date. Styling alterations included a more raked nose with a deeply set-back chin spoiler plus a molded-in spoiler for the tail. Weight was reduced by some 250 pounds at the curb, and rated power was up fractionally on the optional L82 V-8. Base price was now over $13,000. Center spread and near left: The '81 Corvette was mostly a repeat of the '80. New were a revised L-81 version of the 350-cid small-block and a rear transverse leaf spring made of reinforced fiberglass.

Opposite page, top: Still tops in style even after 13 years, the 1981 Corvette displays its aggressive snout. Above: Last of the fifth generation appeared for '82 with new L83 twin-TBI fuel-injected engine and four-speed overdrive automatic transmission. Below, near left, and opposite page bottom: Limited-run Collector Edition '82 featured unique silver/beige paint with "shadow" stripes plus frameless lift-up hatch window and 1963-style finned wheels.

Both pages: The 1984 Corvette was unquestionably the most eagerly awaited new car in recent memory when it was announced in early 1983. Chevy skipped a model year—and thus a 30th anniversary edition—because of federal regulations and the desire to be "first" with an '84. Slick body was brimming with new features, such as one-piece lift-off roof panel, grille-less nose, lift-up hatch window, and head-turning contours boasting an impressively low 0.34 drag factor. Inside were shapelier bucket seats and futuristic electronic digital/analog instrumentation. Revised chassis featured heavy use of aluminum to save weight. "Uniframe" integral body/chassis construction was also new to Corvette, and helped Chevy engineers realize a 250-pound reduction over the '82 model. Not surprisingly, the '84 met with overwhelming response.

Both pages: The 1984 Corvette has an enduring style that should last well past the turn of the century. Combined hood/front fenders aid service access to 205-bhp V-8. Instrumentation is colorful and very comprehensive.

Bearing '84 design influence, this mid-engine, Lola-chassis racer was built for IMSA's 1983 GTP series.

continued from p. 192

headed the Pontiac studio in the 1930s. Other luminaries like Frank Hershey, Art Ross, Ned Nickles, and William L. Mitchell learned their craft from Earl, making their marks at Cadillac and Buick. Clare MacKichan, who would later create the "classic" 1955 Chevy, was yet another Earl pupil. Mitchell, of course, went on to become Earl's successor.

Earl's impact on the shape of GM cars was enormous. In fact, it may be said that for most of his 31 years with the company the GM design philosophy and Earl's philosophy were one and the same. He was exuberant for an artist and unexpectedly playful. "I often act merely as prompter," he admitted in a 1954 interview. "If a particular group appears to be bogging down over a new fender or grille or interior trim, I sometimes wander into their quarters, make some irrelevant or even zany observation, and then leave. It is surprising what ef-

The experimental Olds Cutlass (below) and F-88 roadster from 1954 and the artistic Harley Earl (bottom).

fect a bit of peculiar behavior will have. First-class minds will seize on anything out of the ordinary..."

This elfishness contrasted sharply with Earl's physical stature. He was a large man, standing over six feet tall. Because this gave him a visual perspective most of his designers lacked, they would often do their modeling while standing on wooden boxes to view their efforts the way he would see them—though they never did this in his presence. Earl's height explains the distinctive ribbed or "fluted" roof of the 1955-57 Chevrolet Nomad, as well as the use of brushed aluminum, one of his favorite materials, on the roof of the 1957-58 Cadillac Eldorado Brougham and, before that, a variety of show cars.

"That's all I want [my designers] to do, start exercising their imaginations," he once said. "The ideas will soon pop up." Earl's own imagination was formidable, yet it was always tempered by a shrewd understanding of popular taste honed at countless public showings, including the GM Motoramas.

Earl liked nothing better than to work on flashy show cars. He personally designed many of the Motorama experimentals we remember so well today, including the original Corvette. Often in his sketches he would picture himself at the wheel, with a grin on his face. His very first "dream" car may well have been his most significant. The Buick Y-Job of 1938 literally defined the shape of Detroit cars for the next two decades, with its dramatically low body, absence of the traditional running boards, strong horizontal lines, and long boattail rear deck. Though it may not look so modern now, the Y-Job boasted features that still aren't that common even today, such as hidden headlamps.

His other show models were equally striking. The experimental Oldsmobile F-88 from 1954 had seven nerf bars nestled in between twin tailpieces instead of a rear bumper. The Oldsmobile Cutlass shown that same year was marked by a fastback roofline severely tapered in plan view, plus twin chrome-accented tailfins and a louvered backlight that predicted today's popular accessory rear window slats by almost 20 years. The two-seat LaSalle II featured abbreviated rear fenders, as on an early-1900s runabout, along with exhaust pipes routed through the sills to exit immedi-

Earl's last show car design was the rocket-like Cadillac Cyclone bubble-top two-seater displayed at the 1959 Motorama.

ately ahead of the rear wheels. Earl's last show car, the Cadillac Cyclone of 1959, was a wild-looking concoction, more like a fighter plane than a car.

Aircraft design practice is seen in much of Earl's work. For example, the trend-setting tailfins that first appeared in production on the 1948 Cadillac were inspired by the twin-tail Lockheed P-38 Lightning, a World War II pursuit powered by GM-built Allison engines. During the war years Earl took his designers to see the plane, then under development at the Lockheed plant in California. They then returned to their studios, where Earl had them adapt a number of the aircraft's design elements for GM's first postwar cars. According to Irwin W. Rybicki, who succeeded Bill Mitchell as head of GM Design Staff in 1977, Earl favored rounded, massive forms like the P-38's, and these showed up in the "pontoon" fenders, fastback roofs, and heavy chrome accents that came to characterize GM's postwar look. Even the first Corvette sported rocket-like vestigial fins.

In essence, Harley Earl liked to do things his way, and usually had the wherewithal to accomplish them. He never lost his enthusiasm for cars during his long career with GM. Of course, it was toward the end of that career that he fought so long and hard for the production Corvette, and he kept on fighting for it during its difficult infancy. Right on to his retirement in 1958 he continued looking for new ways to keep his cars exciting, yet always within the bounds of public acceptance. As the chief designer for the world's largest automaker, Earl put his personal stamp on more different cars than any other single individual up to that time. History has already recorded the Corvette as one of his best efforts.

William L. Mitchell

Few automotive designers have been as powerful or as influential as William L. Mitchell. Certainly none have been more outspoken. In 1958, Mitchell became head of what was then called the General Motors Styling Staff, taking over for another larger-than-life figure, his mentor Harley Earl. Over the next 20 years he would be responsible for the design of more than half the cars and trucks sold in the U.S., not to mention a host of other GM products ranging from refrigerators to diesel locomotives. If for no other reason than the sheer volume in which his designs were produced, Mitchell would have been a very important person in his field.

Of course, no one could hope to attain such enormous responsibility without talent. And even his detractors readily admitted that Mitchell was blessed with that in abundance. Some have even gone so far as to credit him with raising industrial design from profession to fine art, and there is ample evidence to support that view. His very first

production automotive design, for example, was the 1938 Cadillac 60 Special sedan, recognized today as one of the most significant styling achievements of the late prewar era. Later, Mitchell would be the creative force behind such memorable production cars as the 1963 Buick Riviera and stunning show models like the Corvair Monza GT and SS. But perhaps his greatest achievement—certainly his greatest love—was the Corvette, specifically the Sting Ray of 1963.

Like his predecessor, Mitchell devoted a good deal of time and energy to the Corvette. In fact, of the many projects he supervised at GM it was his favorite by far. This is hardly surprising given the personality of the man, who has been described with many of the same adjectives applied to the car: brash, flamboyant, even "beefy." For

William L. Mitchell, GM styling chief from 1958 to 1977.

Mitchell, as for Earl before him, the Corvette was his opportunity not only to have fun as a designer but also to make a personal statement about what a high-performance American automobile should be.

Controversial, highly visible, and never given to half-way measures, Mitchell pulled few punches in his work, his arguments over policy with GM managers or, as we see in this exclusive interview, his public pronouncements. He remains a man who revels in making his opinions known and, though now retired, is still one of the most quotable designers in the industry.

Bill Mitchell ended up designing automobiles almost by acci-

dent. As a youth he was no doubt at least partly inspired by his father, who operated a Buick dealership in Pennsylvania. During the early '30s, young Mitchell secured a job as an illustrator for the Barron Collier advertising agency in New York City. He would spend some of his spare time drawing cars although, as he now says, his father hoped he would start drawing other things too. "That's why I was going to the [Art Students] League at night."

After he got to know Mr. Collier and his three sons, Mitchell began spending time with them at the race track they owned at Sleepy Hollow in upstate New York. "These were social events more than anything else," he recalls, but there's no doubt these early experiences kindled the love of auto racing in the young artist that was to influence some of his later work. It was at one of these races that he met someone who saw his sketches and asked if he would be interested in designing cars. "He said, 'I know a big fellow named Harley Earl who's the head of styling at General Motors.'" Before long, Mitchell sent some of his sketches to Detroit, and received a letter from Earl asking what the young illustrator thought cars "ought to look like in the future."

This was in the summer of 1935 and, Mitchell recalls, "in December of 1935, I was at work at General Motors. And in six months I was chief designer of Cadillac Studios. Now that sounds great, but there were only a hundred of us then at the whole place. When I left General Motors [in 1977] I had 1600 people."

Q: How long were you with Cadillac?

A: Until I went into the Navy in the war. I came back in '49. After that, I was taken out of General Motors. Earl wanted me to run a business for his sons; he wanted to put them in design. So I took over Harley Earl Design. I did that for four years and got big accounts like Clark Equipment, General Electric, Westinghouse, Parker Pen. Oh, I really went. I didn't like the products, but the newness of it was good for me.

Q: How did you return to GM?

A: Earl brought me back as director. I didn't love [Earl Design] but it was good background for me, because when I came back... I didn't have to take any lip from any general manager. He [Earl] told me four years ahead I was going to take his job. He talked to [then GM board chairman Alfred] Sloan and [then president Harlow] Curtice. I guess you can't do that any more; committees have to put you in.

Q: When did you first get involved with the Corvette?

A: Harley Earl; this was his idea. After the war, he was a good friend of [General Curtis] LeMay. They had these activities at the bases to keep the uni-

212

formed men happy. They started sports car racing. They got GM and a lot of different companies to put a lot of money into it to give them some fun. We built a Jeep with a Cadillac engine in it for LeMay, I remember. He said, "Harley, why don't you build an American sports car?"

We showed the first Corvette to a group at the proving grounds, and Earl told Sloan he'd like to put it in the [Motorama] show at the Waldorf. This was a prototype—no engine, nothing. It went over so good, Chevrolet said they'd build it.

Q: What were some of the problems with the early Corvettes?

A: It didn't have a good engine. There wasn't a good V-8 then.

Q: How did the decision to use the V-8 come about?

A: [Former chief engineer Edward N.] Cole became the head of Chevrolet, and he was a young fireball. He liked to race. He shoved that ahead. Prior to that, people started to try to race [Corvettes] and they weren't any good. But when you got the V-8 in it, boy, she started to go. When we beat the Jaguars— that was something. And then we beat the Mercedes and we were made. From then on it was all hell to pay. It was like a Ferrari: it looks good, but it's got to go. Performance is part of the act.

Q: What was the closest the Corvette came to being halted?

A: There were times when [James M.] Roche [distribution vice-president 1960-62, later GM president and chairman] wanted to discontinue the Corvette. I raised hell. I knew Roche well, but he was a Cadillac man. I said, "God damn it, the Corvette's got far greater owner loyalty than any damn Cadillac made." And the sales manager backed me up. That was before the Sting Ray got going.

Q: What was your involvement with racing?

A: I did a lot of bootlegging at GM. I had a studio right down underneath my office. I called it Studio X—[it's] where I'd bootleg all the kinds of cars I wanted to do. Chevrolet was racing on a scale, and then that stopped. I knew they had three chassis they didn't use [after the 1957 Sebring race]. So I went to Cole and he gave [one] to me for 500 bucks. I did [the racing Stingray] down in Studio X; nobody knew about it.

Q: When did you have to take the Corvette SS chassis out of GM?

A: I raced it first in Washington with [Dr.] Dick Thompson [in early 1959]. At the engineering policy committee [then president John F.] Gordon made a statement: "I thought everybody realized we're not going to do any racing." After the meeting I said, "Were you talking to me?" and he said, "I sure as hell was." He was tough. Instead of taking it lying down, I got a couple good friends of mine who could write better than I could, and we wrote a letter to him, saying, "I got my job racing with the Collier boys; racing is in my blood."

In those days they'd come out in those big limousines. He came out one day and I said, "Jack, did you get my letter?" And he

said, "You're a pretty damn good salesman. Go ahead." But he said, "Keep it off [GM Tech Center] property and spend your own money." So I did, and I raced for two years until he said, "Stop it, they're getting back after me for racing." [Ed. note: The racing Stingray never ran as a "Chevrolet" or a "Corvette."] So I had a little bit of my own way, and on my income tax I got away pretty good.

Q: Where did you keep the race car outside of the Tech Center?

A: I've got a shop on Twelve Mile Road that's just five minutes from my office, and I did the work out there. But I got GM engineers and I had a lot of talent at GM helping me. I got good mechanics to go to the races with me. I got a lot of things I wanted.

Q: How did the race car affect the production Corvette?

A: I went to the races in Europe and saw the cars there. I didn't

want a car that looked like everything that came out of Europe. I noticed all the young designers would get the magazines and their cars all looked like Ferraris or Maseratis. They didn't have any sharp identifying features. I wanted a car that if it went to Europe, by God, you'd know it a mile away. That was my whole theme. If it went to Le Mans, you'd know, by God, that was an American car. And it did have identity.

I just took all those lines and turned the Stingray, which is what I called the racer, into [the production 1963 Sting Ray]. That made the Corvette. And overnight the sales just boomed. So I knew I had something. I fought like hell to get that strut down the back [window]. Duntov didn't want it. And it was a hazard to the rear vision, but I liked windsplits going clear through a car. The next year we had to cut it out. But it really started the identity of the Corvette.

Q: Did you object to the re-

Bill Mitchell at home with his Stingray racer and the Manta Ray and Mako Shark show cars.

moval of the windsplit on the '64?

A: I had to admit it was a hazard. Duntov won that one. By the way, I stole that back line from the Porsche. I wasn't above stealing things from European cars. Not American cars—nothing over here to steal. There isn't anything today—unless you want a cake of soap, and then you get a Ford. You need identity on a car. Like, if you took the antlers off a deer, you'd have a big rabbit.

Q: What was your relationship like with Duntov?

A: Well, anyone with a foreign accent can get away with arguments because they're hard to understand. He'd mumble around. But he was a good guy.

Q: How much of your time was actually spent with the Corvette?

214

A: Well, that was my pet. Nobody bothered me with that. There was no high power in Chevrolet interested. The volume and high profit wasn't there. You could sort of do that the way you wanted to without anybody monkeying around. In the other divisions, when you'd have a showing, you'd have the chief engineer and six assistants [plus] an audience in the studio that'd drive you nuts. Committees, committees, committees. The first Camaro and Firebird were so "committeed" I don't remember what they look like. They were just nothing. The other ones we got done so damn fast they never saw 'em. With the [Corvette] they'd leave you alone.

Q: Which is your favorite car?

A: At Elkhart Lake a couple years ago we had the Corvette Corral, and on that four-mile track they'd be bumper to bumper all the way around and I wouldn't want to judge. They all looked good. They're like Ferraris. In fact, I ached after the Ferraris to get some of that swoop [into the Corvette]. I took my daughter out on the road one day and I saw one on the road for the first time and she said, "Dad, what's the matter with you? That's a Corvette." I'd never seen one on the road. I have this saying: a car in a studio is like a horse in a kitchen; you can't evaluate it. You've got to see it on the road with other cars.

Q: Where did you get your ideas for the Corvette?

A: I love sharks because, in the water, they're exciting. They twist and turn. I caught a mako shark in Bimini and it's in my studio in Palm Beach. I've got pictures of my Corvettes below it. That's where I got the impetus to do the [experimental] Manta Ray and those things. I'd do a lead car on my own. Then we built things off of it.

Q: How did the Sting Ray get its name?

A: I just did those names. Gordon never liked those names of mine, the fish names. They didn't like those, but we'd get them out anyway. Everything had to be a "C". I don't know how [Stingray] got to be that way; I meant it to be two words.

Q: Why was the Corvette always made of fiberglass?

A: I've always been in the middle of what should we do. You can only make, say, 70,000 at the most. What they like about fiberglass is [that] you can change it. You can't do that with metal. One of the big things about a Corvette—every Corvette you see around here is different because you can do that. That's where DeLorean screwed up. That thing he had— half metal, half plastic—you couldn't do anything with it. This new little [Pontiac] Fiero, that's the beginning. Half of that's plastic. You can make a whole different car, and they ought to because the one they have looks like a soap box.

Q: Where did you think automotive design is going now?

A: I think fins are going to come back. Even down at Daytona, at the races, your Porsches have fins on them. In that sports car class just about every car has fins. Now I don't think they'll be high. You need wings, you need that stuff on there or you've got a pickle. A Porsche to me was always—there was a word they used in Germany—like a loaf of bread. If it spun out you didn't

Mitchell's 600-bhp Can Am-powered custom Corvette, photographed at his Florida home.

know which end was coming. There's a lot of stuff going on now that's called functional. But you've got to have aesthetics. You can't sell a guy a car that looks like hell and tell him it looks that way because it's aerodynamic.

Q: How important were the show cars to production plans?

A: That's how you'd find out what people wanted. That's how the Eldorados were born and the Toronados and all that—at the Motorama. Now they don't make those anymore. Show cars were more fun to work on [because]

you didn't have a bunch of committeemen telling us, "you can't do this, you can't do that." We did it, and if people liked it they'd say, "go make it." It would do more for us in the studio to see one come out of the shop. People want to see something new.

Q: What do you think of the 1984 Corvette?

A: I think the new Corvette looks like a grouper—a blunt look. I think the Camaro and Firebird are sharper. Although—I'll eat my own words—on the highway it looks pretty damn good from the front. But I don't like this lack of whip in the side view; it isn't exciting. And the big taillights look like it was done for A.J. Foyt. I think it should have been done for women as well as men. I like more interest in the car. You look at watches: there's millions of them and they look different all the time. You don't want cars all looking alike.

Q: What would you have done differently with the 1984 Corvette?

A: I'd have put more accents on it. But my day is over, though. Earl never bothered me when he left. Earl was a dynamic man, more Hollywood. He looked so out of place in Detroit it was unbelievable. He had power, politically and physically. And he was a salesman like you never heard of. He could win. Styling ran the world, not design, not engineering...He made it his way. I tried to follow him, and I did a pretty good job. But the boys that followed me are getting pushed off the map. I love 'em, but they haven't got it. Engineering is running it. The new Corvette is engineering perfect, but design? No. The engineers ran the whole damn show. They wouldn't have done that with me.

You need two things in a car: you need road value and show-room value. You need a little sparkle in a car. On a little mis-

ty day they all look dull. You don't want to put chrome on with a trowel like we did in '58, but you need some. There isn't showroom value in these cars today. If I had one, I'd touch it up. You have to have enough interest to keep looking at it. That goes for all the cars.

Q: What are some specific changes you would make?

A: I'd put more flow in the line. I wouldn't have the sideline straight through. I know it wouldn't be as aerodynamic, but I'd put some curve in that. Like a shark is so much more interesting than a grouper because there's so many little things happening to it. This [Corvette] is a big potato. On the road, yes; but you walk up to it—blah. Black rubber around everything. It needs detail. I think the new little Pontiac [Fiero] is a dead duck; it's just a little box. I think that Fiat [X1/9] that's been out for years is much better. I shouldn't be talking about my company like that; they're still good to me.

Q: What are some of the cars you own now?

A: I've got some pets of mine I love. I've got a Jaguar roadster, the old Jaguar 12. Everything is copper on it, the body and all the chrome is copper. I've got a Firebird I did over with a Ferrari engine, and all the metal on that is gold and it's striped in gold. My Corvette is pearl white with two fins on the back like a race car, with a blade going through it. The Corvette has a 600-horsepower Can Am aluminum-block motor in it. I like to have a car that when I pull up, somebody says, "Jesus Christ, whose car is that?" I want a car that, when it's stopped, people walk around it for an hour. Exciting automobiles.

Zora Arkus-Duntov

Although many talented GM people have played a part in the Corvette's 30-year evolution, none has played a larger role than Zora Arkus-Duntov. Within the company and among the 'Vette's millions of fans he was known as "Mr. Corvette." In fact, he still is. It is a title he rightfully deserves. More than any other individual, it was Duntov who transformed what had started out as a mild-mannered tourer into a true-race-and-ride sports car able to stand comparison with the best high-performance machines built anywhere in the world.

Duntov became involved with the Corvette relatively late in his professional career, at age 43. However, he had already achieved a measure of recognition before joining GM in May 1953. The Belgian-born engineer had worked as a technical consultant for Sydney Allard in England, where he developed the famous "Ardun" cylinder head conversion for the Ford/Mercury flathead V-8. After a stint with Fairchild Aviation, Duntov sent a copy of a research report he

Duntov (left) and "Uncle Tom" McCahill discuss the fuel-injected 1957 Corvette on the grounds of the GM Tech Center.

had written on high-performance engines to Ed Cole, then head of Chevy engineering. On the basis of that, Duntov was offered a post with GM Research and Development. After lengthy dickering over salary and benefits, he accepted.

The Corvette was being launched at about the time Duntov arrived. Though he generally liked the car, he found its handling left something to be desired, and started "fiddling" with it on his own time. It wasn't long before management noticed his tinkering and began to give him regular Corvette assignments. The rest, as they say, is history.

Duntov was not only an excellent engineer, he was also quite capable as a race driver. In 1956, for example, he and Betty Skelton drove modified Corvettes to better than 150 mph at the Daytona Speed Weeks (which, incidentally, marked the birth of the so-called "Duntov cam" that boosted popularity of Chevy's small block V-8 among hot rodders in the '50s). The following year he assisted with track testing the futuristic Corvette SS racer at Sebring, although the effort failed due to an overly tight bushing that forced the car to be retired after only 23 laps. When the Automobile Manufacturers Association agreed that its members should cease all racing activities and performance-oriented advertising—the infamous "anti-racing edict" of 1957—Duntov advocated supporting competition in "secrecy," and became a key figure in GM's well-known "closet" NASCAR program and

its other under-the-table competition efforts in the '60s.

Throughout his 25 years as chief Corvette engineer, Duntov approached his work with the energy of a much younger man. His accomplishments are many and important. He helped to develop Chevy's "Ramjet" fuel injection system, created the prototype for the aborted mid-engine Q-model Corvette, and designed the 1963 Sting Ray chassis, which remained in production basically unchanged for an unprecedented two decades. Though he retired from GM in late 1974, Duntov remains very active professionally, and is still very much involved with Corvettes. Among his recent ventures is the turbocharged Duntov Corvette, a conversion that turns the stock post-1975 coupe into a rip-snorting powerhouse with full roadster bodywork. In this interview we catch up with this remarkable personality.

Q: What was your first project at Chevrolet?

A: Research and Development. Corvette was not significant by itself then. I tried to make a better car. 1956 was the beginning of performance.

Q: When did work begin on the first Sting Ray?

A: It began in '59, both chassis and engine. Before that, I was named Director of High Performance Vehicles. I took pride in the small-block Chevrolet engine. The whole car was good, though. Ergonomics were very good. It was quite adequate as an envelope, with such things as a shift lever location that would fall into the hand readily, good legibility of the gauges, and performance that was *non pareil* overall.

Q: Was the Corvette ever in danger when the Thunderbird came out?

A: I used this argument: we cannot pull out of the market with Ford in the two-passenger competition. The demise of the Thunderbird as a two-passenger car opened a prospect to produce more cars to fill the void.

Q: Did you have any problems with the Sting Ray chassis design?

A: No problem: everything worked as designed. And as testimony for that, the Sting Ray chassis has lasted up to the 1982 model. In '62 we produced the Grand Sport Corvette with the disc brakes, vented in front, solid at the rear. In '64, we had the [Girling Brake Company] throw their hands in the air and say we cannot make them because Corvettes have the combination of high weight and high speed. I worked with Kelsey-Hayes, and they succeeded in providing excellent brakes for the Corvette. Kelsey-Hayes did not get the contract because Delco [Division of GM] used their leverage. Delco produced a brake identical to [the] Kelsey-Hayes [design]. For '65 we produced four-wheel disc brakes, and they [too] were so good they stayed until 1982. With the mid-engine Corvette we used a Bendix brake identical to the Delco Moraine brake, four pads per caliper.

Q: What was your opinion of Mitchell's styling?

A: Overall, we were on the same wavelength. I only remember one disagreement, the split window on the '63 Sting Ray

Duntov gives the SS racer a final inspection before the start of the 1957 Sebring 12 Hours. Car completed only 23 laps before retiring.

[coupe]. We took it out [on the '64 model].

Q: What was your opinion of the 1968 Corvette styling?

A: As a whole, design-wise, it was a very good car. Something got lost in the ergonomics, though. You had to move to operate the gearshift. At that time Bill Mitchell was impressed by supersonic jets. The first thing I did was to provide more shoulder room. It was so pinched you couldn't drive it without leaning. To gain a half-inch per side I spent $120,000 retooling door inners. This half an inch was very significant.

Another consideration: the '63-'67 car was a terrible "lifter" aerodynamically. The subsequent design was also a lifter, but not to that extent.

Q: How important was racing?

A: At that time, very important. I considered that it was necessary. To establish the sports car, you have to race it. After a car gets established, like the mid-70s, the racing is second place. We had all the optional items to enable people to race. CERV 1 [an experimental open-wheel single-seat racer] was the progenitor of the Sting Ray suspension-wise.

Q: What were some of the most important racers?

A: The '57 SS Corvette was the one car built specifically to race. Unfortunately, the automobile manufacturers concluded a pact not to race and [we] abandoned the whole plan to race the car. The highlight was when [Juan Manuel] Fangio and Stirling Moss drove this car at Sebring. They broke a track record. At the race itself the SS did not do too well. We were going to produce four more SS cars to enter Le Mans, but that fell into nothing. We entered under a fictitious name and had three cars in Le Mans. In May, [GM management] decided not to race and I had two cars already prepared. I gave one chassis to Styling. That ultimately became the racing Stingray. [This was the "mule" car that was rebodied in Mitchell's styling studio.].

Q: What was your involvement with the SS mule car?

A: I drove the car at the proving grounds. It was really a terrible

One of Duntov's more esoteric projects was the CERV I, which provided valuable experience with the mid-engine layout and aluminum-block engines. Car never raced.

lifter. Right away I lost interest in this car. It's beautiful alright, but [it has] a profile of a wing. I drove the Corvette SS racer at the proving grounds at 183 mph and I ran about 155 mph at the opening of the Daytona track in 1959.

Q: Did you like GM's experimental rotary engine?

A: Not at all. But as things began to shape up in '71, I had either a mid-engine car and a rotary engine or not at all. Therefore, I had to accept the rotary engine. [GM President] Ed Cole was enamored with the rotary engine. Therefore, I showed him the two- and four-rotor Corvettes. The four-rotor engine was interchangeable with a reciprocating engine; it could easily be replaced with the small-block V-8. When GM got off the Wankel kick, they went back to a reciprocating engine. The Aerovette [the four-rotor design] got a 400-cid small-block engine. It also had the space to accept four-wheel drive. I told them . . . four-wheel drive [would be important in the future]. First with rear-wheel drive and, two years later, four-wheel drive. If you look at the Aerovette, you see a big tunnel to fit four-wheel drive. But it was just a styling exercise. The

mid-engine Corvette minus energy-absorbent bumpers was under 3000 pounds with the 400 or 350 small-block. Torsional stiffness was in the area of 6000 pounds-feet per degree. It was a very good car; it had good luggage space. When I think about it, it's a pity it did not come about.

Q: Who killed the mid-engine design?

A: In '74 I had a conversation with the chairman of the board [Thomas A. Murphy]. He said, "Let's wait. Right now we cannot build enough cars to satisfy the demand. When we see the demand will slacken, we'll bring the mid-engine car out." I disagreed with him. I thought Chevrolet should be at the forefront, but he had the last word.

Q: What do you think of the new Corvette and what would you have done differently with it?

A: Very good. I tried to promulgate the mid-engine car. If I was not forced to retire [the new model] would probably be a mid-engine car. The mid-engine design in '69 and '73-'74 was in the picture on and off. I think I would have won the fight given time but, unfortunately, I was forced to retire.

Styling-wise, aerodynamic-wise [the '84 is] excellent. It is ergonomically well thought out. The chassis is not as good as I wish it were. But second guessing is unfair. I'm confident the '85 will be much better than the '84. Digital gauges I don't care for at all. They're good for slow-moving processes, like fuel gauge, clock or oil level. But the speedometer and tach should [have analog] round faces to show where you have been and where you are going. Instantaneous readouts have no place in a sports car.

Q: Can they race the car?

A: They're not man enough. That's a break in tradition with Corvette.

Q: What do you think the next Corvette will be like?

A: By the time they get the money I will be already dead and buried. . . Chassis-wise, the previous Corvette [Duntov's own design] lived from 1963 to 1982. The amortization of the tooling happened in one year. In subsequent years it was gravy. The '84 Corvette will live maybe 20 years—I don't know. As for product costs, the '63 Corvette [came in] less than the '62 Corvette. It sounds incongruous with independent rear suspension and everything, but with the front suspension I made up the cost of the independent [rear] suspension. Using suspension pieces of earlier cars was very cost-effective.

Q: After the first Corvette, was it always intended that the car would have a fiber-glass body?

A: At one time steel was considered in a design study—in about '56 or '58—when considering a new transaxle, which did not materialize. At one time we thought it was possible to produce fiberglass for just 10,000 cars. But we learned. I have a '74 I park all the time on the street and it has no signs of rust.

Q: What do you think of the Pontiac Fiero?

A: Good, really good. Underpowered. Overall, it's good, but this will not compete with the Corvette.

David R. McLellan

David R. McLellan replaced Zora Arkus-Duntov as the head of Corvette engineering in 1975. He, too, is a unique personality and the 1984 model is the first Corvette to reflect it fully. With his tousled, sandy hair, McLellan has an almost elfin look that belies his technical expertise.

He was born in the Upper Peninsula of Michigan in the mid-1930s, about the time Har-

David R. McLellan: The new "Mr. Corvette."

ley Earl was designing LaSalles and Cadillacs. His family then moved to Detroit, where McLellan grew up. He remained there for his college education at Wayne State University, where he majored in mechanical engineering. He went to GM in 1959, fresh out of school, and worked first at the corporation's Milford proving grounds. He spent the better part of a decade there, during which he obtained a master's degree in engineering mechanics from Wayne State.

In 1968, McLellan was transferred to Chevrolet Division, where he worked on the second-generation Camaro. He was also involved with John DeLorean's proposal for a common chassis intended for the Camaro, the compact Nova and possibly, he says, for the Corvette. Fortunately for the two-seater, it never materialized, but McLellan did contribute to the X-body Nova/Camaro chassis.

McLellan's next career step came in 1973, a year's sojourn at MIT as a Sloan Fellow sponsored by Chevrolet. This was an important experience: it gave him the opportunity to learn first-hand about the automotive industry in other countries. He returned to Chevrolet in '74, and was given his first Corvette assignment as a staff engineer under Duntov. Just six months later, Duntov retired and Mc-

Lellan was named chief Corvette engineer.

Though the proposed mid-engine production car derived from Bill Mitchell's Aerovette design was nearly ready at that point, McLellan favored the traditional front-engine/rear-drive configuration for the next-generation Corvette. Significantly, a series of owner surveys supported his position. By now, McLellan had clearly established himself as a clever and capable designer. He had to be: he had the formidable challenge of engineering and overseeing development of the first all-new Corvette in some 20 years. Here, McLellan talks about his career and "his" new Corvette.

Q: What was the first Corvette model you worked on?

A: The first program I had any impact on was the '78. As chief engineer there are some aspects that are under my direct control, some things not under control. The engine and transmission are not under direct control. The '78 program involved many things besides moving on emissions and fuel economy. From a design standpoint, we had devised a hatchback Corvette, which was never approved. That was a hatch with a large frame around it. For '78 we reassessed why we were having problems getting stuff like that approved. The '78 design was originally conceived as a frameless hatch design. This was the one that appeared in the Collector Edition in 1982, its first production appearance.

Q: When did you realize you would be able to build a new Corvette?

A: We realized in that 1977-78 time frame [that] we had to do a new Corvette or the product would be in serious jeopardy. There was general recognition it was time to take a major step with the Corvette. The big issue in that time frame was what should that step be? The options ranged from carrying out the midship V-8 Aerovette-based design to doing a V-6 midship car to taking the front/mid-engine

McLellan's first Corvette project was the reworked '78 model, shown here with the special Silver Anniversary package option.

design we had and doing a thorough reassessment of it.

We started the process with the midship variation as our mainstream. It occurred to us only as we got into detailed assessment to look into the front/mid-engine design again. About that time, Porsche came out with the 928, a front-engine V-8 sports car. We looked again at the benefits and it emerged as a very strong candidate and, as you know, ultimately emerged.

Q: What was the downfall of the mid-engine Corvette?

A: After all this energy Chevrolet had poured into convincing everybody that a midship car was the way to go. . . But when you get to a high-performance-engined car that carries two people and has some kind of creature comforts, the mid-engine gets very tough to deal with. Nobody had—and still

222

hasn't—come up with a mid-engine design that is a fully marketable car. All these mid-engine cars are not without their difficulties.

Q: Is this also true of the new Pontiac Fiero?

A: The Fiero has a little bit different market. It has to do with the smaller engine. We were showing these aerodynamic low cars and saying these are mid-engine cars. There is a certain amount of cubic volume that is consumed by all those functions to transport two people and achieve a level of creature comfort. To make the midship cars look so slick, we had been ignoring the people issue. There was no utility or luggage space at all in those cars. That's where you get into trouble with the larger engine. The front/mid-engine design offers more benefits at that point. Then it comes down to what can we do to reconfigure [it]. So we set about doing that by repackaging the details, putting the front suspension around the engine, putting the engine in at a completely different attitude, designing the rear suspension to configure it around the occupant requirements. Generally we were able to make the car a little bit shorter and lower, though a little bit wider.

Q: What was important to change on the Corvette?

A: As we analyzed the old car, a lot of things, we felt, were right... That was reflected in its performance in the marketplace. We really look at this new Corvette as an ultimate performance statement by Chevrolet. What I mean by that is, in all respects that are important to a Corvette, the car needs to be king of the hill. If it's worth doing, it's worth doing better than anybody else. With the old Corvette we had kind of let things slip a little bit. We had not been pounding the table with our management as hard as we should have. We certainly are

today. In fact, we are being pressed by our own management.

Q: What changes in automotive technology have affected the Corvette?

A: It had been updated year by year. It progressed dramatically in '81 and '82 when we moved production from St. Louis to Bowling Green. It was Jerry Palmer and the design team who worked closely together.

One of the first things we laid down [for the '84 model] was the tire size. For the kind of performance we wanted, the only tire available in that size was a Pirelli P7. Much of the design was done around that tire. We brought Goodyear in early in [the program] and gave them the specifications and they worked hard on it. We're very pleased with the results. The tires have been trouble-free. [Even with their wider footprint] they have better hydroplaning performance than previous tires. Goodyear is X-raying 100 percent of the tires for quality control and is testing a sampling using a holographic technique.

Q: Why the use of the unidirectional wheels on the '84?

A: Basically for aesthetics. It's kind of a non-issue. If that is what the designer wanted and it's reasonable to give it to him, then we'll give it to him.

Q: Is your relationship with Design much like it was between Bill Mitchell and Zora Arkus-Duntov? Mitchell told us that he thinks Engineering is running the show more now than he let them when he was in charge. Is that happening?

A: Certainly Bill Mitchell is a very flamboyant guy. The only way we really got our act together on this car was by waiting until Bill Mitchell retired. The previous car was never really accepted outside the U.S. The new car carries the cues that make people recognize it as a Corvette, but [are] not so exag-

gerated. As we got into the aero aspect of it, this car was really designed in the tunnel. [It] has a coefficient of drag of .34, and we know how to get it down to a .31 or even .30 in honest production trim.

Q: What effect did the wind tunnel have on the '84's styling?

A: Top speed and fuel economy have a lot to do with aero design. Probably the most critical piece of the car from an aero design standpoint was the backlight and the way the taillights were formed. We looked at a variety of ways to terminate the rear of the car.

I can't think of any great disagreements we had with Palmer. The only thing I recall was that we had to redo the taillamps without visible screws. Once we laid down where the engine and people were, it was Jerry fine-tuning the design. I think Jerry was very satisfied with the design, and so were we.

Q: Why is the Corvette still as heavy as it is?

A: I can't tell you how many pounds are tied up in open [Targa-roof body] design, but it's a lot. Structural integrity is important. For light weight, coupe construction is the way to go. To my way of thinking, a ... "ragtop" design is a throwback. We wanted an open feeling, in contrast with the DeLorean. That's the ideal of a closed-in car.

Q: Was any material other than fiberglass ever considered for the '84 body?

A: We never considered anything other than reinforced plastic. It has the ability to absorb minor impacts, and is nearly as light as aluminum.

Q: Why aren't other cars made that way?

A: It's expensive. But you are seeing more and more use of reinforced plastics. Cars such as the Fiero and Honda CRX are using it.

Q: The new Corvette has taken a lot of criticism for being a hard-riding car. Tell us why it was made that way.

A: There are two schools of thought in the press, and we obviously don't side with those who say the car is too harsh. It is a tough car. It was never intended as anything else. It was intended to allow you to get out on a race track and not wallow all over the place. It was intended to enable you to get out and set lap records, and the car has set a number of production lap records at various race tracks. That's one aspect of the car we wanted to optimize and—no question about it—we did.

When you get onto some of the terrible concrete we have in the frost zone, the car gets kind of tough. In response to those kind of inputs, we are looking into softening up the ride. But we're doing it very carefully so as not to jeopardize the handling performance that is inherent there. It's going to be evolutionary, and it's going to be done without degrading the handling performance we've already demonstrated.

Q: What was the rationale behind having a separate export model for the first time?

A: The car was designed not just for Canada and the U.S. market but for the export market from the ground up. The export requirements were taken into consideration very early in design, so changes were kept to a minimum. We're producing the export car in the Bowling Green plant so it doesn't have to be retrofitted at point of sale. The car is export-certified for or is now in final stages for (and I think I'll get all the countries here, but I may miss a few): Germany, France, Switzerland, Austria, the low countries, Sweden, England, Spain, Italy, Saudi Arabia and that whole Middle East area, and Japan. The initial export volume will be low, around 1000 cars. The continuing demand in this market

is so high we would have to forego deliveries here to get the car to Europe. With the dollar so strong and all the economic barriers, the price in Europe will be at 928 levels. That car is cheaper there, so the two converge.

Q: Will we see much factory support of Corvette racing?

A: Our support of racing is a technical support, a position we have taken for a long time. We won't be out there racing the car ourselves.

Q: Do you think racing is still important to the success of the Corvette?

A: I think it's a very important adjunct to it. There's the overall statement on Chevrolet performance we're making with the Lola turbo V-6 GTP car project. That's a joint venture between ourselves and Ryan Faulkner, who is doing the turbocharged V-6 motors. We did the aero work on the car. When that car is all together shortly, it will be a test bed development tool to wring out the vehicle system as a competitive prototype vehicle. Then it's up to various private racers to take replicas of that car and turn them into successful racing cars. We're doing the part of that venture that we do best, which is supporting engine development and doing the aerodynamic development.

Q: Will we see twin-turbocharged, aluminum-block V-6s in racing 'Vettes?

A: That's certainly a possibility. But that's up to [the private racers] given the rules of the series. We really feel the production car is itself a viable competitor. At this point in time the SCCA and their production racing class has not recognized any of the high-performance sports cars. It's kind of a spooky situation. I think they're pretty close to doing that. We've encouraged them to come up with a classification that recognizes the Corvette, 928, [Ferrari] 308, and the Lotus Esprit Turbo, because all of

those cars are roughly equal competitors. We're fairly comfortable that the [Corvette] just driven to the race track is competitive.

Q: What is the purpose of the bulge on the dashboard facing the passenger seat? Was it originally designed to house an air bag?

A: The car is designed around an interior concept to make the car more "friendly" to the occupant in the event of a crash situation. It was developed somewhat like the driver's side, where you have a steering wheel in front of you that absorbs some of that energy. That's why the instrument panel comes out in that padded area the way it does. It was not designed to house an air bag.

Q: What is the future of the Corvette?

A: We're still basically dealing with the [1984] design in the short run. Our short-term philosophy is to make it do what it does even better: going, stopping, cornering, all the sports car objectives. We're making more of those. We're looking at what it takes to make it go faster and improving ride quality.

Long term you'll see a thread [that's characterized] the history of the Corvette: it is a very evolutionary process. Maybe the '62 to '63: there was a dramatic step, other than the '82 to '84. But in terms of the mission of the car there has never been an abrupt discontinuity. To have done the '84 Corvette as [something similar to the Pontiac Fiero] P-car would have been a very abrupt discontinuity. We have a basic chassis that is capable of 150-mph speed, capable of braking from those speeds, tires capable of those kind of speeds. The drivetrain is designed for an engine torque output of around 350 lbs/ft, so we have a little room there. There are just lots of things we can do now incrementally to really stretch the envelope of the car. And these things seem to be the kinds of changes or improvements that the Corvette market is looking for.

Q: How important is improving the ride?

A: It's a secondary objective.

Q: Will we see a different engine anytime soon, such as a V-6?

A: Probably not. We're not going to see them in the short run, period. We'll see them only if we see a benefit. If we can see a V-6 turbo that would outgun the V-8, and had fuel economy and what other benefits it would need to have to be viable, we would consider it. Part of it is that we have such a damn good engine in the small-block V-8. Its evolutionary progress outstrips anything we can demonstrate in a competing alternative . . . That engine in NASCAR form is putting out over 600 horsepower. We are continuing to evolve the engine. You'll see an evolutionary process over the next few years where you'll look back and say, step by step, "they radically changed that engine."

Q: How long will the '84 Corvette's production life be?

A: You have to look at the viability of the configuration. As long as fuel prices do not become outrageous in terms of [buyer] income, and all other things being equal, the current configuration has a long potential life. We will continue to evolve the present configuration. If there is some dramatic shift in consumer demand, we'll have to reconsider what we're doing.

Q: Do you see the Fiero becoming a serious competitor?

A: We've designed the Corvette with drivetrain robustness that will make it a serious ultimate competitor in the marketplace. I look at the Fiero as a very complementary car at best. I don't see the Fiero outgunning the Corvette. There is nothing they can do that we can't do or do more of.

Q: What about the weight differential?

A: But [it's] not that much. We're looking at a curb weight now of about 3150 pounds [on the Corvette]. Over the next two or three years we'll probably see that break in right under 3000 with program developments we have underway. That's kind of a clue as to where we're headed right there. The weight of the car is scaled around the high-speed capability, the powertrain requirements, the structural requirements. Competitors weigh about what we weigh. The new Nissan 300ZX weighs in just over 3000, and that's a coupe with a much small motor and aluminum cylinder heads. There's a penalty you have to accept to have that open motoring capability over a closed car.

Q: Are there any mid-engine or rotary-engine Corvettes still in development?

A: No, not at all.

Q: What sort of Corvettes might we see further down the road?

A: There may be turbine powerplants by then that are viable. That would open up dramatic new opportunities in terms of vehicle design.

Q: Will the Corvette continue to employ plastic or fiberglass construction?

A: Yes! I see the plastic family of materials evolving themselves. There's a great revolution going on in . . . composites.

Q: Many manufacturers are looking at four-wheel-drive for road cars. Is there a 4WD Corvette in the future?

A: Duntov did a four-wheel-drive Corvette back in the '60s. In fact, the first of the mid-engine production designs was conceived such that it could have a four-wheel-drive variation. It's not out of the question [but] it's not very pertinent to the short term.

Q: When the press was first shown the four-speed manual transmission used in the '84s, the electronic overdrive couldn't be locked out. But it can be on the production version. How did this happen?

A: We intended it all along. Everybody just had to bear with us until we worked out all the negotiations with EPA. Somewhere around February of '83, about the time we were getting underway with automatic production, we got all the approvals on the manual worked out.

Factory line drawing highlights the '84 Corvette's new "uniframe" construction.

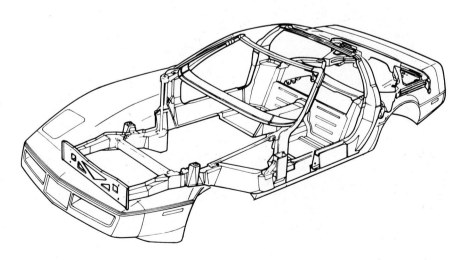

Q: Why was the new Corvette designated a 1984 model and not an '83?

A: According to government regulations, the only way you can sell cars is to meet all the government regulations in effect. At the time of the press show we were working with the federal government to publish the '84 regulations. We wanted to call it an '84, but they had not officially published all the '84 requirements we'd have to meet.

Q: But why give up the idea of marketing a 30th anniversary edition?

A: Well, [Chevrolet General Manager Robert C.] Stempel said it. He had two choices: he could have the last '83 into the marketplace or the first '84. Everything we built [on an experimental basis] we called an '83. Bob made the decision that, nope, it's going to be the first '84. The government rule is that you can have only one January 1 in your model year...Since we were not going to sell the cars to the public until March 24, we fell well within that criteria.

We went out of production with the old one back in mid-October [of 1982]. We had shut down production and cleared the plant out and rebuilt the assembly facility to handle the '84

Jerry Palmer guided '84 design development.

Corvette. The first production car that was a salable vehicle, VIN00002, is in the Sloan Museum in Flint. VIN00001, which is the lowest serial number, was raffled off by the National Council of Corvette Clubs for charity. It was car #1 of '84 production, but it was not the first car built. It was built a couple days later, after they had the production line up and running smoothly. VIN00002 was part of a family of cars, about the first 70, we are not selling because we use those cars to get the build of the vehicle up to standard.

Jerry Palmer

Beginning with the all-new 1984 model, the Corvette's future would be entirely in the hands of a younger—yet no less capable—generation of GM professionals. Jerry Palmer is one of the most important members of the new breed. Since 1974 he has been the head of Chevrolet's production Studio Three, where the '84 Corvette took shape. More importantly, he has had overall responsibility for Corvette design since his redoubtable predecessor, William L. Mitchell, retired as GM's vice-president for design in 1977. Thus, Palmer "inherited" an exciting yet formidable job in much the same way Dave McLellan did in taking over for Zora Arkus-Duntov on the Engineering side. Both men and their teams faced the challenge of not only maintaining the tradition of America's sports car but improving on it. Judging from the results, Palmer is admirably suited to the job.

Not that the job was easy. For one thing, Palmer is an articulate, thoughtful, soft-spoken man succeeding one of the most flamboyant and outspoken designers in the industry. Second, Mitchell had been the sole arbiter of Corvette styling for more than 20 years, itself a very tough act to follow. Although the fifth-generation 1968 design had remained quite popular through

its extraordinarily long production run, it was also quite dated by the mid-'70s. Clearly, its replacement would have to be more modern both in appearance and in function. Yet as development work proceeded on what would become the '84 model, it was equally clear that any new Corvette would still have to be instantly recognizable *as* a Corvette. Palmer also faced the problem of giving the new car enduring style—a look that would still seem fresh in, say, the 1990s—because the next generation would almost surely be in production for about as many years as its long-lived predecessor.

Finally, there was this thorny question: how do you update the future? Remember all those mid-engine experimentals wearing the Corvette label? GM tantalized 'Vette fans with these dream machines in the early '70s, and one of them—Mitchell's stunning Aerovette—had been readied for 1980 production, only to be canceled at the last minute. All these cars still looked wild and exotic some 10 years later, and many enthusiasts still remembered them. Thus, Palmer had to come up with styling that would not only be practical for production but also at least as eye-grabbing as these show cars. Anything less could have been detrimental to sales.

It is a tribute to his creativity and artistry that Palmer managed to reconcile these issues in the 1984 design. In fact, he and his staff have produced what may well be the most handsome car of the 1980s. Certainly there can be little disagreement that the '84 model is one of the best-looking Corvettes ever built.

Palmer claims to be one of the few designers in the domestic industry who's a native Detroiter. His experience with GM Design goes all the way back to 1964, when he spent a summer there as a student. After graduating from the Center of Creative Studies in Detroit the following year, he joined GM permanently, completed the company's internship program, and then served briefly in the Advanced Studios at Design Staff. After a stint in the Army during 1966-67, he returned to Chevrolet and has been with that division ever since, except for brief assignments at GM subsidiaries in Europe and Japan. His first Corvette involvement came in 1969 when he assisted Mitchell in creating several show models.

Jerry Palmer's affable, easygoing personality belies an intense enthusiasm for his work, about which he is uncharacteristically modest for such a high-ranking executive. He's always eager to talk Corvettes despite an always-hectic schedule. We're pleased he took time out to talk with us.

Q: When did you first get involved with the Corvette?

A: My first production involvement came in the '73 and '74 car. I was the assistant chief designer, and we were doing only the front and rear of the car.

Q: What were your thoughts about the previous Corvette design?

A: I thought it was an exciting car. I was really enamored by the show cars, such as the Mako Shark, that led into that body style. Even today you see an '81 or '82 on the road—I know they're dated but they're still exciting and have a lot of personality. They are definitely Corvettes.

Q: When did you start working on the new Corvette?

A: We're always working on a new Corvette. We started on [the '84] in '77, but there were designs before that which were part of the program. We literally laid out the package starting with a clean sheet of paper. The only thing that was a given was the engine and transmission and need for additional ground clearance. We really started

with a package. There's a lot of time and effort spent finalizing the rest of the architecture.

Q: At this point there were no further thoughts of a mid-engine design?

A: When the decision was made to go front-engine, the mid-engine responsibility went downstairs to the Advanced Studio. [Studio Three] had mid-engine responsibility until that time. We are the production studio, so when the decision to go front-engine was made, the mid-engine design went downstairs to an Advanced studio.

Q: Would you have preferred a mid-engine car?

A: The mid-engine design offers different proportions, more unfamiliar proportions. Based on the components available at that time, we made the right decision. The P-car was essentially what we were looking at, V-6 powered. I also had [1982] Camaro responsibility, and we were going to come out with a pretty wild Z28 package. There's no way a 60-degree V-6 Corvette in the form we were working on could compete with the Z28 we were working on. Then Porsche came out with their front/mid-engine [928] design. All those decisions made back in that late-1970s time frame fortified Chevrolet's direction. The mid-engine car is an exciting car, but the [latest] Corvette is a fantastic car for the money in handling, braking, performance. It's right there. We didn't have to apologize for anything. The car is very forgiving. It's hard to screw up in a Corvette; you can screw up in a Ferrari or a rear-engine Porsche very easily. Those considerations were very strong on the engineering side. Plus, the mid-engine car offers less packaging flexibility.

Q: What is your working relationship like with Dave McLellan?

A: We have a very good relation-

ship. Dave knows enough about what we [designers] do to understand or challenge. We are very knowledgeable about each other's bailiwick and can challenge each other. I would say Chevrolet was very creative in helping us achieve the package we wanted. To come up with the idea and make it look good is one thing; to make it work is another. There is more integration between the two [disciplines] than there was 15 years ago. There has to be. I think engineers are a lot more open-minded than they were 10 years ago. We have a better understanding of what has to be done to make the product people are demanding out there. We're closer getting together.

Q: Bill Mitchell has criticized the '84 Corvette in some respects. What is your reaction?

A: We've talked about it. Bill and I are still good friends. He really didn't like the car at first and said so. Then, after he saw the car out in the real world and saw it in motion, he called me up and said, "Goddamn it, I gotta tell ya, that thing really looks aggressive. I still don't quite like the back end, but it looks like a Corvette." I think the thing is [becoming more familiar to] Bill. It doesn't have the exaggerated statement that the previous Corvettes had, but I'm sure if Bill were running the studio I don't think the Corvette would be a lot different than it is today. The shapes are Corvette, but the shapes are also aerodynamically tuned. We didn't conceive the design to aero, but we certainly had aero in mind. We had to meet targets.

Q: Mitchell told us he thought the '84 was more an engineer's car, not a stylist's car.

A: I was not controlled at all by Engineering. In fact, Engineering bent over backwards to give us what we wanted. I think Bill would have probably done things a little differently. However, I don't think it would be a lot different. The 16-inch wheels, the 65-degree windshield, those things are all designer's wants, like the flip-open front end, the "T-less" T-top. Engineering didn't make those things. They made them happen, but the concepts originated here at Design Staff. For some of those design features we paid penalties...in cost and in mass. But the appearance or aura of that car is the thing we wanted. Engineering didn't back off. In fact, I can't think of anything Engineering demanded we have that we're not happy with. I think the days [are gone when Engineering compromises] what we want. They want as exciting a car as we do.

Q: What is the limiting factor in production numbers with the current car?

A: It gets down to how many people you want to employ at Bowling Green and how many shifts. We are very reluctant to go into a double shift until we are satisfied the demand is there, not an artificial demand because of the newness of the car. If the demand is there, I'm sure Chevrolet will consider another shift. I feel with a double shift we can make 60,000 cars with the quality the car has to have. We will not pump out cars and detract from the quality. We are still gaining on the quality of the car. I see the car leveling out at around 40,000 units a year. That's a gut reaction.

Q: The previous body design lasted 15 years. How long do you think this new one will be around?

A: I don't think it's going to last anywhere near that long. But I think it will take us into the '90s; in fact I know it'll take us into the '90s. That's not to say the car will not be injected with new technology wherever possible or [if] we discover something better appearance-wise or function-wise. We'll implement

that, but it won't be a total new design.

Q: What changes do you foresee to keep the car current?

A: At this point in time I don't have any definite plans. I would have to change quite a few parts to make a significant change appearance-wise and aero-wise. Right now we're just sniffing around [to see] what those parts might be. A lot of this has to do with what we do with the driveline. We have tuned port fuel injection coming for '85. When you do a car—I don't care whether it's a Corvette or a Cavalier— there is so much time and effort spent on basic engineering. All these things are so costly to engineer and design that those are there for quite a while. Improvements are made, but the basic design is there. I see us working around the architecture that's been established. If we find a different front or rear that will enhance the appearance and, at the same time, reduce the drag, we'll consider it very seriously.

Q: What's the next change for the Corvette?

A: If we get into the program, it would be the front and rear. The one thing you're going to hold is the passenger capsule—the windshield, side glass, backlight, the main body of the car. In '85 we'll spell out the different fuel

injection. And we have to comply with the new federal law that a [third] brake light be mounted on the centerline of the car no lower than three inches below the base of the backlight and no higher than the opening of the backlight. You'll see this grotesque light wherever we feel we can make it work. You'll see a Corvette with this cancerous growth on it. That's how you'll be able to spot a new one.

Q: Do you know where the light will go yet?

A: No, because where we feel we'd like to have it [is] illegal. We have to challenge the regulation. That's not an exclusive Corvette problem; a lot of other cars are in the same boat. We're looking at all avenues. Inside the window meets our requirements: however, there's a lot of glare we can't control because of the angle of the backlight. That's the immediate major challenge this year for anyone who is going to bring a car into the United States.

Q: Will we see any changes in instrumentation?

A: There have been some refinements made relative to the angle of the readout, because of the revealing glare, and the size of the numerals.

The mid-engine Lola-chassis Corvette GTP was designed by Palmer and his staff.

Q: Is there a possibility of bringing in analog instruments?

A: Analog was [to be] standard and electronics were the option at one point in time. But that's all been shelved. I was probably one of the bigger critics that we should have analog gauges. [Now] I don't have any problem with it.

Q: Are you working on any show cars now?

A: Yes. We did the bodywork for the Trans-Am Corvettes that are starting to find their way onto the track. We have just completed a PPG pace car Corvette. And the GTP mid-engine Lola-chassis car was a major job for us.

Q: What kinds of things are you trying out with the show cars?

A: The PPG pace car is another extension of ground effects, again aero being the prime consideration. How slippery can we get the Corvette? It's a kind of a high-styled Trans-Am race car. We haven't taken the chassis and done an all-out design theme car yet.

Q: Are you planning an all-out theme car?

A: No, not really. You have to understand when you do a show car it's almost one of these things you do with your other hand in your spare time. We're so busy with production programs we can't use the manpower necessary to produce a whole new car, not the way we used to.

Q: Is there a convertible in the Corvette's future, a revival of the fully open roadster?

A: We did a convertible [version of the '84, but] we are not going to build one.

Q: Do you have a favorite Corvette of the past?

A: I have several. The 1956-57 are favorites of mine. Of course, the '63 split-window coupe has been identified as the classic Corvette and I have to agree with that. The '65 convertible, '68, '69 cars. Didn't like the rounded-off rear end [on] the '61. I think the '80 car was an improvement over the 1974-79 car. Those are some high points.

Q: Do you keep an eye on the aftermarket to see what other designers do with the Corvette?

A: Sure, but there hasn't been anything that's gotten me to say, "Hey, look at what they've done here. Let's try that." We've been through this thing for so many years [and] we've tried a lot of things. I really get a kick out of seeing the competition cars, because [altering the design] becomes functional.

Q: Do you ever have a desire to do something that's done in the aftermarket that Chevrolet can't do?

A: A convertible would be one, a well-done convertible. There are very few well-done convertibles. Most of them are compromises. To see a well-executed convertible is a rarity now. Cars are getting smaller, and you just don't have the real estate to package the way you'd like to. The [1984 Cadillac] Eldorado convertible is a case in point: the backlight is so small. In the old Eldorado we had much larger cars, so you could package a backlight that was more appropriate for the car.

Q: What is your opinion of the Pontiac Fiero?

A: I think it's a neat car. The car looks good on the road, better than I thought it would. It's not a Corvette, and I don't think it has to be a Corvette. For the money, it's a hell of a car.

Q: Would you be interested in working on the Fiero?

A: I guess I'd like to work on anything that presents a challenge.

Q: Will Chevrolet have its own version of the Fiero?

A: No. Just as Pontiac won't have a version of the Corvette. Those are unique cars for the respective divisions. I think the fact that we can do that is a great plus for both divisions. I think it would be a mistake for Chevrolet to [offer its own version of the] Fiero and Pontiac to offer a Corvette. [Other GM] divisions have wanted to get in on the Corvette action over the years. But it's an exclusive, and I think that's a neat thing about the Corvette. And now the Fiero—I think that's great. Pontiac can do a lot of things with that car, but it will never be a Corvette.

Q: Could the Fiero ever threaten the Corvette?

A: If they start to up the power of that to the point where they become a threat to the Corvette, we also have the ability to turn the wick up.

Q: Do you foresee a V-6 Corvette?

A: It's an interesting package. I'm sure it's one of the options we'll be looking at in the 1990s if the gas guzzler problem stays with us and we have to maintain or achieve higher performance levels.

Q: Would a V-6 work in the current chassis, and what kind of styling options would that offer you?

A: I really don't know, because when you get the V-6 to put out the kind of power needed to match or surpass the performance levels we know now—and will experience in 1985—all that room vacated by the two cylinders will be absorbed by intercoolers. The secret to the V-6, obviously, is turbocharging. I don't think there's any question the V-6 is going to be the performance engine of the future. But we're not planning any styling changes around that possibility now.

THE SHOW CARS AND EXPERIMENTALS

Fastback "Corvair" was shown at the '54 Motorama. It was a production prospect, but was killed by slow Corvette sales.

From the beginning, show cars and experimentals have figured prominently in the evolution of America's sports car. The very first machine to bear the Corvette name was originally created for the 1953 Motorama shows. And, as we know, it met with such highly favorable public response that it convinced General Motors management to go ahead with a production version.

Nowadays, the one-offs we see at auto shows seem little more than ordinary assembly-line cars with some fancy add-ons and maybe a new engine. But in the Fifties and early Sixties, show cars were something else: unique, often flamboyant dream machines, completely different from anything on a real-world road. Typically they boasted very radical styling, envisioned advanced engineering concepts, and were loaded with futuristic gimmicks. Though they were—and still are—glamorous and fun, they served a very serious purpose. They were built to test the feasibility of new design ideas and—most importantly—what the public thought of them. Today most automakers conduct product clinics, which accomplish much the same thing but in greater secrecy. But in the show car's heyday hundreds of millions of dollars often depended on viewer reactions, particularly if the show model had styling or some new feature that was already approved for production. You can bet that had the EX-122 prototype bombed at the Motorama, the Corvette would never have made it to the street.

Though GM discontinued its Motoramas after 1961, it continued to build show cars and experimental models that gave tantalizing clues as to what might lie ahead. A good many of the most memorable and inventive ones were inspired by the Corvette. As a high-performance two-seater, it was the sort of concept that appealed to both stylists and engineers, an exciting basis for such projects. And as the production models gained in fame and prestige, it was only natural GM would showcase its best and most advanced thinking under the Corvette label. Not surprisingly, many elements of concept vehicles like the Mako Shark II would show up in later production 'Vettes.

In this chapter we present the most famous Corvette-based experimentals. Most of these toured the auto show circuit, but you'll find a few that didn't. They're a fascinating group, and help us to better understand the forces that have made America's sports car what it is today: a dream machine for enthusiasts of all ages.

231

Opposite page, top: Early arrival of the Corvair coupe suggests GM was aware of the need for greater comfort and convenience in the production Corvette roadster. The car was repainted for later '54 shows. Bottom: The EX-122 Motorama prototype in a ritzy European setting. This page, above: The '54 Motorama hardtop prototype forecast the lift-off roof option and roll-up side glass of the production '56. Left: Also from 1954, the Corvette Nomad sports wagon, a nonrunning blue-and-white showpiece. Fluted, hardtop-styled roof was stretched to mate with the '55 Chevy lower body to create the production Nomad. Below: One of the two SR-2 racers built in 1956, this one for Harley Earl's son Jerry. It was later acquired by driver Jim Jeffords.

Opposite page, top: Originally a roadster built in 1958, Bill Mitchell's XP-700 was again seen in 1960 with a narrower grille, longer tail, and a wild see-through canopy with periscope. Bottom: Seen first in late 1960, the mid-engine CERV I (Corvette Experimental Research Vehicle) was conceived as a cross between an Indy and a hillclimb car. A variety of engines were tested in this platform, including V-8s with single and dual superchargers. Center spread: Mitchell's racing Stingray (right) led directly to the XP-755 Shark of 1961, an evolution of the XP-700. It was later retitled Mako Shark I. Above: A mildly customized '63 roadster from GM Design. Below: The Mako Shark II from 1965 previewed the production '68 'Vette. Two were built. This is the running Mark IV V-8 version.

This page, above: Built in 1967, the mid-engine XP-880 was shown as the Astro II, and fired rumors that the next generation production 'Vette would be a midships design. Left: The mid-engine Two-Rotor car, built as part of GM's stillborn Wankel engine program in 1973 and also known as XP-987GT. Below: The mid-engine XP-882 as it appeared at the 1970 New York Auto Show. Opposite page, top and center: A companion to the Two-Rotor was this Four-Rotor study styled by Bill Mitchell and built on an XP-882 chassis. Car was later fitted with a conventional 400-cid V-8 and shown as the Aerovette. It nearly made 1980 production. Bottom: The Astrovette was based on a stock 1968 platform.

CORVETTE IN COMPETITION

Winning, as we all know, is something of an American national pastime. For many of us "it isn't everything, it's the only thing," as football coach Vince Lombardi phrased it so long ago. In the world of automobiles there's a maxim that says "Win on Sunday, Sell on Monday," and it's just as true now as it was in the early days of dirt tracks, duster coats, and Mercer Raceabouts. It refers to the fact that people tend to buy cars that win—especially those makes that win most often or in the most grueling contests. And why not? The race winners are the cars that go fastest, handle best, and don't break, so why shouldn't that manufacturer's road machines be just as durable and speedy? Today, the expression applies not just for the cars but for all manner of racing components, from tires to shock absorbers to oil additives. Perhaps the best example of this philosophy in action is Ford Motor Company's "Total Performance" competition program of the Sixties.

America's sports car showed it could win very early on, and over the next three decades would compile one of the most enviable track records in the world. In light of this, it's odd that most Corvette fans aren't all that interested in their car's competition history. Oh, some are, to be sure. They're the ones largely responsible for the 'Vette's victories over the years. In fact, the single most striking fact about the Corvette's racing record is that virtually all of it has been forged by privateers, unlike that of other marques, notably Porsche. There's a very good reason: GM's own direct competition efforts were cut short by the Automobile Manufacturers Association "anti-racing edict" of June 1957, which came just as the Corvette was beginning to realize its full potential. And though GM continued to provide support to those who wished to race its sports car, the factory never again campaigned Corvettes itself.

But let's start at the beginning. The Corvette wasn't conceived with racing in mind, although Harley Earl had a notion that people would race it. As we

know, Earl's original concept of a spartan, lightweight, dual-purpose two-seater got side-tracked, and the Corvette emerged as more of a sporty touring machine that didn't look at all like it was cut out for the track.

Still, the temptation to tape the headlights and stick on some numbers proved irresistible, and even the earliest 1953-54 'Vettes saw limited action. The car's earliest victory came in 1955, when it set a new record in the stock car class at the annual Pike's Peak Hill Climb in Colorado. Apparently the record was unofficial, though, because the United States Auto Club (USAC), which would sanction the event in future years, had yet to be formed.

As we've seen (in Chapter 2) the Corvette was far below expectations in sales during its first few years on the market. Understandably, Chevy management began looking for something—anything—to reverse the situation. Thus, they were receptive when a newly hired engineer, Zora Arkus-Duntov, suggested that establishing a competition image would do just that. Duntov had done some racing himself. Though he wasn't the world's greatest driver (he failed to qualify at Indy on two occasions), he certainly was not lacking in technical expertise. He knew the Corvette had potential, and he was excited about the advent of Chevy's high-winding small-block V-8. Management was intrigued, and told Duntov to get cracking.

And he did. One of the first results of his Corvette improvement program was the decision to slot the new V-8 into the mostly carryover 1955 model. It made a tremendous difference, of course, and soon the "buff" magazines began taking the car more seriously as true race-and-ride material. But this new-found performance needed to be highlighted in a dramatic fashion, and it was with introduction of the completely restyled second generation for 1956. As noted previously (see Chapter 2), Duntov himself set a new record for the flying mile on the sands of Daytona Beach in 1955—a blistering 150.583 mph. A few weeks later, at the prestigious and well-publicized Speed Weeks competition in January 1956, Betty Skelton set a new speed record for American sports cars, and John Fitch drove a Corvette to take the sports-car class in the standing-mile run. The 'Vette was off to the races.

That spring, a dentist from Washington, D.C., Dr. Richard Thompson, began campaigning his Corvette in the C-Production class of the Sports Car Club of America (SCCA). With help from Duntov and others, he went on to take the national championship that year, which was a big boost to the car's fortunes. Part of his winning formula was a special hot camshaft developed by Duntov and also used in the Daytona cars. Corvette advertising soon began trumpeting this go-faster part—and the car's mounting number of wins. One now-famous ad, headlined "Bring on the Hay Bales!", contained a prophetic bit of copy: "But that's only the start. Corvette owners may enter other big racing tests in the months ahead—tests that may carry America's blue-and-white [international racing] colors into several of the most important European competitions." By changing the word "months" to "years," this statement serves as a neat summary of the Corvette's entire competition history.

In the mid-Fifties, of course, the most important international event for sports cars, aside from the legendary 24 Hours of Le Mans, was the 12 Hours of Endurance run on the old airport course at Sebring in central Florida. It attracted competitors from around the world, and the most prestigious marques were usually well represented, all vying for the acclaim and prestige associated with a Sebring win. Duntov knew a good showing at this one event would help the Corvette's prestige. He wanted more than anything else for the car to be taken seriously and not thought of simply as a toy, which is what some had called the 1953-55 car.

In early 1956, Duntov immersed himself in a purpose-built racer, which became known as the Corvette SS (Super Sport). The inspiration for this experimental project (XP-64) was the racing D-Type Jaguar, which would be one of its track competitors. At one point, GM considered sneaking one of its own V-8s into the D-Type chassis and actually racing it with new bodywork. Ultimately, however, a new design was okayed.

In final form the SS looked a bit like the Jaguar, a smooth cigar-shaped body sporting a rear dorsal fin. But GM couldn't resist giving it some Corvette styling flourishes, so the SS appeared wearing a wide toothy smile plus a modified version of the bodyside "cove" indentations from the production '56. Underneath this slick exterior was a

complex multi-tubular space frame, de Dion rear suspension, and a hopped-up, fuel-injected version of the just-released 283-cid small-block V-8, putting out 307 bhp at 6400 rpm. Bodywork and many chassis components were made of lightweight magnesium, and the whole car was quite a bit smaller than the production 'Vette. The SS wheelbase, for instance, was just 72 inches versus the road car's 102 inches, and overall length was a compact 168.6 inches. The SS stood just 48.7 inches high with its removable bubble canopy, designed for long-distance events. In open form it sat about three feet high.

The SS would be entered in the prototype class at the 1957 Sebring race, along with a brace of production models running in the sports car category. John Fitch was selected as team manager, though Duntov would be on hand to supervise the entire operation, and preliminary track testing got underway in mid-February. Originally, the incredibly talented Juan Manuel Fangio had been signed to drive the SS, but he feared the car

Opposite page: The racing Corvette SR-2 in 1957. Below: The ill-starred SS at Sebring.

wouldn't be ready in time and asked to be released. It wasn't and he was. Duntov, meantime, had been reworking a "mule" testbed car, driving it around the airport course himself to sort out handling problems. At the end of 60 days, Fitch and his mechanics declared the SS ready, though it would have to run without the magnesium body initially planned. Fangio saw the car with the large number "1" on its flanks and was intrigued. He asked to drive it in practice. He promptly went out and, unofficially, beat the Sebring lap record. Suddenly, the pits were abuzz about the new Corvette racer.

Duntov's long-range game plan was to use Sebring as a shakedown for the SS, then go on to Le Mans in June. But this idea would be derailed. The SS was forced to retire at Sebring after completing only 23 laps, the victim of an over-torqued bushing. Victory also eluded the production entries, though both finished respectably enough. In fact, Thompson and co-driver Gaston Andrey managed 12th overall and first in class. The second team car, driven by Bill Kilborn and Jim Jeffords, took the checkered flag in 15th position.

As it turned out, the production cars' placings may have done far more for the Corvette's image among sports car aficionados than the fancy SS ever could have. The SS was, after all, an exotic experimental no one could buy. But you could have one of the stock models, which had done very well in a formidable field. Suddenly the Europeans were forced to admit that America's sports car was indeed a true dual-purpose machine and one to be reckoned with—a car of style, but with stamina, too. As if to confirm that, Dr. Thompson won another SCCA championship in 1957, this time in the B-Production class where the 'Vette now qualified owing to its larger-displacement standard engine. And J.R. Rose captured the B-Sports/Racing crown with his modified 'Vette that same year.

The AMA resolution to abandon factory-sponsored racing and to deemphasize performance-oriented auto advertising spelled the immediate end of the SS program, as well as Chevy's stock car efforts in NASCAR and USAC. As events would prove, we had not exactly seen the last of the SS, but for now it was time to adopt a low profile. Yet with enthusiasts like Duntov,

Bill Mitchell's Stingray racer was painted red initially. It's shown here in its silver show car form as seen in early '61.

Ed Cole, and Bill Mitchell around, there was no question that race assistance and new components would continue to issue from GM. The only difference was that, under the AMA resolution, it would now have to be of the "under-the-table" and "back-door" sort. From this point on, GM would never be "officially" involved with racing again, a bit of public posturing that everyone recognized as exactly that.

The spotlight accordingly shifted to the privateers beginning with the 1958 season. As in the stock car field, most racing Corvettes this year were the more competitive 1956-57 cars, not the bulkier, heavier '58s. And, America's sports car racked up some notable wins. Perhaps the highlight was this year's Sebring classic, where a near-stock Corvette finished 12th overall. The car, driven by Jim Rathmann and Dick Doane, also scored first in the GT class, sprinting to the line 20 laps ahead of the nearest Mercedes-Benz 300SL. At the Pike's Peak Hill Climb, Ak Miller took his 'Vette to a first place

in the sports car division with a time of 15 minutes, 23.7 seconds and a speed of 48.392 mph for the 12.42-mile course, which rises from 9402 feet to 14,110 feet through 230 curves. Jim Jeffords gave the 'Vette its second consecutive B-Production crown in SCCA with his "Purple People Eater" car, actually one of two SR-2 racing machines created for Sebring. Built during the summer of 1956, this car featured a rounded nose, a single central rear tailfin with faired-in headrest, and a paint job reminiscent of the kind used on racing airplanes. A highly modified stock model, it was raced by Curtis Turner, Dr. Thompson, and Harley Earl's son Jerry before Jeffords acquired it. In 1959, Jeffords again took the national B/P crown.

The 1960 season witnessed several Corvette triumphs. The first came at Sebring, where Chuck Hall and Bill Fritts added another class win for America's sports car in the 12-hours enduro. But it was left to wealthy sportsman Briggs Cunningham to give the Corvette the moral victory Duntov had so longed for—a good showing at Le Mans. Cunningham was no stranger to the French circuit, of course, having won in

class at the 1950 event with his fabled near-stock "Le Monstre" Cadillac and the next year with his Chrysler-powered C-1 sports car. For the 1960 running he entered a trio of Corvettes in the big-engine GT class and a Jaguar prototype. Although one of the 'Vettes retired during the race (which Mike Kimberly spun out on the rain-soaked track; he was uninjured), the car driven by Fitch and Bob Grossman came in eighth overall, completing 3782 kilometers. At one point, this machine was timed at over 151 mph down the long Mulsanne Straight. Though the winning Ferrari of Oliver Gendebein and Paul Frere was much faster (170 mph maximum, race average of 109.128 mph), the Corvette had conclusively proven its mettle in the world's most demanding test of speed and endurance.

Back home, William L. Mitchell had taken over for Harley Earl as GM's chief stylist. "Racing's in my blood," he once told a fellow executive, and naturally he was familiar with the Corvette SS. One day, while poking around the company vaults, he discovered the old "mule" development car from that 1957 assault. Mitchell couldn't stand the thought that the car might be

destroyed, and he didn't like the idea of it just going to waste in some dusty warehouse. With his considerable clout and some finesse, he arranged to buy the "mule" for a mere $500. In exchange, he agreed "that I'd keep it off the Tech Center property, and spend my own money to run it." Yes, he thought the SS deserved a second chance to race and win.

But the old body wouldn't do. It was only a cobbled-up affair anyway, and by the time Mitchell found it the car was in pretty sad shape. So, he designed a new body, put it on the chassis, and called the whole thing the "Sting Ray Special." He enticed Dr. Thompson to drive, and the "flying dentist" flew it all the way to the SCCA C-Modified national championship in 1960. Said Mitchell: "It cost me quite a bit, too. I financed it all out of my own pocket. I couldn't afford to build

and race the Sting Ray today. But back then, it pleased me no end to go up against Cunningham and those boys with the faster cars and take any of them." Mitchell's car could reach 60 mph from a standing start in just four seconds. At one point he equipped it with four Weber carburetors and exclaimed it would "tear your head off."

The racing career for Mitchell's "kit car" would be short: just two seasons. Once Thompson had won the championship, the Sting Ray Special was retired from the track to become a showmobile. Up to this point it had never worn Corvette emblems, nor was it listed as a General Motors entry because GM wasn't racing. But when it made its first off-track appearance—at the Chicago Auto Show in February 1961—it sported Corvette script on its shapely tail. There was a reason for this: Mitchell had decided to

use this basic shape for the next new production Corvette, the 1963 Sting Ray, and GM wanted to test public response. In fact, the production styling had been approved in more or less final form by the end of 1960. Needless to say, most people liked what they saw. As for those who didn't, at least the racer/show car allowed them to become accustomed to Mitchell's aggressive lines long before they began appearing on the street.

During 1961 it seemed Corvettes were winning everywhere you looked. On July 4, Ak Miller repeated his 1958 win in the Pike's Peak Hill Climb by hurling his 'Vette up the mountain in 14 minutes, 28.6 seconds at an average speed of 51.462 mph. The third through sixth spots were also held by 'Vettes. Dr. Thompson continued his winning ways in SCCA and claimed another B-Production national title. At Sebring, Delmo Johnson and Dale Morgan drove to a first place finish in the GT class, the fourth such victory for America's sports car.

It was in late 1961 that Duntov began work on yet another Corvette racer he hoped would be a world-beater. This was Chevy's last "openly" supported factory competition car, the fearsome Grand Sport. Designed by Duntov, along with Walt Zeyte and others, the GS was his reply to the challenge of the Ford-powered Cobra, a lightweight rocketship created by ex-racer Carroll Shelby and employing a British AC roadster body stuffed full of Ford 289 V-8, an engine that was already beginning to show its muscle on the tracks.

Duntov had hoped to complete 125 Grand Sports, the number needed for it to qualify as a production sports car under international racing rules. The car appeared in late 1962 bearing a specially built body made of woven fiberglass with lines very close to those of the just-released Sting Ray split-window coupe. The chassis was a special tube-ladder affair with stock suspension mounting points. The drivetrain consisted of a four-speed gearbox hooked to a special 377-cid racing version of the Chevy V-8, with aluminum head and block and two spark plugs per cylinder. Power output was reported to be 550 bhp, though the actual figure was probably higher.

The Grand Sport program was carried out in great secrecy, deep within the confines of GM and away from disapproving managerial eyes. Duntov took the first prototype to Sebring in December 1962 to test the car's general competitiveness and its brakes in particular, which he hoped to improve. There remains controversy today over whether these tests and the car itself were actually approved by his superiors. Apparently they weren't, because when word of the tests reached GM headquarters the company publicly restated its opposition to racing

in January 1963, and the entire project was halted after only five cars, all of which had been completed the previous summer. All were engine-less, so quickly did the axe fall.

But the Grand Sport wasn't dead yet. Two Corvette enthusiasts, Grady Davis and Dick Doane, somehow managed to get hold of two of the cars. (One story says they were delivered in unmarked trucks.) Davis, a Union Oil official, and Doane, a Chevy dealer, dropped in stock Corvette engines, and Dick Thompson raced the Davis car throughout 1963, winning at that year's Watkins Glen race. The other three cars wound up

in the stable of Texas oilman John Mecom, Jr., who took them to the Nassau Speed Weeks in 1963. Roger Penske led virtually all the way in the 25-lap Governor's Trophy Race, finishing third overall and first in the prototype class out of a field of 58. In the main event, the Nassau Trophy Race, 56 laps and 62 entries, Grand Sports finished fourth and eighth overall and first and third in class.

In early 1964 the first two cars were returned to GM to be prepared for that year's Daytona Continental, at which time they were converted from coupe to roadster configuration. But management again didn't want to know and decreed the roadsters be moved to a warehouse, where they sat for three years before being purchased by Penske and George Wintersteen in 1966. The Mecom cars contested Sebring in March 1964, but the results proved disappointing. Delmo Johnson and co-driver Dave Morgan endured numerous mechanical breakdowns to finish 32nd, while Penske and Jim Hall put their white GS across the line 18th overall.

It was a sad finale for the Grand Sport. The roadsters saw limited action in 1966, but scored no major wins. Even so, this car was, as Karl Ludvigsen summarized, "a reminder to Ford, then on the way up in its historic assault on the racing world, that the way would not always be easy."

While the factory was having one last fling with a racing machine, numerous privateers continued to put production Corvettes in victory circles all across the country. During 1962, Dr. Thompson took the A-Production championship in SCCA with his newly homologated 327-cid car. Following in his footsteps in B-Production was Don Yenko, who would win the national class crown this year and next. A Corvette also took first in class at Daytona in '62. The highlight of the 1963 season was Yenko's repeat in B/P and Penske's prototype-class victory at Nassau. The following year, the B/P title was claimed by Frank Dominianni, and a Penske 'Vette ran to first in the GT category at that year's Daytona Continental, piloted by Wintersteen, Dick Guldstrand, and Ben Moore.

Such victories were heartening for Corvette fans, who really had very little to cheer about in the mid-Sixties. Most of

the truly important events now fell to the Cobras, even though they were far from the "production" sports cars Carroll Shelby said they were. But they had the SCCA's blessing and that's what counted, so the Corvette's dominance in road racing was stymied in these years.

Ironically, the Cobra might have been powered by Chevy and not Ford. Shelby had approached Ed Cole in 1962 with a request for engines. But Cole declined and the rest, as they say, was history. Duntov certainly knew the score: "It was clear as day to me that the Cobra had to beat the Corvette. The Cobra was very powerful and weighed less than 2000 pounds. Shelby had the configuration, which was no damn good to sell to the people, except a very few. But it had to beat the Corvette on the tracks."

Cobra production would cease after 1967, and by the end of 1968 those cars still racing were tired and worn out. Until then, Corvette pickings were slim, though the car would roar back in the Seventies. But even in the Cobra era there were a few bright spots. For example, the Sting Ray entered by Roger Penske finished 12th overall and first in the GT class at the 1966 Daytona Continental and ninth overall and first in GT at that year's Sebring 12 Hours. The following year, Don Yenko teamed up with Dave Morgan for another Sebring win in GT. And at Le Mans '67 the Corvette of Bob Bondurant and Dick Guldstrand ran a strong first in class until its engine failed toward the end of the marathon. A little reported triumph came at that showplace of speed, the Bonneville Salt Flats, where Bob Hirsch ran to a record-setting 192.879 mph.

Corvettes came back in SCCA events beginning in 1969. Chevrolet engineer Jerry Thompson (no relation to the racing dentist) and driver Tony DeLorenzo teamed up to take the national A-Production crown, ending the

Corvette drought in this class that had begun back in 1962. That same year, Allan Barker captured the B-Production title, and would go on to take it in each of the next three seasons. After 1972, he sold his 'Vette to Texas racer Bill Jobe, who won the class with it in 1973 and again in 1974, giving this car six national B/P titles. As recently as 1978 this car was still being campaigned.

In 1970, Corvette repeated as A-Production champ, with a young John Greenwood doing the honors. He won again in 1971, a year when he teamed with TV personality Dick Smothers to come home first in GT at Sebring. At that year's 24 Hours of Daytona contest, De-Lorenzo and Yenko scored yet another GT victory while finishing a surprising fourth overall. Greenwood moved on to Le Mans in 1972, where he qualified faster than any other GT contender. He led the class for hours during the race itself until a blown engine forced him out. Filling in for Greenwood as SCCA national A/P titleholder that year was Jerry Hansen.

The energy crisis put a temporary damper on racing in 1974, but by 1975 things were more or less back to normal. Like the Sting Rays before it, the fifth-generation Corvettes were too big and heavy to compete effectively against the likes of Porsche and BMW in international enduros. And Corvette campaigners couldn't hope to match the large sums of money spent by the European companies. So the 'Vette's biggest successes continued to come in SCCA club racing. America's sports car would be A-Production champion in 1973 through '78, B-Production champ in 1973-74 and 1976-79. Corvettes also did well in the new sport of autocross, winning the B-Stock Solo II crown every year from 1973 to '79, except for '75. Though GM still wasn't racing, America's sports car would figure prominently in the reconstituted

Above: An Owens-Corning team car in pre-race trials at Daytona, 1971. Opposite page, top: J. Marshall Robbins in the 1973 Road Atlanta Trans-Am. Bottom: A much-modified Sting Ray in B-Production.

Trans-Am series. In 1973, for instance, the Corvettes of J. Marshall Robbins, Greenwood, and Jerry Thompson were third, fourth, and fifth in the overall standings. Two years later Greenwood took all the marbles, and the 'Vettes of Babe Headley, Jerry Hansen, and Paul Misuriello came in right behind. A couple of lean seasons followed, but Corvette again claimed the series in 1978's Category II with Greg Pickett's wild racer, and Headley finished a somewhat distant second to Bob Tullius' Jaguar in Category I. The next year, Gene Bothello took the Category I title, and 'Vette pilots Frank Joyce and Gary Carlen finished third and fourth in the point totals. Pickett finished second in 1980's consolidated series. And in 1981 it was Eppie Wietzes who ended up the point leader in a season described as one of the most exciting and competitive in the Trans-Am's 16-year history. In International Motor Sports Association (IMSA) competition, the Corvette has been a consistent contender and frequent winner. Chevy captured the IMSA's All-American GT manufacturer's crown for 1978, a

fitting tribute for "USA-1."

The Corvette has much more competition history to write. The cars are still running well in both SCCA and IMSA. For example, a 'Vette finished first in the GT-1 category at the 1982 SCCA runoffs. And competition-prepped 1984s are already appearing in various events—all under private sponsorship, of course. An interesting new development is Chevy's support—via "technical assistance" only—for an exciting mid-engine prototype-class racer destined for IMSA. It features a long-tail body with ground-effects skirting and a nose vaguely reminiscent of that on the '84 production model. Underneath is a sophisticated new chassis engineered by Lola of England. How this car will fare remains to be seen, but its mere existence seems certain to add new luster to the Corvette's reputation as a consistent, classy champion.

THE INDUSTRY THAT SERVES A CAR

Corvette fandom has always taken many forms, from the traditional to the exotic. For proof, look no further than the industry that serves America's sports car. Today there are literally dozens—maybe even hundreds—of companies whose business depends largely or entirely on the Corvette. They're found in most every state, including Alaska. Among them, they offer a bewildering array of products and services— everything from floormats to engine hop-up kits to restoration assistance to Corvette Christmas tree ornaments. And we're not even talking about the general-service parts and accessory houses, shops, speed equipment stores, or the thousands of Chevrolet dealers. No doubt about it: if there's something you need for your Corvette or something special you want to do with it, chances are somebody's already thought of it and will be only too happy to take your money.

Of course, an industry is not unique to the Corvette. Similar enterprises have grown up around marques like Jaguar, Ferrari, MG, and BMW as well as certain model groups like the early Ford Mustangs and the "classic" 1955-57 Chevys. But nowhere will you find a more diverse group of people than those devoted to the 'Vette. They range in age from teenagers to septuagenarians and are found in all walks of life. They enjoy their cars in many different, often sharply contrasting ways. Some prefer to keep their 'Vettes in pristine original condition, while others load up their cars with accessories, soup up the engine, and add maybe a wild paint job or fender flares. Some owners never take out their cars except on sunny days, while others never take out their cars except to go to the local race circuit or dragstrip. Some Cor-

vettes haven't put a tire to a real road in years, while others are used as everyday transportation. Some owners belong to one or more of several national Corvette clubs and affiliated local chapters, some don't. But all these folks have one thing in common: they're just nuts about Corvettes and anything that has to do with their car.

None of this should come as a surprise, because the Corvette has always been many things to many people. Almost from the first, it has been a car that can be enjoyed in several ways, and it has always had the sort of personal character that seemed to invite even further personalization in the hands of an imaginative owner.

As one example, consider the fiberglass body. GM originally chose fiberglass because it was easier and less expensive than steel for a low-volume model like the Corvette. More practically

Two decades of Corvettes, represented here by the 1973 coupe (left), the '53 production roadster (center), and the 1963 Sting Ray coupe (right).

speaking, GRP could be quickly and inexpensively modified when it came time for a style change, which made sense to the accountants. 'Vette owners discovered the same thing, and many went about restyling their cars, especially since fiberglass molding and bonding techniques filtered down quickly to the general public. The Corvette remains a natural for customizers today. A large number of replacement and substitute fiberglass pieces is available for most every Corvette ever made—fender flares, special hoods, scoops, fins, and spoilers. The manufacture and sale of these items constitutes one of the largest and most profitable segments of the aftermarket Corvette industry.

As for mechanical alterations the possibilities are near limitless. Few engines have been honored with as much bolt-on speed equipment as the Chevy small-block V-8, and there's still a wide choice of goodies available from any number of sources, items like special heads and cams, lightweight pistons and flywheels, less restrictive exhaust systems and freer-breathing manifolds. If you'd rather go the straight cubic-inch route, upping displacement of your 283 is as simple as taking it out and replacing it with a 327 or 350. The block is the same size on all of these engines, so where one fits, the others will, too. Similar performance pieces for the big-inch mills are only slightly less plentiful. Of course, too many mods and you run the risk of making the car untractable for the street, so it's usually wise to take things one step at a time. You can also move in the other direction—toward better fuel economy—by exchanging differential gears for a more long-striding ratio. And indeed, those who aren't so concerned with all-out speed may want to investigate this.

Corvettes have long been famous for roadability, but there's room for considerable variation here, too. Hi-jacker rear-end kits, traction bars, and air-adjustable shocks are available for the drag crowd, while the tweed-driving-cap set will prefer to install a set of Koni or Bilstein shocks and perhaps fiddle with various-diameter sway bars. Tires run the gamut from racing slicks to all-season radials, and you can play with steering gears and power steering valves depending on what kind of helm control you're after.

Then there are the accessories, which are so numerous as to boggle even a devoted parts

249

counter employee. Just a sample will have to suffice here. If you do a lot of long-distance traveling, consider a deck-mounted luggage rack. Replacement T-tops are available in both steel and glass for the fifth-generation models. They're expensive and, partly because of this, quite popular with thieves, so invest a little more in a set of key locks for them. Most Corvette specialists carry a good inventory of replacement door panels, carpeting, and upholstery. Those concerned about authenticity in a restoration will want to ensure that they're getting either new-old stock or an accurate reproduction.

Then there's a whole slew of Corvette clothing—jackets, T-shirts, caps, belts, buckles—even Corvette underwear in one catalog we've seen—all emblazoned with the name, the crossed-flags logo, or various slogans, some of which border on the crude. And if you're not content to stop there, you can go on to Corvette towels, mugs and glasses, sunglasses, camera straps, desk sets, wall clocks and thermometers, mirrors, memo pads and—no kidding—Christmas tree ornaments.

For the more adventuresome who own a late-model T-top coupe, a number of firms will be glad to convert it into a roadster. It's difficult to generalize about the quality of such conversions, but they can be carried out fairly simply since most of the pieces used in the 1968-75 roadster will fit the later coupes. At least one firm, Convertible Concepts, Ltd., of Blaine, Washington, has tried its hand at an open-air 1984. We can't comment on its workmanship since we've not been able to examine one first hand, but we will say the sixth-generation design looks every bit as handsome in this form as you'd expect.

With the great scope in Corvette modifications and accessories, it pays to be informed. One of the best ways to do that is to join a club. Currently, there are at least three national clubs devoted exclusively to America's sports car (see below). In addition, several general-interest organizations like the SCCA welcome Corvette owners. Most of us in the publishing game know that almost anything about Corvettes sells well, and there are a number of excellent books and periodicals around to slake your knowledge craving. One of the best-known magazines is *Corvette News,* put out by Chevrolet Public Relations. Articles on America's sports car are always appearing in nationally distributed publications, including *Collectible Automobile,* a bimonthly magazine produced by the editors of this book. On the subject of collecting, club membership is probably the best way to plug into information not only about availability and prices of cars but also about sources of parts and restoration assistance. Most clubs also publish technical and service hints as part of their newsletters on a regular basis. And, belonging to a club offers the satisfaction of meeting other enthusiasts like yourself to enjoy group activities and exchange hard-learned lessons.

The Corvette industry is hardly glamorous for the most part, but it could not exist without the continuing enthusiasm of hundreds of thousands of 'Vette lovers. And this brings up an interesting point. Over the past 30 years Chevrolet has built nearly three quarters of a million Corvettes, a huge number compared with the volume of prestige marques like Porsche or even Mercedes-Benz. No one knows precisely how many of these cars survive, but it's likely a high percentage, which testifies to the Corvette's enduring and broad-based appeal. Equally significant is the high number of non-owner 'Vette enthusiasts, a figure that probably exceeds total production by a factor of three. There is probably no other car that inspires such intense, widespread interest—certainly none that appeals to so many different types of people. It's no wonder so many firms have jumped *so* wholeheartedly into the "Corvette business."

And that business is, by and large, the stuff of dreams. Making one's car just a little bit different, maybe even a little bit better than the other fellow's, has been an American preoccupation since automobiles were called "horseless carriages." The desire for individuality coupled with the quest for more power and speed were what gave us the first sports cars—the Stutz Bearcats, the Mercer Raceabouts, and all the rest—the forerunners of the Corvette.

In today's impersonal, computerized, mass-production world, dreams and the expression of individual tastes have become more important than ever. Perhaps this is why an industry flourishes around the Corvette and why the car itself thrives. America's sports car remains as much a symbol of freedom and the pursuit of happiness as it did 30 years ago. It's a car as timeless as the emotions it stirs, as irresistible as the dreams it fulfills.

Clubs for Corvette Enthusiasts

National Corvette Owners Association
P.O. Box 777A
Falls Church, VA 22046
(703) 533-7222
Founded 1975. Current membership: 22,000. Publication: *For Vettes Only*

National Council of Corvette Clubs
P.O. Box 325
Troy, OH 45373
Founded 1957. Current membership: 9000.

Western States Corvette Council
2321 Falling Water Court
Santa Clara, CA 95054
Founded 1965. Current membership: 3000. Publication: Quarterly newsletter.

BRIEF SPECIFICATIONS AND PRODUCTION

Year	Body Type	WB (in.)	Length (in.)	Width (in.)	Curb Wt. (lbs)	Price	Production
1953	rdstr	102.0	167.0	72.2	2705	$3513	315
1954	rdstr	102.0	167.0	72.2	2705	3523	3640
1955	rdstr	102.0	167.0	72.2	2799	2799	674
1956	rdstr	102.0	168.0	70.5	2764	3149	3467
1957	rdstr	102.0	168.0	70.5	2730	3465	6339
1958	rdstr	102.0	177.2	72.8	2793	3631	9168
1959	rdstr	102.0	177.2	72.8	2840	3875	9670
1960	rdstr	102.0	177.2	72.8	2840	3872	10261
1961	rdstr	102.0	177.2	72.8	2905	3934	10939
1962	rdstr	102.0	177.2	72.8	2925	4038	14531
1963	coupe	98.0	175.2	69.2	2859	4252	10594
1963	rdstr	98.0	175.2	69.2	2881	4037	10919
1964	coupe	98.0	175.2	69.2	2960	4252	8304
1964	rdstr	98.0	175.2	69.2	2945	4037	13925
1965	coupe	98.0	175.2	69.2	2975	4321	8186
1965	rdstr	98.0	175.2	69.2	2985	4106	15376
1966	coupe	98.0	175.2	69.2	2985	4295	9958
1966	rdstr	98.0	175.2	69.2	3005	4084	17762
1967	coupe	98.0	175.2	69.2	3000	4353	8504
1967	rdstr	98.0	175.2	69.2	3020	4141	14436
1968	coupe	98.0	182.5	69.0	3055	4663	9936
1968	rdstr	98.0	182.5	69.0	3065	4141	18630
1969	coupe	98.0	182.5	69.0	3140	4781	22154
1969	rdstr	98.0	182.5	69.0	3145	4438	16608
1970	coupe	98.0	182.5	69.0	3184	5192	10668
1970	rdstr	98.0	182.5	69.0	3196	4849	6648
1971	coupe	98.0	182.5	69.0	3190	5536	14680
1971	rdstr	98.0	182.5	69.0	3200	5299	7121
1972	coupe	98.0	182.5	69.0	3190	5394	20496
1972	rdstr	98.0	182.5	69.0	3200	5168	6508
1973	coupe	98.0	182.5	69.0	3416	5635	28881
1973	rdstr	98.0	182.5	69.0	3460	5399	5583
1974	coupe	98.0	185.5	69.0	3420	6002	32873
1974	rdstr	98.0	185.5	69.0	3475	5766	4629
1975	coupe	98.0	185.5	69.0	3420	6810 ⌐	38465
1975	rdstr	98.0	185.5	69.0	3475	6550 ⌐	
1976	coupe	98.0	185.5	69.0	3400	7605	46588
1977	coupe	98.0	185.2	69.0	3529	8648	49213
1978	coupe	98.0	185.2	69.0	3530	9322	46776
1979	coupe	98.0	185.2	69.0	3530	10220	53807
1980	coupe	98.0	185.3	69.0	3336	13140	40614
1981	coupe	98.0	185.3	69.0	3330	15248	45631
1982	coupe	98.0	185.3	69.0	3370	18290[1]	25407
1984	coupe	96.0	176.5	71.0	3120	21800	NA

1: Base model; Collector Edition: $22538

CORVETTE ENGINES: 1953-84

Type	Bore x Stroke (in.)	CID	C.R. (:1)	Bhp @ rpm (SAE gross)	Induction	Available
ohv I-6	3.56 x 3.94	235.5	8.0	150 @ 4200	carb	1953-54
ohv I-6	3.56 x 3.94	235.5	8.0	155 @ 4200	carb	1955
ohv V-8	3.75 x 3.00	265.0	8.0	195 @ 5000	carb	1955
ohv V-8	3.75 x 3.00	265.0	9.25	210 @ 5200	carb	1956
ohv V-8	3.75 x 3.00	265.0	9.25	225 @ 5200	carb	1956
ohv V-8	3.88 x 3.00	283.0	9.5	220 @ 4800	carb	1957
ohv V-8	3.88 x 3.00	283.0	9.5	245 @ 5000	carb	1957-61
ohv V-8	3.88 x 3.00	283.0	9.5	250 @ 5000	FI	1957-59
ohv V-8	3.88 x 3.00	283.0	9.5	270 @ 6000	carb	1957-61
ohv V-8	3.88 x 3.00	283.0	10.5	283 @ 6200	FI	1957
ohv V-8	3.88 x 3.00	283.0	9.5	230 @ 4800	carb	1958-61
ohv V-8	3.88 x 3.00	283.0	10.5	290 @ 6200	FI	1958-59
ohv V-8	3.88 x 3.00	283.0	11.0	275 @ 5200	FI	1960-61
ohv V-8	3.88 x 3.00	283.0	11.0	315 @ 6200	FI	1960-61
ohv V-8	4.00 x 3.25	327.0	10.5	250 @ 4400	carb	1962-65
ohv V-8	4.00 x 3.25	327.0	10.5	300 @ 5000	carb	1962-68
ohv V-8	4.00 x 3.25	327.0	11.25	340 @ 6000	carb	1962-63
ohv V-8	4.00 x 3.25	327.0	11.25	360 @ 6000	FI	1962-63
ohv V-8	4.00 x 3.25	327.0	11.25	365 @ 6200	carb	1964-65
ohv V-8	4.00 x 3.25	327.0	11.25	375 @ 6200	FI	1964-65
ohv V-8	4.00 x 3.25	327.0	11.0	350 @ 5800	carb	1965-68
ohv V-8	4.00 x 3.48	350.0	10.25	300 @ 4800	carb	1969-70
ohv V-8	4.00 x 3.48	350.0	11.0	350 @ 5600	carb	1969-70
ohv V-8	4.00 x 3.48	350.0	11.0	370 @ 6000	carb	1970
ohv V-8	4.00 x 3.48	350.0	8.5	270 @ 4800	carb	1971-72
ohv V-8	4.00 x 3.48	350.0	9.0	330 @ 5600	carb	1971-72
ohv V-8	4.00 x 3.48	350.0	8.5	195 @ 4400*	carb	1973-74
ohv V-8	4.00 x 3.48	350.0	9.0	250 @ 5200*	carb	1973-74
ohv V-8	4.00 x 3.48	350.0	8.5	165 @ 3800*	carb	1975
ohv V-8	4.00 x 3.48	350.0	9.0	205 @ 4800*	carb	1975
ohv V-8	4.00 x 3.48	350.0	8.5	180 @ 4000*	carb	1976-77
ohv V-8	4.00 x 3.48	350.0	9.0	210 @ 5200*	carb	1976-77
ohv V-8	4.00 x 3.48	350.0	8.2	185 @ 4000*	carb	1978
ohv V-8	4.00 x 3.48	350.0	8.9	220 @ 5200*	carb	1978
ohv V-8	4.00 x 3.48	350.0	8.2	195 @ 4000*	carb	1979
ohv V-8	4.00 x 3.48	350.0	8.9	225 @ 5200*	carb	1979
ohv V-8	4.00 x 3.48	350.0	8.2	190 @ 4400*	carb	1980-81
ohv V-8	4.00 x 3.48	350.0	9.0	230 @ 5200*	carb	1980
ohv V-8	3.74 x 3.48	305.0	8.6	180 @ 4200*	carb	1980 (Cal.)
ohv V-8	4.00 x 3.48	350.0	9.0	200 @ 4200*	FI	1982
ohv V-8	4.00 x 3.48	350.0	9.0	205 @ 4300*	FI	1984
ohv V-8	4.09 x 3.75	396.0	11.0	425 @ 6400	carb	1965
ohv V-8	4.25 x 3.76	427.0	10.25	390 @ 5400	carb	1966-69
ohv V-8	4.25 x 3.76	427.0	11.0	425 @ 6400	carb	1966
ohv V-8	4.25 x 3.76	427.0	10.25	400 @ 5400	carb	1967-69
ohv V-8	4.25 x 3.76	427.0	11.0	435 @ 5800	carb	1967-69
ohv V-8	4.25 x 3.76	427.0	12.5	430 @ 5200	carb	1969
ohv V-8	4.25 x 4.00	454.0	10.25	390 @ 4800	carb	1970
ohv V-8	4.25 x 4.00	454.0	12.25	465 @ 5200	carb	1970
ohv V-8	4.25 x 4.00	454.0	8.5	365 @ 4800	carb	1971-72
ohv V-8	4.25 x 4.00	454.0	9.0	425 @ 5600	carb	1971
ohv V-8	4.25 x 4.00	454.0	9.0	270 @ 4400	carb	1973-74

*SAE net horsepower

INDEX

Corvette for 1962, last of the "classic" roadsters.

America's sports car for 1968--and the inevitable admirers.